Modern Fiction
and the Art of Subversion

American University Studies

Series III
Comparative Literature

Vol. 60

PETER LANG
New York • Washington, D.C./Baltimore • Boston
Bern • Frankfurt am Main • Berlin • Vienna • Paris

Jonathan Quick

Modern Fiction and the Art of Subversion

PETER LANG

New York • Washington, D.C./Baltimore • Boston
Bern • Frankfurt am Main • Berlin • Vienna • Paris

Library of Congress Cataloging-in-Publication Data

Quick, Jonathan.
Modern fiction and the art of subversion / Jonathan Quick.
p. cm. — (American university studies.
Series III, Comparative literature; vol. 60)
Includes bibliographical references and index.
1. American fiction—20th century—History and criticism. 2. Fitzgerald, F. Scott
(Francis Scott), 1896–1940—Technique. 3. English fiction—20th century—History
and criticism. 4. Faulkner, William, 1897–1962—Technique.
5. Hemingway, Ernest, 1899–1961—Technique. 6. Conrad, Joseph, 1857–1924—
Technique. 7. Joyce, James, 1882–1941—Technique. 8. Social norms in
literature. 9. Modernism (Literature). I. Title. II. Series.
PS374.M535Q53   813'.5209—dc21   98-18025
ISBN 0-8204-4097-3
ISSN 0724-1445

Die Deutsche Bibliothek-CIP-Einheitsaufnahme

Quick, Jonathan:
Modern fiction and the art of subversion / Jonathan Quick.
–New York; Washington, D.C./Baltimore; Boston; Bern;
Frankfurt am Main; Berlin; Vienna; Paris: Lang.
(American university studies. Ser. 3,
Comparative literature; Vol. 60)
ISBN 0-8204-4097-3

Cover design by Lisa Dillon

The paper in this book meets the guidelines for permanence and durability
of the Committee on Production Guidelines for Book Longevity
of the Council of Library Resources.

Printed in the United States of America

For Elaine

TABLE OF CONTENTS

Introduction   The Art of Subversion:
                   Five Modern Writers   1

Chapter 1   Joseph Conrad's Blank Maps:
                   The Art of Inversion   13

Chapter 2   James Joyce's Material Language:
                   Art and Regression   41

Chapter 3   F. Scott Fitzgerald's New World:
                   Transfiguring America   67

Chapter 4   William Faulkner's Civil War:
                   Transposed History   97

Chapter 5   Literary Hemingway:
                   Subversion and Influence   129

Conclusion   A Community of Writers:
                   Modernists, Realists, Postmodernity   155

Works Cited   159

Index   167

INTRODUCTION

The Art of Subversion:
Five Modern Writers

In a poem from the 1950's titled "Church Going," Philip Larkin anticipates a central trait of the postmodern temper with the question, "And what remains when disbelief has gone?" He does not presume to answer it, but describes the feelings stirred by his intimation of a massive withdrawal of religious culture: the sense of theological realities giving way to formless material, the empty and silent church becoming "A shape less recognizable each week" with "A purpose more obscure." It arouses his surprising but unsatisfied "hunger to be more serious." Shunning the trite declaration that there is nothing left to lose, Larkin appears content to realize that no belief is left to require rejection, no intolerable dogmas to overturn, and only a strangely serene sensation of vacancy and indifference remains. "Church Going" further surprises by its inference that the historical spread of disbelief that left the church nearly abandoned was itself, for the greater part of those whose lives it touched, perhaps a less wrenching matter than has commonly been supposed. The poem tells of a world that ended without the bang and, indeed, scarcely with the whimper of Eliot's *The Hollow Men* (1925). Instead, its evanescence brings Larkin a paradox-rich wonderment at loss and silence, and at the gathering shadows of meaning. It gives him a curious satisfaction at being "sure there's nothing going on."

Larkin's undramatic presentation of the waning of spirituality at mid-century suggests a revision of the more drastic views of the earlier modernist writers' immediate reactions to it. His meditative sobriety commends a quizzical look at the canonization of the "high modern" authors that proceeded in tandem with the early development of academic criticism after the Great War. Largely as a consequence of the special status accorded by the New Criticism to complex and "well-wrought" literary works, virtually heroic personalities were conferred on their authors in the classroom, and for the reading public they became "literary giants." For many, the modern masterworks were blows struck by revolutionaries in the cause of resisting, undermining and supplanting the materialistic culture that was despiritualizing people's lives. An adjustment of that view can be made by demonstrating the various forms of regressiveness found in some of the most conspicuous texts of modern fiction. The present argument does not seek to denigrate the superlative achievements of these works, but rather regards them primarily as prodigies of style that were parlayed critically into classics. Further, it stresses their authors' attempts, never wholly successful, to overcome the deficiencies of their material, their craft and their own temperament. From this perspective, these writers stand out prominently among their contemporaries by writing effectively enough, consistently enough, to enlist their own negation and self-subversion, their sense of severe artistic limitation, and even their erroneous execution in the service of fictive creation. It is hoped that such a critical assessment can to some extent free their works from the appearances of elitism, mystification and inaccessibility they acquired over the decades. This image has exaggerated the well-disposed reader's difficulties in approaching much of modern fiction;. it has prompted harmful attacks from the Left; and it has led to overstatements of the antagonism between "high modern" writing and the arguably more populist subversive fiction of postmodernity.

Critical attempts to draw broad distinctions between modernist and postmodern writing have commonly implied the monumentality of the former as opposed to the self-subversiveness of the latter. The theoretical work of Ihab Hassan is a conspicuous example of this tendency, seeking to define the contemporary avant-garde by a contrasting exaltation of the modernists. Typical of his view of their eminence is his assertion in the 1970s (repeated recently in *Rumors of Change: Essays of Five Decades* [1995]) that "the spirit of anti-art is foreign to their spirit." Their aesthetic temper, he finds, is characteristically aristocratic and authoritarian in its reaction against cultural decay (112). Opposing two of the most noted writers representing the modernist/postmodern split, he perceives the "quest for a total verbal consciousness in Joyce, the quest for a minimal verbal consciousness in Beckett" (116). (Hugh Kenner anticipated this opposition in his early study *The Stoic Comedians: Flaubert, Joyce and Beckett* [1962]: Joyce's "competence" and "total control" find their counterparts in Beckett's "comedy of incapacity" [106]). In his 1985 article, "The Culture of Postmodernism" (*Theory, Culture and Society* 2/3, 123), Hassan's inclination toward binary opposition of the two movements produces thirty-two pairs of opposing terms to typify them: romanticism and "pataphysics" are followed by form and anti-form, purpose and play, centering and dispersal, transcendence and immanence, creation and decreation, and so forth. Such dualities as these may appear to be considerably less persuasive if they are seen to project images of greatness shaped by the canon-forming standards of the New Criticism. The notion of solitary grandeur—of the transcendent modernist genius—requires the assumption of the "finished" *oeuvre*; thus it excludes the rather more modest estimation of the work as a makeshift assemblage, anti-artistic in its partly conceded defects, truly modern in the traces of a ruinous culture that mark it and constitute much of its author's basic material. Thus circumscribed, the principal modernist compositions are placed in greater continuity with their successors than has usually been recognized.

Richard Ellmann's work on James Joyce is a salient example in American literary criticism of the development of the figure of the modern writer as cultural hero. His critical biography (1959, revised 1982) accomplished Joyce's induction into the modern canon and, indeed, in view of later biographical research on the unpalatable aspects of Joyce's character that Ellmann slights or overlooks, it now reads like a work of secular hagiography. *The Modern Tradition* (1965), which he subsequently edited with Charles Feidelson, gathered some two hundred background texts to serve as bases for theoretical statements about the "untraditional tradition" that Joyce and his contemporaries had brought to a high state of development. Literary modernism thus became further established as a contemporary aesthetic orthodoxy. Its central defining trait was the consciousness of "some sort of historical discontinuity, either a liberation from inherited patterns, or, at another extreme, deprivation and disinheritance." Its exuberant experimentation was heavily weighted by what Henry James called an "imagination of disaster" (vi). In this atmosphere of both emancipation and crisis, modernist writing took on the aspect of a refuge from an incoherent historical reality, and its producers, in large part by inference of the critical attention they drew, were sometimes portrayed as visionary prophets. T.S. Eliot's essay, "*Ulysses*, Order, and Myth" (*Dial*, November 1923), an early instance of such estimation, claims that Joyce's use of myth provides "a way of controlling, of ordering, of giving a shape and a significance to the immense panorama of futility and anarchy which is contemporary history." It takes "a step toward making the modern world possible for art" and does so "in a world which offers very little assistance to that end" (Givens 202–203). Issuing from his saintly isolation—with which Eliot and others identified—Joyce's writing was received as intercession and benediction.

The chapters that follow provide a view of the modernist canon that either counters this heroic image or suggests its qualifying ambiguity. By means of close attention to patterned detail, often latent and sometimes unintended, it examines works of five writers in terms of some limitation, some persistent idiosyncratic technical lapse, or an impulse of self-effacement that their narration discloses. An argument for painstaking textual analysis is thus implied, but in a way that resists the formalist tendency to lavish fetishistic attention on the work of art. The most remarkable technical features of the modernist text—the radically disjointed or associative narrative of *Absalom, Absalom!*, for example, or the bravura monologues in *Ulysses*—are regarded for the greater part simply as imposing craftsmanship that offers little of the subtle conflict to be found in less conspicuous and less impressive places—the misplaced settings of *The Great Gatsby*, for instance, or the inaccurate chronologies of William Faulkner's Civil War fiction. Turning aside for the time being from the modernists' brilliant innovations and bold transgressions, we may see them in less gigantic postures—in their growing sense of belatedness, for example (Harold Bloom's term used without his emphasis on Oedipal confrontation, here and in the chapter on Ernest Hemingway). With the exception of Joseph Conrad, the writers studied here reached maturity in the 1920s, after the foundations of modernist art had been laid (most notably by painters in pre-war France). Their most typical assessment of their own achievement—as the works themselves reveal it—tends accordingly to dispel the idea that their writing was intended in some way to intervene directly in the historical calamity invoked by Henry James's phrase. Rather, to the extent that their writing was conceived and executed, more or less consciously, as *part* of this disaster, the historical situation itself becomes by association paradoxically less significant and more illusory. Unlike the deconstructive view of writers as Quixotic over-reachers caught in a naïve and futile struggle against the conflicting and dissipating forces within their texts, they use subversion as part of the creative process; they are implicated, in a certain sense, in their own works' immolation. Their authority as autonomous creators is thus partly preserved, enabling them to confront the extra-textual disaster of modern history by both reflecting and enveloping it in their writing. Ultimately, the aesthetic and ethical integrity that they retain despite their adverse historical circumstances conveys a measure of redemptive vitality. By means of its inevitable flaws, the modern writer commends his art to the sympathetic reader not as the revelation of a prophet but as the narrative of a survivor.

As modernism abandoned the main literary traditions of the nineteenth century and continued its ascendancy after the Great War, its expressions of a sense of discontinuity with the past gradually ceased to take the form of revolutionary gestures. Its writers typically evolved a style of attentive, stolid reflection on the strange, reversed states of being that anticipate those in Philip Larkin's "Church Going." It is a question worth asking whether the subversive impulses of modernist writers may have arisen largely from their experience of such a vestigial and inverted reality, characterized increasingly by a paradoxical absence of disbelief rather than disbelief itself. To the extent that this is so, their critics should be wary of a tendency to over-state the subsequent affirmative conception of spiritual emptiness as space cleared for creativity.

The conflict between unyielding fact, whether historical or material, and the constructs of the literary imagination was intensified for the modernists by their commitment to a mode of fiction that was anchored in this hollowed-out empirical reality. Their break with the main conventions of novel writing of the eighteenth and nineteenth centuries was to a great extent a rejection of the literalism—the surface realism of journalists and photographers—that had mirrored the complacencies of middle-class life and exposed the plight of the socially abused. What was needed instead was a psychological complexity of fictive analysis that could explore the inwardness of the Self and build a better model for an understanding of its social circumstances. These writers sought, for the greater part, to transfigure the photograph-like recordings of the particular conditions of existence made by novelists more or less closely associated with the naturalist movement, which tended to depreciate the metamorphic energy of the fictive imagination that makes every book, from their anti-naturalist perspective, a "book of changes." James Joyce stated the artistic problem succinctly: "In realism you are down to facts on which the world is based: that sudden reality which smashes romanticism to a pulp" (Power 98), and his friend and advocate, Eugene Jolas, spoke for the opponents of the consequent literary materialism in his "Manifesto: The Revolution of the Word" (1926), declaring, "Narrative is not mere anecdote, but the projection of a metamorphosis of reality" (Ellmann 588). In a similar vein, Virginia Woolf saw the absence of this transformative intimacy as a crippling flaw in the fact-obsessed fiction of Arnold Bennett, H.G. Wells and John Galsworthy, whom she attacked in "Mr. Bennett and Mrs. Brown" (1924): "They have laid enormous stress upon the fabric of things," she charged. "For us those conventions are ruin, those tools are death" (110, 112).

The main difficulties that this aspect of the modernist aesthetic created for writers of fiction stemmed from its lack of clear alternatives to the widely rejected romantic quest for metaphysical reality; and their concessions to factuality were countered by irrationalist currents in the arts such as Dada and various modes of absurdist writing because of the false documentary quality that they believed it imposed on literary style.

Nevertheless, the spirit of compromise with empirical epistemology served to assure a large measure of compatibility between fictional and practical truth-telling and therefore sustained a plausible, chastened reflection of human character and circumstance. One important result was the development of the characteristic technical features of modernist writing, including its resistance to closure, its substitution of discontinuous narrative structures for elaborate plotting and its internalization of consciousness as the principal method of fictive characterization.

This complicated deference to the given-ness of reality in modernist fiction accordingly tends to mask the tensions it creates with a pervading air of plausibility. Conflicts rarely occur in relatively large-scale narrative movements and overt character traits, and they are usually detectable only in patterns of incongruous detail and apparent mistakes whose significance appears to be minor. The familiar dailiness of the main narrative material is commonly marked by traces of the writers' resistance or even outright hostility to a standard of factuality that is in some sense dictated—by dogma, by official history, by social, financial and legal pressures, and by the cultural encrustations of the literary conventions and language they use. An important result of this reaction was the emergence of an intermediate or collateral order of fictional reality in which writers could achieve a plasticity of time and space, at times straining the principle of verisimilitude to a point not of breaking but of indeterminacy resulting from the disfiguring pressures they exerted on it.

The "mistakes" that writers make in deviating from actuality sometimes present a case in point, and this is especially so when these deviations recur as patterned elements resembling leitmotifs. Three of the following chapters demonstrate such patterns: the distorted New York settings of Scott Fitzgerald's fiction; the erroneous history of the Civil War pieced together in the fiction of William Faulkner; and, viewed from a more subjective angle, Ernest Hemingway's apparent misreading or mishandling of literary models he used for his novels. In most cases these contradictions appear to be of little consequence when considered individually, and the critics who have noted them have tended to dismiss them as the kinds of flaws that are probably inevitable in those otherwise masterly creations that have won so much critical approval. In doing so they have passed over opportunities to examine what may in fact be read as coherent structural elements, albeit of an unusual and largely unintended kind. Slips of the pen can add up to more than exposure of a writer's fallibility, and their significance need not necessarily be defined—as they have tended to be—from a clinical or pathological perspective alone.

A useful and unexpected example of a series of apparent errors of this kind appears in *Madame Bovary* (1857), the novel Flaubert called "a world of attentive observations of the most humdrum details" (*Selected Letters* 127). In the second chapter he begins to compose his exceedingly painstaking portrait of Emma by focusing on her most striking feature: "Her real beauty was in her eyes; although they were brown [*bruns*], they seemed black [*noirs*] because of the lashes" (38; Garnier 15). In the numerous descriptions of her eyes that follow, they continue to change colors, appearing in some shade or intensity of either blue or black, depending on the light and on her emotional state, but the original farm girl's brown eyes never recur. Although Flaubert was perhaps being simply accurate in noticing that dark eyes like Emma Bovary's could in actuality appear variously black or dark blue, the extreme chromatic contrasts that he introduced appear at moments to risk outright contradiction. In a late scene a tear forms in her eye "like a raindrop [*l'eau d'un orage*] in a blue flower cup" (289, Garnier 288); earlier, however, "Her eyes had never been so large, so black, nor of such depth. She was transfigured by some subtle change permeating her entire being" (163). Since it is hardly possible that these variations would also extend to brown, the conclusion that Flaubert was being reckless or simply mistaken in a matter of detail seems inescapable without resort to some credible critical alternative. Another look at his eye imagery shows that at times he indicates the color only indirectly or not at all: in one scene, when Emma's lover, Rodolph, makes her cry, her eyes "sparkled like flames under water" (190); and in the next her "indefinable beauty" is expressed thus: "Her eyelids seemed purposely shaped for her long amorous glances, in which the pupils disappeared" (191); in anger "her large flashing eyes" were "clouded by tears" (264); and consummately, horribly, in death, "her eyes were beginning to disappear under a viscous pallor, as if spiders had spun a web over them" (306). The great range of passions expressed visibly by Emma Bovary may finally lead Flaubert's reader to the conclusion that her eyes really have no characteristic color. The physiologically incongruous instance of her brown eyes may dramatize, by an inversion of likelihood, the truly indefinable quality of her beauty—the mysterious, irrational, confusing quality that cannot be pictured except in a cluster of incomplete, paramorphic images.

Just prior to Emma's tearful scene with her lover, Flaubert modulates his voice to convey Rodolph's jaded thoughts, deploring "the eternal monotony of passion, which always assumes the same forms and speaks the same language" (178). He implies that the deficiency lies in the forms and the language and not in the emotions themselves: "The human language is like a cracked kettle on which we beat out a tune for a dancing bear, when we hope with our music to move [*attendrir*] the stars" (188, Garnier 178–79). Introducing a principal reflexive theme of modernism, Flaubert's acknowledgment of the incapacity of language for full emotional expression anticipates later writers' willingness to depart from standards of truthfulness that had themselves become doubtful. In a critique of what he took as the excessive regard for objective truth in Zola's *L'Assomoir*, Flaubert wrote, "To be truthful does not seem to me to be the first requirement for art. The main thing is to aim for beauty and to attain it *if you can* [emphasis added]" (Troyat 296). Elsewhere he declares that the "goal of art . . . is exaltation of some kind" (Troyat 213), again through carefully chosen words warily avoiding overstatement of what words can be expected to achieve.

Flaubert's skepticism about the writer's ambition to overcome the weaknesses of his craft can therefore be understood to arise from his perception that they are to a great extent a function of the language he is forced to use. Subsuming the partly willed errors he commits are the patterns of apparent linguistic breakdown that betray his futility but can also be read constructively as gestures of integrity—of the sincerity of his determination not to overestimate or oversimplify his literary means and achievements. As the following chapters on Conrad and Joyce attempt to show, these patterns demonstrate that language cannot finally sublimate reality. As with its susceptibility to error, a more general vulnerability of literary language calls attention to the writing process as a self-subverting action that reverses expectation, performing virtual acts of erasure, decomposing words to opaque fundamental units, and—ideologically, as postmodern theory has always asserted—exposing the constructedness of established verbal norms, particularly in their claims to authoritative priority.

This is perhaps the most important way the authors of modernist fiction developed a verbal plasticity to convey their vision of a collateral reality that could to some degree resolve the antagonism of the literary materialism of the nineteenth century realists and the spirituality they had virtually excluded. Two recent writers on modernist and postmodern theory, David Nicholls and Paul deMan, have addressed this conflict from the perspective of Charles Baudelaire, whose critical writings they position at the opening of the debate about modernity. Nicholls describes Baudelaire's conception of anti-bourgeois art as a daemonic inversion of the values that led to the ascendancy of realist art. Baudelaire exposes its obsession with the "unceasing reproduction" of commodities that are passed off as perpetually new creations by means of an illusion generated by "the conjunction of greed and inertia" (7). Both Nicholls and deMan refer in particular to Baudelaire's essay, "The Painter of Modern Life" (1859–60), which analyzes a picture of a coach in motion painted by his Dutch contemporary, Constantin Guys. For deMan, Baudelaire's essay anticipates modernity by presenting Guys's picture as a successful attempt "to freeze what is most transient and ephemeral into a recorded image"; because of the ordinariness of the image, it varies radically from the traditional, classical frozen moment: "The painting remains steadily in motion and exists in the open, improvised manner of a sketch that is like a constant new beginning." In this manner it counters the realists' fraudulently imaged reproduction (157–58).

Baudelaire regarded the anti-naturalist styles of sympathetic writers such as Flaubert as weapons attacking the realists' "debased forms of cultural imitation" (Nicholls 20). He saw that poetic language increasingly reflects, and at the same time assails, this debasement as it becomes "a body of inert and reified signs from which the human guarantee of meaning has fled along with the divine" (Nicholls 22). Baudelaire's critique thus introduces the central paradoxes of modernism: it asserts the creativity of negation that transforms hollowed-out cultural forms to the blank pages and white canvases of artistic creation. Corrupted language thus becomes the malleable material that the writer/artist can use to bear witness to, to escape, and to celebrate the self-annulment of aesthetic materialism.

James Joyce's epiphanies, composed at the beginning of this century, are instructive early examples of modernist writing that reflects Baudelaire's and Flaubert's art of continuous resistance to all forms of closure, especially finality of interpretation. They appear at first to do no more than sketch silhouettes of Dublin characters and settings, but it becomes apparent that the social and psychological realities they communicate remain concurrent with but apart from the literal dailiness they record. In the "Eccles Street Epiphany," which Joyce included in *Stephen Hero* (216), Stephen Dedalus walks past one of Dublin's brown brick tenements and overhears a "fragment of colloquy" between a young woman standing on the steps and a young man leaning on the rusty railings:

> The Young Lady—(drawling discreetly) . . . O, yes . . . I was . . . at the . . . cha . . . pel. . . .
> The Young Gentleman— (inaudibly) . . . I . . . (again inaudibly) . . . I. . . .
> The Young Lady—(softly) . . . O . . . but you're . . . ve . . . ry . . . wick . . . ed. . . .

The young woman's coy manner makes it questionable whether she has truly been at the chapel—or been there in good faith—and the young man's muffled response to her explanation of her movements intensifies the doubtful mood she sets, tingeing it with an unascertainable wickedness. The recorded facts of the scene are so vestigial that they cannot be lodged in any final, static composition; on the contrary, they are drawn into a subversive process that continuously preserves the epiphany from the interpretive finality of rhetorically crystallized metaphor. The fluidity thus achieved provides an aesthetic quality that is essentially different from the perceived stillness of the "timeless moment" or "moment of being." It seeks no transcendence, no sense of "arrival" (the term "epiphany" can be misleading in this respect), nothing like an apotheosis; rather, it confers consciousness of liberated motion among the objects of perception which, like the couple in the epiphany, are capable of no such movement when portrayed in their paralytic condition from a conventionally realistic perspective. The image juxtaposing their liberation and their entrapment is paradigmatic of the modernist writer's resistance to forms of oppression through a permanent and inclusive refusal.

The unarticulated dialogue of the young couple in Joyce's epiphany does not, on the other hand, yield the infinity of interpretations that postmodern theorists tend to see as being potentially generated by all literary texts. In an unusually intrusive rhetorical moment he indicates that the woman is standing "on the steps of one of those brown brick houses which seem the very incarnation of Irish paralysis"; and so the scene is clearly presented in the light of a socially problematic, specifically Irish condition, defined approximately by the unsettling juxtaposition of "chapel" and "wicked." Joyce therefore retains control of the referential energy of his material by verbally delimiting the range of admissible readings. The relatively broad latitude of interpretation that remains does not lead to a radical indeterminacy—the postmodern "perpetual flight of the subject"; nor is the disfiguration that enters this process—the largely inaudible dialogue of the "Eccles Street Epiphany," for example—fairly characterized as a symptom of the inevitable falseness of the products of the literary imagination. It is true, of course, that the modernists' rejection of imposed interpretive conclusions to their texts can lead to regressive states of incommunication, as parts of Joyce's *Finnegans Wake* or Ezra Pound's *Cantos* illustrate abundantly. Moreover, the ironic stance of the writer as a creator by negation can lead to an overwhelming destructiveness, as it did in some of the anarchical extremes of Dada, or in the futuristic exaltation of kinetic violence. At the core of the modernist movement, however, constructive purposes translate its subversiveness into the fundamental impulses of mental emancipation. This is the "exaltation" that Flaubert wrote of as the goal of art. In *Jean Santeuil* Proust calls it as the "transmutation of memory, into a reality directly felt" (408). The Russian formalist critics, in many respects originators of modernist theory, saw in the literary arts the power to reintroduce a rich strangeness to a habituated, dictated sense of reality, to "de-familiarise" it through distortion, divergence, deviation from the norm, through "creative deformation" (Erlich 176–80). Finally, Virginia Woolf, a principal witness of the modern, wrote in *A Room of*

One's Own (1929) that the artist's transforming mind becomes "incandescent" in "the prodigious effort of freeing whole and entire the work that is in him" (56).

The discussions of the five writers that follow attempt to give some sense of their careers as they reveal changing attitudes toward the subversive function of their writing. Since a comprehensive treatment of their work would have produced a far longer work, with perhaps only moderate substantive enrichment, each chapter focuses the discussion on two or three novels or short stories, most of them landmarks in the critical history of their authors' achievements. They have been chosen from the many authors who might just as well have represented the modernist canon at its supposed peak of verbal competence. Joseph Conrad serves as a representative of the precursors of modernist writing in English, and James Joyce as one of its principle founders. The three Americans then demonstrate in related ways the culmination of this subversive period. All Caucasian, all male, they reveal in the infirmities of their art a less imperious patriarchal authority than has often been alleged. The central argument implies continuously, by discovery, that the main currents of British, Irish and American modernist writing would have flowed in very different directions and with considerably less power had its authors lacked the fundamental will to transgress and decompose all forms of oppression and injustice. It attempts, moreover, to define points of resolution of the ideological contention that has embroiled modernist aesthetics over the past two decades. The central issues of this controversy have coalesced around its writers' perceived aestheticization of historical realities by mystifying their intentions and meanings, making fetishes of their works and reputations, and otherwise manipulating critical response from the vantage of male authority.

Most vocal among critics who have participated in this attack is Terry Eagleton, who states his position characteristically in his chapter titled "Capitalism, Modernism and Postmodernism":

> The modernist work brackets off the referent or real historical world, thickens its textures and deranges its forms to forestall instant consumability, and draws its own language protectively around it to become a mysteriously autotelic object, free of all contaminating truck with the real. Brooding self-reflexively on its own being, it distances itself through irony from the shame of being no more than a brute, self-identical thing. (139)

To the extent that Eagleton's critique can be referred to individual cases, it is not only persuasive but it also poses difficulties for their defenders by implying—accurately, in essence—that the modernist writers were often conscious of the defensive proclivities for which they have been assailed.

As the following chapters seek to demonstrate, their representative works betray a susceptibility to various forms of emotional and ideological regression. The affirmative impulses that prompted their subversion of dogmatic cultural forms were liable to diversion toward historical nostalgia and reaction, and they were in some instances blocked by racism and misogyny based—particularly in Joyce's case—on an unsublimated infantile association of language and matter. By referring to the pained self-awareness arising from these and other artistic shortcomings as "shame," however, Eagleton associates his argument with those that tend to confine the debate to questions of self-seeking motivation and therefore pass over opportunities to explore the range of meaning that may be perceived in the modernists' self-critical, reflexive irony. The deficiencies of their art are evident both in the sense of personal limitation that they express in producing it and in their consciousness of intractable historical realities. It is this conflicting sense of the artistic Self that results in an alertness to the unanswered questions of identity that history poses and concedes the indeterminacy of those states of being that might one day realize social justice.

CHAPTER ONE

Joseph Conrad's Blank Maps:
The Art of Inversion

In the introduction to J. A. Hammerton's *Countries of the World* that Joseph Conrad wrote a few months before his death in 1924, he looks back over his writing career and recalls the English explorers' books that first stirred his literary imagination. When he was ten he discovered Leopold McClintock's *The Voyage of the Fox in the Arctic Seas* (1857), an account of the doomed attempt to rescue the expedition led by Sir John Franklin in his search for the Northwest Passage. Not only did this work give Conrad the notion of some day composing his own adventure tales, but it also sparked his life long interest in English exploration and what he calls its "militant geography." Reprinted posthumously as "Geography and Some Explorers" in *Last Essays* (1926), this brief memoir reveals that his desire to write fiction derived less from the exploits of characters in the novels he read as a boy than from the histories of the people who entered and mapped regions of the world where Europeans had never been. Since his childhood was passed in the years of the exploration of Lake Tanganyika and Victoria Nyanza in eastern Africa, he was particularly drawn to the achievements of those who led the way there—gigantic figures such as Mungo Park, Richard Burton and David Livingstone. In the light of their accomplishments Conrad even acquired a personal sense of identity as "a contemporary of the Great Lakes." He kept his childhood faith in these pathfinders' idealism throughout his life, insisting even near the end that their "only object was the search for truth." "The great spirit of the realities of the story" of their accomplishments, he adds, "sent [him] off on the romantic explorations of [his] inner self." They appealed powerfully to the "romantic feeling of reality" which he characterized in a note to *Within the Tides* (1915) as an "inborn faculty" that "in itself may be a curse, but, when disciplined by a sense of personal responsibility and a recognition of the hard facts of existence shared with the rest of mankind, becomes but a point of view from which the very shadows of life appear endowed with an internal glow" (vii-viii).

Much of "Geography and Some Explorers" is cast in this elevated style, recalling the romantic effusions of Conrad's early fiction. He envisions the legendary "landsmen investigators . . . each bearing in his breast a spark of the sacred fire," a rhetorical echo of a passage near the opening of *Heart of Darkness,* written a quarter-century earlier (1902), in which the narrator evokes those same "messengers of the might within the land, bearers of a spark from the sacred fire" (29). As he turns to his own experience in Africa, however, he assumes a sober manner more reflective of "the hard facts of existence." He reconstructs the moment in September 1890 on the Upper Congo near Stanley Falls when he experienced the "unholy recollection of a prosaical newspaper 'stunt' and the distasteful knowledge of the vilest scramble for loot that ever disfigured the history of human conscience and geographical exploration. What an end to the idealized realities of a boy's daydreams!" This outburst was provoked by what he had witnessed of the commercial exploitation of the Congo Basin of equatorial Africa in the aftermath of the expeditions led by Henry Morton Stanley, whose second much-publicized adventure on the Congo had concluded in the previous year. Stanley first won international African fame in 1871 by publicizing an image of himself as the rescuer of the Scottish missionary David Livingstone, who was presumed lost among the Great Lakes in his quest for the source of the Nile. Although Stanley actually found that Livingstone considered himself neither lost nor in need of deliverance, he persisted nonetheless in portraying himself as his savior in *How I Found Livingstone* (1872). His activities during the following two decades in what came to be called the "Congo Free State," now the Democratic Republic of the Congo, were always motivated in part by the quest for celebrity in connection with colonialist schemes that had played a central role in the Livingstone episode. Chief among these later exploits were, first, the expedition from 1874 to 1877, which made Stanley the first white man to descend the Upper Congo. The subsequent expedition from 1887 to 1889 was similar to the Livingstone mission in its professed intent to bring relief to a notable and reportedly imperiled figure—in this instance Emin Pasha, the governor of the Anglo-Egyptian "Equatorial Province of Egypt," historical antecedent to the present Republic of the Sudan. Emin had been isolated near Lake Albert by a Mahdist rebellion, but, as had been the case with Livingstone, his plight was hardly the dire emergency that Stanley's publicity had declared. This unheroic actuality notwithstanding, Stanley again succeeded in casting himself as a rescuer on his return to Europe. By the closing years of the century, however, when Conrad wrote his principal African story, *Heart of Darkness,* the venal motives and brutal methods condoned by Stanley and his sponsors in the Congo, including his employer, King Leopold II of Belgium, had been widely exposed, giving rise in the West to the kind of disillusionment and indignation that Conrad expressed at Stanley Falls.

The corruption of greatness is the central tragic theme of Conrad's fiction. H. M. Stanley figured prominently in his imagination as he drew his portraits in *Heart of Darkness* of the corrupters of what he persisted in seeing as the great tradition of African exploration. Stanley's leading role in this sorrowful history can be inferred from the depiction of the aging Livingstone in "Geography and Some Explorers." Although Conrad calls him "the most venerated perhaps of all the objects of my early geographical enthusiasm," he concedes that Livingstone's stature declined as his later years brought him into the era of far less subtle colonialist intrusion. His quest for the headwaters of the Nile, beginning in Conrad's adulatory estimation as a heroic enterprise, eventually deteriorated to an obsessive "passion [that] changed him in his last days from a great explorer into a restless wanderer refusing to go home any more." Like the portraits of high-minded, romantic adventurers of Conrad's fiction, his image of Livingstone as the triumphant revealer of unknown worlds becomes dimmed and disfigured by the vague impulses of modernity. They particularly recall Kurtz in *Heart of Darkness,* the erstwhile idealist whom Marlow envisions as "this wandering and tormented thing . . . the lone white man turning his back suddenly on the headquarters, on relief, on thoughts of home—perhaps; setting his face towards the depths of the wilderness" (107, 64). Although Conrad does not appear to suggest that Stanley's exploits had any direct bearing on Livingstone's decline, he evidently held the view of many of his contemporaries that Stanley was mainly responsible for confusing "militant geography" with armed aggression. As the historian Felix Driver puts it, Stanley's critics saw him as "everything that Livingstone was not . . . Stanley's famous encounter with Livingstone at Ujiji in 1871 might . . . be seen as a moment of transition: the old imperialism giving way to the new" (165–66).

Although Conrad's sorrow over such devolutions of the heroic world that his youthful imagination had conceived is plainly evident in these images of Stanley and Livingstone, the complexity of feeling that shapes his writing about them has not been fully examined. Neither nostalgia for the romance of boyhood nor righteous anger at the Europeans' brutality can be said to dominate the tone of *Heart of Darkness.* Satirical derision— unmistakable, for example, in Conrad's portrait of the greed-besotted "pilgrims" of the "Eldorado Exploring Expedition"—is an equally inadequate characterization of his critique, which was tempered by his rather credulous faith in the putative civilizing potential of Europe's colonialist "idea." *Heart of Darkness* departs markedly from Conrad's romantic manner of narrating travel adventures in other early works such as *The Nigger of the Narcissus* (1898) and *Youth* (1902). Its authorial tone can be characterized most accurately as that of the parodist, whose method is based on ironic formal imitation and distortion but whose critical stance is less specific and topical than a political satirist's would normally be. The main objects of Conrad's parody were, in this case, Stanley's two books on his Congo expeditions, *Through the Dark Continent* (1878) and *In Darkest Africa* (1890). In *Heart of Darkness* he constructs an extended literary analogue that not only attempts to discredit Stanley's reports of his African adventures by means of a deflating parallel narrative, but seeks to erase them imaginatively. Through this process of fictive reversal, inversion and even obliteration, Conrad's novel radically recomposes the fictions that Stanley had foisted off on an unsuspecting public as history; but it does so at a price. Its negations entail so much un-naming and un-making, such hollowing out and silencing, that the narrative tends to reduce itself to a ruinous simulacrum of the texts it confronts. As the discussion of *Under Western Eyes* (1910) later in this chapter demonstrates, Conrad extends this inverting process to the point where the text and its narrator are mired in incompetence. A key early-modernist trait of these novels is that they exhibit the identifying symptoms of the contagions they encounter and therefore cease to figure simply as triumphant expressions of revolt. They take on the additional aspect of verbal failure caused by real and inevitable deficiencies that the author must nonetheless contrive to enlist in the service of his art.

As a historian, Stanley was a more important and more difficult target for Conrad than the easily parodied fiction of colonialist writers such as Rudyard Kipling and H. Rider Haggard. Jacques Darras has observed that Conrad's European empire is "Kipling's world turned upside down and inside out, a world where all roads no longer lead to Rome" (62); and Brian Spittles shows how *Heart of Darkness* undermines the popular subgenre of the "rescue novel" that shaped English readers' view of Africa in such popular works as Haggard's *King Solomon's Mines* (1885) (81). As false as their imperial worlds were, it was Stanley's writing that offered Conrad the most immediate and vivid examples of the colonialist idea corrupted. Ian Watt suggests that "to create a character who revealed the brutal discrepancy between the colonising ideal and the reality, Conrad needed no other historical model than the two founders of the Congo Free State, Leopold and Stanley. . . . Stanley is probably of central importance, though not so much as a basis for the character Kurtz as for the moral atmosphere in which he was created" (145).

Although Conrad's experiences during his employment by a Belgian trading concession on the Congo River in 1890 are the primary factual bases for the main story he tells in *Heart of Darkness*, they match Stanley's in so many respects that it is often impossible to distinguish clearly between his fictionalized autobiography and his parody of his famous precursor's books. Because Conrad's novel appears to reflect his interpretation of his own African experience as something of a formal parody of Stanley's— even, at moments, as a travesty of it—it would be useful to detail their parallel adventures at some length.

With respect to biographical fact, his work for the *Société Anonyme pour le Commerce du Haut-Congo* took him to many of the scenes that Stanley was the first white man to see. There must have been many moments when Conrad sensed that his introduction to Africa was but a negligible re-enactment of the feats of the celebrated explorer. He heard Stanley's African moniker, Bula Matari—the Rock Smasher—uttered wherever he went, whether in Africa or in Europe; it seemed to be on everyone's lips and in every newspaper. Even as he rushed between London and Brussels in hasty preparation for his departure from Bordeaux for the Congo in early May 1890, excited reports of Stanley's return to Belgium and of his hero's reception at Dover only days earlier were still in the air. On April 28 the *London Times* reported his "triumphal entry into Antwerp" three days before; there he assured the Belgians that the "destinies of the Dark Continent" were in their hands, and he "drank to work and progress" in the Congo. The next day he sailed from Ostend amid jubilation, "every ship being draped with flags, and the quays . . . lined with people." *The Spectator* extravagantly but typically compared Stanley's march toward Emin Pasha to Xenophon's journey to extricate the Ten Thousand Greeks—thrilling sentiments of the sort that Conrad, with his romantic "inborn faculty," would have hardly resisted in any event, and least of all in these moments when his own adventure was getting under way. He cannot have missed or ignored the commotion on both sides of the Channel and in the press. A year later, in retrospect, it may well have seemed to him that he had been cruelly set up for the disappointments that awaited him.

Even though the Belgians were well-established on the Congo by 1890, the river route was still the only approach to the company's furthest inland trading station at Stanleyville. Conrad's itinerary was therefore essentially identical to Stanley's three years earlier. Like his precursor (but moving in opposite directions), Conrad sailed to Boma, the capital, near the mouth of the Congo, and continued by steamer to the head of navigation at Matadi, about one hundred miles inland. Because the next 220-mile stretch descends through a series of cataracts, Conrad and his party had to advance on foot (Stanley had ridden on a pack animal) for the difficult trek to Leopoldville, the depot near Kinshasa on Stanley Pool, now Malebo Pool. From this point at the western end of the navigable thousand-mile reach of the Upper Congo, the trading company's steamers took them deep into the Congo Basin. They reached Stanley Falls on September 1. (In the Emin Pasha expedition Stanley, also proceeding upstream, had left the Congo route 120 miles below Stanleyville, following the tributary Aruwimi River eastward toward Emin's camp.)

At the principal ports on the Lower Congo, Conrad would have witnessed scenes of disorder, ruin and misery. Consequences of the Belgians' virtual enslavement of native and imported laborers, many of them seriously ill, were visible everywhere. Also, because of the poor communications with Kinshasa, large quantities of freight had piled up and rotted at Boma and Matadi. The wagon roads that Stanley had started to build above Boma in 1879 had been poorly maintained, and the railroad line that he had been chartered to build in 1887 had not even been surveyed (Kimbrough 116). Finally, to greatly dim Conrad's prospects for employment, disturbing rumors about the condition of the steamers at Leopoldville were circulating in Matadi: "Bad news from up the river," he wrote in his diary on July 29. "All the steamers disabled—one wrecked" (Kimbrough 115). When he arrived there more than a month later, Conrad took little comfort in discovering that the rumors had exaggerated the problem. The steamer he had been hired to command, the *Florida*, was in fact badly broken down and had been towed to Kinshasa for repairs (Karl 293). This unlucky turn of events led before long to a break in Conrad's already impaired relations with his employers, effectively spoiling his chances for further work on the Congo. He nonetheless accompanied them on the *Roi des Belges*, presumably to study the river in anticipation of the return of the *Florida* to service on the same route. The principal goal of the two-month voyage from Leopoldville to Stanleyville, however, was to bring back one of their ivory traders, Georges Antoine Klein, who was incapacitated by dysentery. Klein died on the way back to Leopoldville. Conrad actually commanded the boat for ten days during its captain's illness on the trip downstream, but he had evidently concluded by this time that his employment with the company was soon to end. The final and crowning misery of the trip was an attack of the tropical disease that would eventually force him to end his career as a ship's captain.

The damage that had disabled the *Florida* had occurred in the mere three years since its hull had been launched at Kinshasa. This for Conrad must have seemed a particularly dismal instance of the ruinous forces hard at work on the Congo. He would nevertheless have appreciated the ironic discovery that the abuse of his boat had begun at the hands of the Rock Smasher himself even before its engine had been installed. When Stanley arrived with his huge expedition at Stanley Pool in 1887 and found none of the state's steamers in serviceable condition, he simply commandeered others owned by the trading company or by the missionaries stationed there (Hall 295). These included even the powerless *Florida*, which he ordered either towed behind his own boat or lashed to it to serve as a sort of barge for transporting his bearers and supplies (*In Darkest Africa* I, 95). With its direct bearing on crucial moments in Conrad's life and career, this typical instance of Stanley's aggressive methods illustrated the realities that mocked Conrad's romantic preconceptions about the Europeans' incursions into Africa.

On his return to Europe at the end of the year, Conrad found that the ruthlessness that Stanley and his associates tried to dignify as firm measures taken in the interests of establishing order in the "Congo Free State" had been exposed extensively by journalists. The celebrations that had taken place as Conrad was about to leave for the Congo had given way to angry controversy. According to the historian Iain Smith, Stanley's African expeditions and those that followed were viewed increasingly as "huge quasi-military affairs backed by powerful commercial interests, and their progress resembled that of an invading army" (297). (Stanley armed both Congo expeditions heavily, even carrying a Maxim machine gun in 1887 [Bierman 269]). According to this increasingly dim view, Smith concludes, they accounted for "the decline and disappearance of the romantic Victorian conception of exploring expeditions led by high-minded Europeans through unknown continents" (299). The benign popular image of David Livingstone, fixed in the public mind as the noble altruist, pressing on through East Africa with his walking stick and his Bible, was giving way to something closer to the grotesquely parodic "pilgrims" who assault the wilderness with their staves and Winchesters in *Heart of Darkness* (80). Written near the end of a decade of controversy, Conrad's African story clearly reflects the revised thinking of the time; as a work of the imagination, moreover, it seeks to penetrate further the darkness of Europe's colonialist ventures.

Conrad's narrating character Charlie Marlow tells of his own parallel journey (41–90): he sails to the mouth of the great river and to the "seat of the government," with its infernal disorder, then to the "Company Station" thirty miles upstream. There he joins a caravan for the 200-mile trek to the "Central Station" where the river again becomes navigable. Following repairs to the steamer that he finds sunk there, Marlow departs with his passengers on the two-month journey to Kurtz's "Inner Station." Apart from this identical itinerary, few of the dramatic episodes of Marlow's journey to Kurtz's station can be traced with any certainty or even probability to Conrad's days on the Congo. The illness and death of Kurtz are clearly based in part on Georges Antoine Klein's last days (Kurtz is even called Klein in the manuscript of 1898–99 [Baines 117]), but Conrad's personal experiences appear otherwise to have provided little more than the broad outline and a few incidental details for the story Marlow tells. For example, according to Conrad's *Congo Diary*, his caravan came across the decomposing body of a tribesman who had been shot on the road to Kinshasa, an episode related briefly and without substantial alteration by Marlow. He also echoes notations in the *Diary* such as the descriptions of abandoned villages and ruined countryside along the river, or the constant worry about snags in the river channels. Otherwise, there is no evidence of extraordinary incidents of any kind during Conrad's voyage, nor were any to be expected. By the time of his arrival the Congo was already a familiar route for many travelers and had ceased in most respects to resemble Stanley's murky, violent world. Norman Sherry draws out the contrasts between Conrad's story and his actual experience:

> Disentangling fact from fiction in the actual journey up-river, we are left not with a mysterious and dangerous journey into the unknown and the primitive during which the passengers are beset by an ignorant greed for ivory, and the captain, Marlow, is the isolated and dedicated workman intent on the immediate difficulties of his job, but with a routine, highly organized venture along a fairly frequented riverway linking quite numerous settlements of trading posts and factories, and with a number of competent and busy men on board, and with Conrad there to learn the route under the guidance of a skilled captain. (71)

The commercialization of Stanley's Africa had been in progress for more than a decade; some fifty Belgian trading stations as well as a number of mission settlements had spread along the entire length of the Upper Congo (Kimbrough 108). The hostile tribes living on its shores had been pacified by "treaties" or otherwise subdued, driven away or destroyed. Accordingly, Conrad drew in large measure on the pristine, unexplored and far more perilous Congo of Stanley's books as the models for most of the more dramatic events and their settings in *Heart of Darkness*. The most overt result of this is, of course, an exciting narrative; but instead of using Stanley merely as a quarry for vivid material, Conrad achieves an intensely ironic evocation of that world as a powerful counter to the one Stanley had depicted. A trading post that Marlow sees on the river bank, for example— an emblem of Stanley's exploits—consists of nothing but a "tumbledown hovel . . . clinging to the skirts of the unknown" as if in infantile helplessness; the white men stationed there have "the appearance of being held there captive by a spell" (67–68). Here and elsewhere, Marlow's rendition of Stanley's Congo invariably suggests transience, breakdown, futility and imminent flight. Everywhere Progress is being reversed by the pre-colonial vitality of the wilderness as it resists the Europeans' encroachment.

Marlow tends accordingly to reduce the ordeals of the kind that Stanley endured hardily to instances of vanity or banality or simple, issueless misery. A telling instance of this reductive process appears in his reactions to the "Eldorado Exploring Expedition" (61–66), in many respects, including its grandiose name, a caricature of Stanley's out-size caravans. Marlow observes its arrival at the Central Station, where he waits irritably for a shipment of rivets to repair his boat: "Instead of rivets there came an invasion, an infliction, a visitation. It came in sections during the next three weeks, each section headed by a white man riding a pack animal and wearing fresh clothing and tan shoes, bowing from that elevation to the impressed pilgrims." This passage recalls descriptions of the Emin Pasha Expedition, which at its outset included more than 800 people stretched out over four miles in a succession of columns led by the Europeans on donkeys and mules. Stanley rode grandly foremost on a henna-stained mule caparisoned in silver (Hall 299), his dress impeccable and unvarying— Norfolk jacket, knickerbockers, high-topped peaked cap and gleaming hip boots (Bierman 272). The personal appearance of the Eldorado Exploring Expedition's leader also caricatures Stanley: he is short and fat and gesticulates with a "short flipper of an arm"—a rendition of contemporary accounts of Stanley's public appearances that commonly describe him with tactful terms such as "thickset" and "stocky." He speaks with Stanley's much-emulated gruff *basso*, a "heavy rumble" peppered with hoarse grunts and growls. The huge quantity of supplies that Marlow sees on the bearers' backs includes "a lot of tents, camp-stools, tin boxes, white cases, brown bales." The list is drawn from the tons of luxuries, including delicacies from the London provisioner Fortnum and Mason (Bierman 269), that Stanley had vainly hoped would keep his party comfortable. For Marlow they are nothing but "the loot of innumerable outfit shops and provision stores . . . an inextricable mess of things decent in themselves but that human folly made look like spoils of thieving." He characterizes the members of the Expedition as "quarrelsome," "sulky," and "disorderly"; their conversation is "the talk of sordid buccaneers":

> It was reckless without hardihood, greedy without audacity, and cruel without courage; there was not an atom of foresight or of serious intention in the whole batch of them, and they did not seem aware these things are wanted for the work of the world. To tear treasure out of the bowels of the land was their desire, with no more moral purpose at the back of it than there is in burglars breaking into a safe. (61)

While Marlow's indignant contempt may seem gratuitous or excessive, or merely peevish, the language he uses suggests his deep-seated desire to eradicate the very idea of the Eldorado Exploring Expedition, confirming the insubstantiality of such a "fantastic invasion" (65). Not content with his exposure of their very evident hypocrisy, their vicious motives, and their fraudulent pretentions—even in their greed and their brutality they are deficient—he is drawn toward images of their obliteration. Their lack of foresight entails equally a lack of hindsight, and they have no conception of the void that both precedes and awaits them as they blunder through the jungle. As the column lurches forward again, it "went into the patient wilderness, that closed upon it as the sea closes over a diver"; nothing more is heard of it, except that "news came that all the donkeys were dead" (66), literally bringing the leaders down from their deluded eminence toward the hollowness of non-being.

Marlow's account of his agonizing difficulties in getting his steamer repaired and then surviving the attack on it below Kurtz's station provides further instances of Conrad's method of drawing on Stanley's Congo books and muting their triumphant tone as he did so. When the Emin Pasha Expedition reached the Congo in March 1887, Stanley was greeted, as Conrad was to be, by reports that the Belgians' state-owned steamboats at Stanley Pool were all disabled. The "Stanley" itself was said to be "a perfect ruin" because "the fool of a captain ran her on shore" and "not one steamer is in service. They are all drawn up on the banks for repairs, which will take months" (*In Darkest Africa* I, 75). Although the actual condition of the boats was not as bad as rumors had led Stanley to believe, again anticipating Conrad's experience, Conrad confirmed them in *Heart of Darkness* by drawing on Stanley's account of a later incident when the hull of the "Stanley" is pierced in four places by rocks upstream from Leopoldville. Stanley notes that "several rivets [were] knocked out and others loosened," but since these could not be replaced, bolts were used to secure new plates cut from oil drums. As the repairs to Stanley's boat proceed, he watches the engineer who directs the crew "up to his waist in water" (I, 103), anticipating Marlow's foreman, who "had to crawl in the mud under the bottom of the steam-boat" (42). When Marlow arrives at the Company Station and finds his command "at the bottom of the river," he reacts with Stanley's exasperated language: he finds the affair "too stupid" for words, the bungling of "some volunteer skipper" (30). The extensive repairs, which "took some months" (30) after the wreck had been "hauled up on the slope like a carcass of some big river animal" (38), were required because "they tore the bottom out of her on stones" (30). "We had plates that would do, but nothing to fasten them with" (40). Just as Stanley characterizes one of the expedition's least reliable steamers, the "Peace," as "good-for-nothing" when it repeatedly slows to a near halt as it loses steam pressure and emits "asthmatic" gasps, so Marlow's is often on the verge of breaking down—"when the steam-pipes started leaking we crawled very slow" (50)—and finally does so on the return trip (110). Although Marlow's infinite worry about the steamer in *Heart of Darkness* may possibly reflect actualities aboard the *Roi des Belges,* the *Congo Diary* says nothing about them, and it is far more likely that Conrad relied on Stanley's descriptions of his ailing vessels.

Through the Dark Continent was evidently Conrad's main source for the natives' attack on Marlow's boat as it approaches Kurtz's station. As Stanley's original expedition made its way down the Upper Congo, it was involved, by his reckoning, in no fewer than thirty-two violent clashes with tribesmen. Each of their attacks with spears and arrows, some poisoned, was repelled with rifle fire. (Marlow anachronistically observes "a deuce of a lot of smoke" from the Winchester rifles fired by his passengers [80]. Since smokeless gunpowder had been introduced in 1885 and would have been in general use on the Congo by the time of Conrad's arrival, the image can be presumed to be drawn from *Through the Dark Continent,* in which Stanley's men were armed with the old Snider rifles that were fired with black powder [*Through the Dark Continent* II, 178–79].) Similarly, both Stanley and Marlow report a "shower" of arrows as an assault begins (II, 222; 66), and in one of these, ten of Stanley's men are killed and their bodies are disposed of in the river "to prevent them becoming food for the cannibals." These are Marlow's means and reason for disposing of his helmsman's body; he is killed by a spear that pierces him "in the side just below the ribs" (66, 74), again evidently echoing Stanley's report of the death of one of his Zanzibaris from a spear wound in the abdomen (II, 262). Drums repeatedly signal the approach of the strangers in both works, and both record the shouts and wailing of the natives along the shore.

In order to dramatize the brooding power of the Congo wilderness, Conrad paid particularly close attention to Stanley's accounts of the more remote and unknown regions he passed through. These included not only the Upper Congo but also the huge Ituri rain forest of the upper Aruwimi and Ituri Rivers—the last large unexplored territory in central Africa— each first described in Stanley's Congo books. Conrad's childhood fascination with such uncharted areas as these are reflected in Marlow's impulse to "lose [him]self in all the glories of exploration" by imaginatively entering the blank spaces on the maps he studied. Equatorial Africa was the greatest of these, "the biggest, the most blank, so to speak—that I had a hankering after" (11). As Stanley prepared to set out for the Upper Congo, he used similar language, recorded in *Through the Dark Continent*: "Something strange must surely lie in the vast space occupied by total blankness on our maps . . . this enormous void is about to be filled up. Blank as it is, it has a singular fascination for me. Never has white paper possessed such a charm for me as this has, and I have already mentally peopled it . . . all in the imagination . . ." (II, 145, 195). At moments he sounds a note of foreboding that also anticipates Marlow:

> What forbidding aspect had the Dark Unknown which confronted us! I could not comprehend in the least what lay before us. Even the few names which I had heard from the Arabs conveyed no definite impression to my understanding. What were . . . . such uncouth names to me? They conveyed no idea, and signified no object; they were barren names of either countries, villages, or peoples, involved in darkness, savagery, ignorance, and fable. (II, 127)

Marlow also comments crudely on the "farcical names" of the coastal African trading villages (20) and shares Stanley's imageless sense of the interior and the man he is being sent to rescue: "What was in there? I could see a little ivory coming out from there, and I had heard Mr Kurtz was in there. I had heard enough about it, too—God knows! Yet somehow it didn't bring any image with it . . . He was just a word for me. I did not see the man in the name any more than you do" (38–39).

The style of Stanley's chapter in *In Darkest Africa* on his journey up the Aruwimi and through the Ituri forest frequently anticipates the lyrical anthropomorphic manner that Marlow assumes when he tries to express the strange moods of the river and the profuse vegetation on its banks. In Stanley's view, the enormous trees resemble "stately kings" who project an "eerie strangeness. . . . It was as if we stood amid the inhabitants of another world . . . massive and colossal" (II, 81); and in one of the dispatches that Stanley sent back from the expedition of 1874, he renders a Manyema forest also as a kind of alien kingdom of "forest monarchs":

> my mind . . . felt overwhelmed by the scene. . . . I gradually felt myself affected more strongly than can be described by the deathly stillness, in the middle of which appeared those majestic, lofty, naked and gray figures, like so many silent apparitions. . . . The atmosphere seemed weighted with an eloquent, though dumb, history, wherein I read, heard, saw and inhaled the record of lost years and lands. For the time I dropped all remembrances of self and identity—all perception of other scenes and reposes. . . . They appeared to say, 'Go and tell your kind you have seen silence.' (*Despatches* 337)

Such passages as these prefigure Marlow's characteristic manner during the trip toward Kurtz on the steamer—"this grimy fragment of another world"—carrying him away from familiar realities:

> Going up that river was like travelling back to the earliest beginnings of the world, when vegetation rioted on the earth and the big trees were kings. . . . you thought

yourself bewitched and cut off for ever from everything you had known once—
somewhere—far away—in another existence perhaps. We were wanderers on
prehistoric earth, on an earth that wore the aspect of an unknown planet. (66)

While it is apparent that this passage exposes Conrad's penchant for
romantic stereotypes of the African Great Unknown, its emphasis on a
quality of alien encroachment serves his parodic intention as well. As
intruders, the "wanderers" forecast their eventual expulsion.

Despite Stanley's elaborate preparations, both Congo expeditions were
beset by illness, injury, starvation and death. Although these hardships
nearly cost him his life on repeated occasions, no matter how desperate his
circumstances became, his writing never betrays the fear of total and
helpless envelopment that seizes Conrad's characters. Indeed, Stanley's
dogged optimism and his capacity for denial of alarming probabilities are
almost always at his service, as, for example, when he tries to imagine the
reality of those blank spaces on his maps representing areas he is about to
enter in *Through the Dark Continent*: "I see us gliding down by tower and
town, and my mind will not permit a shadow of doubt . . ." (II, 195).
Characteristically, "tower and town" supply him with the soothing
European frame of reference to which he resorts whenever the Unknown
becomes too menacing; and rousing slogans like 'Victory or death!' come
to his aid reflexively at such difficult moments. Although he candidly
concedes that his first journey to the Congo is a "desperate" undertaking,
he takes comfort in the idea that its object "is to flash a torch of light across
the western half of the Dark Continent"; and even though that huge expanse
is largely unknown and full of perils, Stanley is braced by the conviction
that "our purpose is lofty" (11, 127). The river, full of snags and
wandering channels, flowing past cannibal villages, and reverberating with
angry drums, is nonetheless a "broad watery avenue cleaving the Unknown
to some sea, like a path of light" (II, 148). He remembers the positive
mood he found himself in on New Year's Day 1877 after a horrendous
year on the Congo: "my heart, oblivious to the dark and evil days we had
passed, resolutely closed itself against all dismal forebodings, and reveled
in the exquisite stillness of the uninhabited wilderness" (II, 209–10). Even
as Stanley and his party, reduced by dysentery and malnutrition to "hideous
bony frames . . . hollow-eyed, sallow, and gaunt, unspeakably miserable in
aspect . . ." (II, 425, 435), are near collapse as they stagger toward their
goal at Matadi, he never appears to flag in his faith in the success of his
conquest of Africa. When supplies are sent out to him by the white traders
there, he receives them as confirmation of that faith: "Never did gaunt
Africa appear so unworthy and despicable before my eyes as now, when
imperial Europe rose before my delighted eyes and showed her boundless
treasures of life, and blessed me with her stores" (II, 458). After three

years in the interior, he is "dazzled" by "the immaculate purity" of the Europeans' clothes (compare Marlow's amazement at the perfect grooming of the company's chief accountant [45–46]). He concludes *Through the Dark Continent* metaphorically with an overview of his journey as a grand procession—divinely assisted—away from Atlantic civilization and back again, with the African continent itself standing as a vast impediment that has been overcome through unstinting heroic effort. As he sails for the Atlantic with the survivors of his expedition, he passes the mouth of the river, "gliding through the broad portal into the Ocean, the blue domain of civilization" (II, 467).

Throughout *In Darkest Africa* Stanley sustains this self-assured manner, with its occasional grandiloquent crescendos. His confidence appears finally to falter, however, when he tries to account for the disaster that nearly destroys his rear column. Particularly disturbing to his composure are the scandalous incidents involving his two chief assistants, James Jameson and British Army Major Edmund Barttelot. In mid-1887 Stanley left them in command of the column camped at Yambuya on the Aruwimi, a hundred miles upriver from the Congo, and proceeded eastward with the others. Jameson and Barttelot stayed behind to bring up supplies that had to be left at Leopoldville because of the shortage of steamers. Once this was done they were to lead the column further up the Aruwimi to rejoin Stanley. Stanley later insisted that these were his orders, but Barttelot found them ambiguous and decided to remain at Yambuya until Stanley should return. (He had promised to rejoin the rear column in November but didn't arrive until the following August.) As they waited, discipline and morale broke down, food grew scarce, and sickness and starvation set in. When Stanley finally reappeared, he not only found most of the survivors desperately ill but also learned that Barttelot had been shot dead by a Manyema chief whose wife he had abused. Jameson, moreover, had succumbed to malaria as he was being taken downstream by canoe. Reports alleging Barttelot's repeated derelictions of duty and atrocious treatment of his subordinates and the Congolese soon spread to Europe. Jameson, lauded at the outset for his idealistic and philanthropic character, was implicated in an incident involving cannibalism. As Stanley made his way back to their camp at Banalya in the summer of 1888, the grisly rumors that began to reach him left him with an impression of "an insatiable love of horror" all along the Upper Congo; "quantities of human bones are said to be found in cooking-pots . . . whole families indulging in cannibal repasts; it is more than hinted that Englishmen are implicated in raids, murder, and cannibalism" (I, 511). He arrives at the camp and is stunned by what he sees: "Pen cannot picture nor tongue relate the full horrors witnessed within that dreadful pest-hole." The survivors are "worn to thin skin and staring bone from dysentery [and] crawled about and hollowly sounded their dismal welcome—a welcome to this charnel yard! . . . I heard of murder and death, of sickness and sorrow, anguish and grief, and wherever I looked the hollow eyes of dying men met my own." His inquiries lead only to confusion: "It was all an unsolved riddle to me" (I, 521–22). Stanley was never implicated directly in his subordinates' atrocious conduct, and his books and lectures continued to be popular throughout the 1890s despite the notoriety that clung to the events they reported. Nonetheless, for many in the West, sordid episodes such as those that plagued the Emin Pasha expedition had tarnished his image and led to widespread condemnation of the kinds of expeditions that had made him famous.

Conrad drew on Stanley's and others' accounts of the rear column disaster for some of the grimmest scenes in *Heart of Darkness*. These include the grove of dying slaves at the company station and the portrayal of Kurtz in his last days. Although he witnessed the illness and death of the Belgian trader Klein on the *Roi des Belges*, and no doubt saw a great deal of suffering elsewhere, he would have had to turn to sources such as Stanley's books and subsequent news reports for the horrifying details of these dismal scenes. Like Stanley's men at Yambuya, the traders' slaves whom Marlow sees are so weak from disease that they can move only by crawling, and their "sunken eyes looked up at me, enormous and vacant, a kind of blind, white flicker in the depths of the orbs, which died out slowly . . . others were scattered in every pose of contorted collapse, as in some picture of a massacre or a pestilence. While I stood horror-struck, one of these creatures rose to his hands and knees, and went off on all-fours towards the river to drink" (44–45). Marlow's description of Kurtz focuses similarly on "the eyes of that bony apparition shining darkly far in its bony head" (85); he crawls away from the steamer in a feeble effort to escape, and with his last words his voice, which had remained surprisingly strong, is reduced finally, like the hollow voices of Stanley's men, to "a cry that was no more than a breath" (111).

In his effort to construct the history of Kurtz's corruption Marlow stops short of unambiguous inferences of cannibalism or any other particularity of atrocious behavior, offering only circumlocutions on his "gratified and monstrous passions" (107) and "abominable satisfactions" (113). Whatever ghastly message Kurtz may have intended to send with the human heads that Marlow sees mounted on posts at the Inner Station is too unclear to lead him to any conclusion about actual deeds. This omission suggests that he wanted to fix his auditors' attention on the corruption itself rather than any one set of causes or means. "All Europe contributed to the making of Kurtz" (86), Marlow asserts, leaving the implication that his loss of contact with that totality must in a sense entail his un-making. The particular causes of such a hollowing out after such a plenitude seem to have mystified Conrad much in the way the similar fates of the leaders of Stanley's rear column mystified him. Although Stanley's biographers agree that he was well aware of Captain Barttelot's manifold shortcomings—they rapidly came to despise one another (Bierman 273)—he nonetheless views his behavior as unaccountable for a man whose "soul was ever yearning for glory" and who was "lavishly equipped with Nature's advantages" (I, 522). He is equally disingenuous about the character of Jameson, who by his own admission, corroborated by a credible witness, arranged for the purchase of a Congolese girl whose cannibalistic dismemberment he then personally observed (Hall 309, Bierman 304). Stanley's elegy for Jameson merely repeats, without qualification, that "all conceded a certain greatness" to him (I, 523). While Marlow is equally disposed to invoke Kurtz's supposedly superior gifts and lofty aims, he has no choice but to accept, as Stanley declines to do, the possibility that the Europeans' appearances of greatness and glory are a sham—that Kurtz is "hollow at the core" (97).

The principal characters and the setting of Conrad's other African story, "An Outpost of Progress" (1896), also appear to be derived from this material. The traders Kayerts and Carlier, like Jameson and Barttelot respectively a civilian and an army officer, are left in charge of an isolated post on a tributary of "the main river." They assume their duties in a glow of rhetoric that echoes Stanley's, proclaiming "the sacredness of the civilizing work" they will perform as they carry out their mission of "bringing light and faith and commerce to the dark places of the earth." Their morale sags rapidly, however; isolation, fever, fear of attack and guilty shame arising from their involvement in slave trading combine eventually to drive them to insanity, murder and suicide. The Managing Director of the "Great Trading Company" who leaves Kayerts and Carlier to this fate resembles Stanley in the silent contempt he feels for his subordinates and in his uncharacteristic emotion when he learns of their fate on his belated return to their outpost: "even he, the man of varied and startling experience, was somewhat discomposed by the manner of his finding."

Conrad's tendency to omit the names and other historical details of settings and characters in *Heart of Darkness* is a further salient feature of Marlow's attempted imaginative obliteration of Stanley's Africa. Just as Stanley had sought, in effect, to erase aboriginal names in the territories he entered by inscribing in their place his own and those of the Europeans he wished to associate with them (he referred to the entire Upper Congo as the "Livingstone" and tried for years to persuade the Royal Geographical Society, Livingstone's sponsor, to adopt the name formally), so *Heart of Darkness* in turn expunges the names Stanley had placed on the map.

Applying this reverse cartography to Stanley's Africa, Conrad strips names from places, rivers and characters and leaves only the wholly anonymous "conquering darkness" (116). In this way he restores the primordial blankness to the maps drawn by the Europeans' "fantastic invasion." The characters of these nameless invaders, along with their accomplices and their victims, are developed principally in terms of their putative functions with the trading company—the "manager," for instance, or the "maker of bricks" or the "helmsman"; but even these traces of individuation are blurred by the characters' incompetence, impotence and insubordination. Whatever sympathetic humanity they might have displayed either fails to emerge or is made to appear absurd, and their emptiness is finally all that is real about them. Marlow sees the feckless brickmaker as a typical case; he lacks the physical means of carrying out his identifying purpose and appears as a "papier-mâché Mephistopheles" with "nothing inside but a little loose dirt," he says, his contempt thickened by a qualifying "maybe" (56). This image of the hollowed-out brickmaker may have occurred to Conrad as a counter to a moment of forced enthusiasm in *In Darkest Africa* when Stanley arrives at Bangala Station near the equator on the Upper Congo and pronounces his delight with signs of progress he sees there: "Bricks were made, of excellent quality: 40,000 had already been manufactured. The establishment was in every way creditable to Central Africa" (I, 107). Bangala is the last location Conrad mentions in the *Congo Diary,* perhaps an indication that this was the place where his dissatisfied employers gave him reason to believe that it would be pointless for him to make further notes on navigation. Accordingly, in keeping with his tendency to invert Stanley's narratives, he imagined not just a paralysis of progress even in the rudimentary business of making bricks, but a nullification of the very idea of the brickmaker, who becomes the obverse of a recognizably human character. Instead of a rendered portrait, he becomes substantially less even than the bricks he is powerless to create. Reduction proceeds in a free fall toward obliteration.

Un-naming as an act of reversal and inversion of Stanley's world reaches a climax in the concluding scenes of *Heart of Darkness.* Marlow returns to the "sepulchral city" (like the unuttered name of London in the framing narrative, Brussels [Utrecht? The Hague?] is expunged by the pervading darkness) and calls on Kurtz's Intended. Her name, he falsely assures her, was his dying word—a word that was in fact not only not uttered, but is also excluded altogether from the narrative. In its place, "the Intended" is a further indicator of a character's blocked function. In echoing Stanley's celebrated return to Europe, including his royal reception in Brussels, Marlow exposes the element of imposture in the figure he cut in his view of Kurtz as being "avid of lying fame, of sham distinction," clinging to a "contemptibly childish" ambition "to have kings meet him at railway stations on his return from some ghastly Nowhere, where he intended to accomplish great things" (110). Marlow learns that Kurtz, like Stanley, had risen from obscurity and "comparative poverty" (119), had been a "journalist" and "wrote for the papers." According to a "colleague" of Kurtz whom Marlow meets, he had shown that his "proper sphere ought to have been politics 'on the popular side'" (115), a couched reference to Stanley's term from 1895 to 1900 as a Liberal Unionist M.P. for North Lambeth. Marlow senses that Kurtz returns to Europe spiritually not as a celebrity but as "a shadow insatiable of splendid appearances, of frightful realities"; he seems to re-enter the home of his fiancée in "an invading and vengeful rush." In this "moment of triumph for the wilderness" (116), the world of darkness dispels the pseudo-heroic "saving illusion" of the Intended's Europe. Her voice is full of its "mystery, desolation, sorrow," and in her gesture of appeal to Kurtz's memory she produces a shadowy reflection of his native woman, "tragic also, and bedecked with powerless charms, stretching bare brown arms over the glitter of the infernal stream, the stream of darkness" (120). Finally, as the figure of the Intended fades, the framing narrative concludes with a vision of the Thames (like the Congo never named) that inverts Stanley's portrayal of his first emergence from the Dark Continent. As Stanley concludes his narrative, the ocean appears to swallow the river he has navigated:

> Turning to take a farewell glance at the mighty River on whose brown bosom we had endured so greatly, I saw it approach, awed and humbled, the threshold of the watery immensity to whose immeasurable volume and illimitable expanse, awful as had been its power, its flood was but a drop. And I felt my heart suffused with purest gratitude to Him whose hand had protected us, and who had enabled us to pierce the Dark Continent from east to west, and to trace its mightiest River to its Ocean bourne. (II, 467)

Marlow's last image suggests, to the contrary, the virtual engulfment of the great European river by that African immensity Stanley believed he had conquered: "The offing was barred by a black bank of clouds, and the tranquil waterway leading to the uttermost ends of the earth flowed sombre under an overcast sky—seemed to lead to the heart of an immense darkness" (121).

In Conrad's parody of Belgian Africa there was clearly more at issue than historical revision. Any effort, in fact, to assign a single intention or even a set of compatible intentions to Conrad's ironic subversions in *Heart of Darkness* would be bound to result in simplistic readings. The present argument has taken into account some of the personal impulses that appear to have led him to write it, among them his nearly overpowering dismay at the Europeans' commercial designs on Africa and the pain of his own misfortunes as an employee of the Belgians who arrived in Stanley's wake. It is of course possible to attribute his sentiments to the nostalgia of a man reviewing his youthful enthusiasms, or, more particularly, to the regrets of an aging mariner unwilling to reconcile himself to the eclipse of sailing ships by steamers and the rest of the new technology that made Stanley's feats possible. Autobiographical explanations such as these, however, are of limited value in the effort to understand the deliberately crafted aspects of *Heart of Darkness*, imagined, written and then read and remembered as a text among texts. In the characteristically modernist kind of battle of books that Conrad wages with Stanley, his gestures of negation—of subversion, inversion and erasure—ironically express the most generative power of his literary imagination.

Other studies have adumbrated the notion of Conrad's method of re-composition in *Heart of Darkness*. Darras comes closest to the argument advanced here, viewing Marlow's journey to Kurtz as an iconoclastic inversion of colonialist mythology: Livingstone/Marlow advances toward Stanley/Kurtz, restoring to the map of Africa the mysterious "symbolic geography" of medieval romance (42, 66, 68). More recently Daphna Erdinast-Vulcan has made the collateral argument that "Marlow's quest is an attempt to reinstate the 'blank space' as the explorer's destination" where he can psychically recover an Edenic "Genesis state of undifferentiated vitality" (93, 98). The work of these two critics and others, including D.C.R.A. Goonetilleke in his 1995 edition of *Heart of Darkness,* is representative of the revisionist readings that have tended to modify attacks, most notably by Chinua Achebe and Edward Said, on Conrad's racism. They seek to demonstrate his subversion of apologist histories of European colonialism. Their theses depart from the present argument, on the other hand, in their emphasis on his search for some prior, serene realm of the psyche—a pre-modern paradisal or romantic state of being— to which Marlow's imagination turns as a refuge from the "horror" uncovered by Kurtz. The main difficulties that theses such as these present are, first, that they can be cited readily in support of a view of Conrad as an ideological reactionary or a decadent escapist; second, they assume too narrowly that Conrad's creative temperament was dominated by his craving for emotional repose, ignoring the positive theme of unrest that pervades his writing. It would be more to the point to suggest that the strong feelings of revolt expressed in the act of writing are what Conrad was after, and that he struggled to realize them without being merely destructive on the one hand, or, on the other, allowing his individuality to be submerged in the ideological currents of his day. He saw that the creative power of negation must be exerted as a continuing artistic process.

It cannot aspire to some final state or "closure" since the vitality of a work of art is felt only as it is being created and actively apprehended or recollected. For a writer with Conrad's aesthetic disposition, what is being negated—a dishonored world, or, by the same token, a spuriously heroic world such as Stanley's—is perceived as massively inert, retaining little vitality of its own for the imagination to draw on. The writer must accordingly supply everything needed to reconstitute an aesthetic whole by means of a parodic reconstruction of the very material he has negated. Later, Conrad's narrating character in *Under Western Eyes* (1911) would state the idea in this way: "For the dead can live only with the exact intensity and quality of the life imparted to them by the living" (304).

Conrad's 1905 tribute, "Henry James: An Appreciation," reprinted in *Notes on Life and Letters* (11–19), closely approximates the quality of creative negation that sustains his own work. James, whom he saw as a sharer in his own ironic aesthetic, is "heroic (in the modern sense) for the absence of shouted watchwords, clash of arms and sound of trumpets" (15). He sees in the "sincerity" and "sacrifice" of James's fiction the idea that "a solution by rejection must always present a certain lack of finality, especially startling when contrasted with the usual methods of solution by rewards and punishments, by crowned love, by fortune, by a broken leg or a sudden death" (18). It is through such renunciations as these, Conrad implies, that a wholly contemporary mode of fiction is crafted, for they are a writer's means of continually resisting the lure of closure:

> the desire for finality, for which our hearts yearn, with a longing greater than the longing for the loaves and fishes of this earth. Perhaps the only true desire of mankind, coming thus to light in its hours of leisure, is to be set at rest. One is never set at rest by Mr. Henry James's novels. His books end as an episode in life ends. You remain with the sense of life still going on; and even the subtle presence of the dead is felt in that silence that comes upon the artist-creation when the last word has been read. It is eminently satisfying, but it is not final. Mr. Henry James, great artist and faithful historian, never attempts the impossible. (18–19)

Underlying the celebratory mood of this essay is the note of anguish that often sounds in Conrad's writing. The regrets he expresses in "Geography and Some Explorers" typify his mood when he faces the possibility that too great a renunciation may be required of the modern writer, that James's sacrificial integrity may leave him too few fictive tools. For Marlow the modern "sickly atmosphere of tepid scepticism" menaces the narrative impulse itself, resisting his struggle to grasp and bear witness to the significance of Kurtz's moral crisis. Even though the "careless contempt" of the manager's boy's "Mistah Kurtz—he dead" repels him, he fears that he himself may have "nothing to say" at the moment of his "last opportunity for pronouncement" (113, 112). The ever-elusive "summing up" is the occasion for a similarly expressed resignation on Marlow's part in *Lord Jim* (1900):

> Are not our lives too short for that full utterance which through all our stammerings is of course our only and abiding intention? I have given up expecting those last words, whose ring, if they could only be pronounced, would shake both heaven and earth. There is never time to say our last word—the last word of our love, of our desire, faith, remorse, submission, revolt. (208)

Paradoxically, Marlow gives virtual "full utterance" to such "last words" in the act of renouncing them, eloquently stirring his listeners—if not heaven and earth—who can surely imagine no fuller utterance at the moment they listen to it. In this familiar exalted mood his voice radiates the "internal glow" of Conrad's "inborn faculty." It reveals itself negatively in somber declarations of bewilderment, in valedictory perorations, or in the rhythmic dying fall of his periods. It recalls another moment in *Lord Jim* when the trader Stein likens Jim's idealism to the unrest of the butterfly, who "will never on his heap of mud keep still. He want to be so, and again he want to be so . . . as he can never be." Shifting to a nautical metaphor, he concludes that the solution lies ironically not in fighting the waves of the "destructive element" but in submitting to them in order to "make the deep, deep sea keep you up. . . . That was the way. To follow the dream, and again follow the dream—and so—*ewig—usque ad finem*" (200–201).

With the exception of a few of the lighter works he wrote late in his life, Conrad's fiction seems always on the verge but never quite at the point of finally relinquishing the brooding sonority that is a key signature of his style. "All adventure, all love, every success is resumed in the supreme energy of an act of renunciation" (16) he said in the tribute that was intended for Henry James but equally describes his own inverted eloquence. Conrad's art of reversal developed out of a growing ideological agnosticism that led him to reject in large measure both the destructive rhetoric of revolutionaries and the propaganda of the autocrats they sought to depose. His resistance to these extremes undoubtedly arose in part from ethical and even patriotic principle, but it also expressed his desire to distance himself and his writing from ideological positions *per se* because of their tendency to harden thought and emotion into dogma. Conrad's politics are difficult to characterize precisely because they were based on his wariness of adopted positions that threatened to halt the artistic process of self-invention by the inversion of dictated ideas.

Conrad continued to develop this process in his later fiction. Perhaps the most revealing example is the political novel, *Under Western Eyes*, commonly rated as his last major work. In this narrative Conrad employs some of the technical devices he used in *Heart of Darkness*, including the corrupted central character and the disinterested but perplexed narrator, and he again reverses conventional dualities, particularly in his symbolic development of images of light and darkness. A brief look at his narrative strategies reveals, in comparison to *Heart of Darkness*, a more radically subversive irony.

The narrating character, an elderly teacher of English living in Geneva, tells the story of the student Razumov, who is unwillingly drawn away from his studies in St. Petersburg and into revolutionary intrigue against the Tsarist tyranny. When he secretly betrays the assassin, Victor Haldin, to the police, Razumov finds himself ensnared in their schemes as well. He is sent to Geneva to gather intelligence on the celebrated revolutionary Peter Ivanovich and his coterie of exiles, who have been led to believe he acted heroically as Haldin's accomplice. The moral anguish he suffers because of his duplicity becomes intolerable when he meets Haldin's sister Nathalie and is moved by her nobility of character. He finally confesses to her and to a meeting of the revolutionists. Their violent reaction breaks him physically, and eventually he returns to Russia in the care of Tekla, the disenchanted secretary of Peter Ivanovich.

Conrad's characterization of Razumov is clearly based to some extent on the "superfluous" character common in Russian fiction of the later nineteenth century. It is also evident that Peter Ivanovich is a composite parody drawn mainly on the lives the anarchist leaders, Mikhail Bakunin and Peter Kropotkin (the latter's recent *Memoirs of a Revolutionist* [1899] anticipates the career of Peter Ivanovich in a number of ways). While these are some of the principal external objects of the kind of parody that Conrad had subjected Stanley's works to in *Heart of Darkness*, the internal narrative structure of the story itself is a complex of contending histories of revolutionary turmoil. Conrad reshapes these into an over-arching narrative that becomes in the end the story of the narrating character's self-effacement—his withdrawal from the activity of self-presentation that his characters have engaged in by telling their own stories.

In his later "Author's Note" (1920) to *Under Western Eyes*, Conrad explains that his purpose in creating this "much criticised" narrating character was to provide an eye-witness who would gain readers' credit through his detachment and fairness; the effect would be to validate his account of Razumov's life, even though it is perceived through Western eyes. He is accordingly prone to self-conscious declarations of sincerity, and he fretfully avoids appearances of dubious artifice, going so far as to spurn transitions between his book's four sections (100). In his resolute unobtrusiveness, he says nothing about his personal history except that he has lived in Geneva for more than twenty years, the son of English parents who settled in St. Petersburg (187–88). Consistent to a fault, he even withholds his name, being in his own estimation an utterly unremarkable character. He concedes, indeed, that he would have had no story to write had Nathalie not engaged him to instruct her in reading English poetry at her home, thus putting him in contact with the Russian expatriates who visit her. Still, not content with this effort to exclude himself as a character, he commences his narrative by admitting his virtual incompetence to tell Rasumov's story in any case:

> To begin with I wish to disclaim the possession of those high gifts of imagination and expression which would have enabled my pen to create for the reader the personality of the man who called himself, after the Russian custom, Cyril son of Isidor—Kirylo Sidorovitch—Razumov.
> If I have ever had these gifts in any sort of living form they have been smothered out of existence a long time ago under a wilderness of words. Words, as is well known, are the great foes of reality. I have been for many years a teacher of languages. It is an occupation which at length becomes fatal to whatever share of imagination, observation, and insight an ordinary person may be heir to. To a teacher of languages there comes a time when the world is but a place of many words and man appears a mere talking animal not much more wonderful than a parrot. (3)

Even if this disclaimer is taken simply to convey his engaging modesty, it actually reveals something quite different about the writer/character who offers it; and it reaches deeper into the art of narrative than the confessions of self-doubt and confusion that Charlie Marlow occasionally makes. It declares categorically at the outset that language itself is a desolate phantasmagoria that can project no real image of the world. Such is the radical skepticism that underlies his plain-spoken manner and his disavowal of all literary distinction. As an actor in his own narrative, he wishes to function almost exclusively as a *ficelle*, a mere presence enabling speeches to be made and encounters to occur among the more consequential characters. "I have done little else but look on" (134), he protests, "a mute witness to things Russian" (381). "Removed [from Nathalie] by the difference of age and nationality as if into the sphere of another existence, I produced, even upon myself, the effect of a dumb helpless ghost, of an anxious immaterial thing that could only hover about without the power to protect or guide by as much as a whisper" (126).

In the long run, as Frank Kermode argues in his assessment of this restlessly passive character, this insistence on self-effacement becomes problematic. Kermode sees him as actually enacting the role of the "diabolical" character whom Razumov suspects of egging him on to steal Nathalie's soul. He causes "a virtually uncontrolled dispersion of souls, spirits, phantoms, ghosts, ghouls, and so forth" to clog his narrative and finally to plunge it back into the Russian murk from which it arose. By mischievously blurring and blocking the sequence of events with his insertion of "irrational figures," he creates a book that in a sense "hates its readers," bewildering them with the "things unseen" that he pits repeatedly "against the page we are seeing." Kermode's discussion draws on Avrom Fleishman's explanation of the narrator's "abnormal interest . . . in the acts and arts of writing" as the expression of his "ultimate despair of written language, and of the art of fiction" (145–48). Although Kermode proposes no clear motive for this strange obstructiveness and perhaps overstates the narrator's disingenuousness, he makes the useful point that the narrative technique of *Under Western Eyes* projects a deeply ironic attitude toward literary writing by composing a narrative that tells the story of its own radical limitations. Beyond expressing mute despair of language and writing, it resorts to Mallarmé's image of "the empty paper sheathed in its whiteness" (*le vide papier que le blancheur défend*, "Brise Marine" [1.7]), leaving only a potentiality of expression that is protected against contamination by the words that have become "the great foes of reality."

As a presence in Conrad's world of exiles, the aged narrator's text counters the cynical inversion of "decent" values caused both by the young revolutionists and by the autocracy that has created them.

> For that is the mark of Russian autocracy and of Russian revolt. In its pride of numbers, in its strange pretensions of sanctity, and in the secret readiness to abase itself in suffering, the spirit of Russia is the spirit of cynicism. It informs the declarations of her statesmen, the theories of her revolutionists, and the mystic vaticinations of prophets to the point of making freedom look like a form of debauch, and the Christian virtues appear actually indecent. (67)

Again, when Razumov's confession threatens to shatter her faith, it appears to the narrator "as if the steady flame of her soul had been made to vacillate at last in the cross-currents of poisoned air from the corrupted dark immensity claiming her for its own, where virtues themselves fester into crimes in the cynicism of oppression and revolt" (356).

Like Kurtz's Intended in *Heart of Darkness*, Nathalie becomes the solitary upholder of a faith that monstrous corrupting forces threaten to destroy, leaving nothing but an invading "dark immensity." The narrator returns to this ominous image repeatedly—"I saw the gigantic shadow of Russian life deepening around her like the darkness of an advancing night" (202). He echoes the somber imagery of *Heart of Darkness* that projects the African continent, darkened by the European presence. For the young Marlow it had appeared as an enticing blank area on the map, an image that also recurs in depictions of snow-covered Russia in *Under Western Eyes*, "like a monstrous blank page awaiting the record of an inconceivable history" (33). The page without words, the featureless map, is the void "awaiting the record" which Conrad's narrator seeks to compose from the fragments of Russian existence presented to him; but as an "inconceivable history," it cannot yet be written. At best, he can only intimate it as the antithetical "debauch" takes its course.

The written record of Peter Ivanovich's life and convictions therefore becomes the principal counter-text for the narrator to confront. As a character he is nothing but words—those "foes of reality" named by the narrator in his opening. His speeches are all theatrical performances— booming sonorities, grave rumbles, entreaties and excoriations. He has become famous as the "heroic fugitive" (125) through the published memoirs that tell of his sensational escape from the Tsar's police; "all Europe was aware of the story of his life written by himself and translated into seven or more languages" (120). His style vigorously projects the image of a vastly prolific mind. His revolutionary plans to foment an uprising in the Balkans are elaborately drawn but immeasurably far from execution.

The reality that undercuts Peter Ivanovich's heroic language is provided by his amanuensis, Tekla. She tells Razumov of her wretchedness and her disillusionment: "The trying part of it was to have the secret of the composition laid bare before her; to see the great author of the revolutionary gospels grope for words as if he were in the dark as to what he meant to say" (148). This is the sole intimate view of Peter Ivanovich's character in *Under Western Eyes*, and it significantly exposes his posturing as a master of language. Tekla reveals that his revolutionary rhetoric is a mask disguising the narrator's "mere talking animal" who becomes lost in the "wilderness of words." Suffering from his despotism, and witnessing the reverse of all her illusions about him, Tekla sees herself reduced to a non-entity: "After taking down Peter Ivanovich from dictation for two years, it is difficult for me to be anything" (147). She says essentially the same thing about Peter Ivanovich when she observes that he "stands for everything" (233), implying that he really stands for nothing. She tells Razumov that "to have one's illusions destroyed—that is really almost more than one can bear" (148); she suffers from the pain of a deeply paradoxical knowledge: "I know Peter Ivanovich sufficiently well. He is a great man. Great men are horrible" (232). The dismantling of the self-constructed image of the "heroic fugitive" is completed at the conclusion when the narrator learns that Peter Ivanovich returns to Russia, his revolutionary views presumably in abeyance, and settles down in unheroic circumstances with an unnamed "peasant girl" (382).

Razumov is the extreme case of the Russian character shorn of an identity by the historical realities of *Under Western Eyes*. Of his lineage he can surmise only that he is the natural son of Prince K—, who intercedes on his behalf with the authorities in Petersburg but does not acknowledge him. He lacks kinship or intimacy with any other person, and he is without an identifying affiliation or creed—apart from what he calls "certain honest ideals" (366) that take the form of a vaguely Nietzschean messianism. Deprived of the image of himself that an academic appointment would have created—"His solitary and laborious existence had been destroyed—the only thing he could call his own on this earth" (82)—he can identify himself only abjectly as a Russian: "this Immensity . . . this unhappy Immensity . . . all this land is mine—or I have nothing" (61). "His closest parentage was defined in the statement that he was Russian" (10–11), but he has no certain claim even to his own patronymic and concedes bleakly, "I have no name" (208). In the ruin of his academic hopes, he senses that his "existence was a great cold blank, something like the enormous plain of the whole of Russia levelled with snow and fading gradually on all sides into shadows and mists" (303). This is a comprehensive image of Russia, moreover, "which his view could embrace in all its enormous expanse as if it were a map" (66).

Thus virtually equated with and wholly defined by his country and its unwritten, uncharted, "inconceivable history," Razumov must himself inscribe a series of identities on the blank page of himself. In his efforts to do this he finds that the self-portrait is always in some way compromised. First, his student notes, on which everything had rested, "neatly sorted" in the service of his academic career, become "a mere litter of blackened paper—dead matter—without significance or interest" (68) after Haldin's disastrous visit. When he tries to write an essay for a prize to regain his standing at the university, his hand seems paralyzed; and as he composes a list of counter-revolutionary slogans "his neat hand lost its character altogether" (66). The police search his room soon after this, leaving his papers in "a ragged pile" with the sheet of slogans placed on top in evident acknowledgment of their exculpatory effect. In this way Razumov haplessly creates the illusion of his transformation from scholar to Tsarist ideologue.

From this point forward Razumov performs a series of scripted and improvised roles, all duly recorded in the journal he begins to keep after his interview with the police official, Mikulin. In what he refers to as his "simulated" (314) escape from St. Petersburg—a travesty of Peter Ivanovich's flight from the Russian police—he views his actions as a "preposterous" charade. He reflects that "nobody does such things" (315–16), but he nonetheless calculates his movements carefully to give them "verisimilitude" (312). Arriving in Geneva, he makes contact with Peter Ivanovich's group and begins sending reports back to Mikulin. His reserved manner among the exiles inspires confidence, masking his hollowness with an apparent probity. Only in writing his journal does he approximate an authentic self and achieve brief respites of calm and of resignation to his anguished circumstances. "I shall write," he resolves; "That's why I am here," he realizes as he makes entries in his journal while he is seated on the island commemorating the earlier writer exiled in Geneva, Rousseau (289–90).

Razumov's journal, begun in St. Petersburg as the furtively composed "book of his compromising record" (375), is transformed ultimately into the confession that he makes to Nathalie Haldin. This is his final text and his last impersonation: he throws his pen away when he finishes it, ceasing to be "a man who had read, thought, lived, pen in hand" (357). In revealing his role in Haldin's death, Razumov cannot finally escape the self-annulling paradox that permits him to tell her only who he is not. By abandoning the false roles he has played, he reveals the true cipher that he has been from the beginning; he finishes his testimony to this fact with the consummate self-contradiction, "I am independent—and therefore perdition is my lot" (362). His reversals of identity finally conclude in his re-absorption by Russia as another non-character in its unwritten story.

Like the greed-driven "pilgrims" of *Heart of Darkness*, the Russian exiles of Conrad's Geneva are a fantastic invasion, their presence based on an egregious delusion. Both intrude briefly on a shadowed world and exist there merely as creatures of their own rhetoric. The narrator of *Under Western Eyes* tries to exempt Nathalie from his general dismissal of these "phantoms" because of her sincere faith in a "merciful future" (353), yet he is unpersuasive in his insistence that this is different from the naïveté of an impossible idealism. In a story of characters who tend to have only textual identities, her identifying script is the letter from her brother naming Razumov—and only Razumov—as one of those incorruptible "right men" whose "unstained, lofty, and solitary existences" will inspire revolution (135). After Nathalie has freed herself from this delusion, the narrator seeks to portray her return to Russia and to some form of earnest humanitarian work as an exception to the general demoralization of the exiles (of the others only the fiery Sophia Antonovna is shown to remain steadfast). It is as though he wishes to believe that she, like the other largely sympathetic characters, Razumov and Tekla, and even he himself, has positioned herself prophetically as an actor in a redemptive history that may one day be written.

Although the map that might locate all of them within such a history is presently featureless and without coordinates, the narrator places them imaginatively in a state of radical contradiction that has its own separate, "inconceivable" reality. This is a late instance of the Conradian darkness that, because of its deeply paradoxical nature, eludes rationalization in his writing. He invokes it strikingly in a review he wrote while *Under Western Eyes* was in progress. "The Ascending Effort," titled after the book by

George Bourne and reprinted in *Notes on Life and Letters* (71–75), dismisses the notion that science and poetry can be reconciled, holding that life and the arts "follow dark courses" and that "art . . . issues straight from our organic vitality, and is a movement of life-cells with their matchless unintellectual knowledge." In the daylight of scientific factuality, modern man has sought to believe in the heliocentric system of Copernicus; but after sunset, he "holds the system of Ptolemy. He holds it without knowing it." Conrad appeals to the old Alexandrian cosmology as another metaphor for the extra-rational realities suggested by his images of blank maps and pages and their darkly inverted worlds. He appears to allude to the neo-Ptolemaic concept of the "equant," a hypothetical point in space where the uniform movement of the planets in their spheres could be observed. The primary significance of this point for Conrad lies in the failure of science to demonstrate its existence, preserving the Ptolemaic cosmos as an artistic figure for the world conceived by means other than the merely empirical reality that it renounces. Beyond the defects of astronomy, it models an antithetical reality "which exposes the depths of our infatuation where our mere cleverness is permitted for a while to grope for the unessential among invincible shadows" (73–74).

Conrad portrayed Leopold's Congo and Alexander's Russia as contradictory absurdities. It was a way of destroying them imaginatively. His blank maps in *Heart of Darkness* and *Under Western Eyes* are parodies of parodies, recognizably modernist in their renunciation of the conceptual closure required by the political satirist and the ideologue. The writing itself is the fullest display of his purpose, with its subversive artistry that continually strips away the illusion of finality. The fictional scars that result bear witness to both the struggle of his "renunciation" and the pained recognition that it may leave him finally with nothing to say. Conrad thus contributes to modern fiction the gesture of immolation, but it is self-sacrifice without a firm altruistic object beyond the aesthetic integrity of the work itself (the admirable enduring female characters in these novels are unconvincing in their idealization). In order for this self-victimization to avoid the appearance of Promethean posturing, it must be seen as the emergence of the modern writer's determination to adapt his manifold deficiencies to artistic purposes.

CHAPTER TWO

James Joyce's Material Language:
Art and Regression

Joseph Conrad's subversive parodies of the rhetoric of European imperialists and revolutionaries are primary instances of the departure of modernist fiction from the heroic subject and the language that attempts to portray it. With greatness of character no longer a tenable theme, he resorts to a self-effacing irony of counter-statement that prefers even silence and error to ideological illusion or mere pragmatic discursiveness. For many of the writers who followed him, the crafting of artistic language itself held out the promise of a sort of surrogate heroism; but the notion of the literary artist as hero was contradicted by the disabling medium he was forced to use. The career of James Joyce continues Conrad's devolution of the modernist text, tracing the regression of its language toward a state of opaque, inexpressive matter.

Critics interested in locating James Joyce's position in literary history have always been divided on the exact nature of his intentions and the extent of his success in turning away from the central aesthetic values of nineteenth-century European art. The various degrees of intensity they have accorded to his rebellion is itself an extension of the uneasiness, confusion and dismay that his works provoked among even his sympathetic early critics. Always concerned about distancing their critiques from the popular reviewers' moralistic banalities, they tended to couch their reservations in aesthetic terms that deplored Joyce's degradation of his talent by his evident concessions to a coarsely materialistic realism. Among the earliest of these partial dissenters was H. G. Wells, who objected to Joyce's "cloacal obsession" in an otherwise approving 1917 review of *A Portrait of the Artist as a Young Man* (1916) in the *New Republic* (157). Even Ezra Pound, Joyce's staunch supporter from early phases of his career, urged him to suppress crudities such as the outhouse scene in the "Calypso" episode of *Ulysses* (1922) (Ellmann, *James Joyce* 442). E. M. Forster's reaction to *Ulysses* in *Aspects of the Novel* (1927) is perhaps best known; he charges that it is "a dogged attempt to cover the universe with mud, it is an inverted Victorianism, an attempt to make crossness and dirt succeed where sweetness and light failed" (121). Although Forster's view clearly absorbed some of the shrillness of the reviews, it also voiced his contemporaries' independent sense of a prodigious talent squandered. Conceding with them that *Ulysses* "is perhaps the most interesting literary experiment of our day" (120), he nevertheless shared a commonly expressed feeling that came close to physical aversion. Virginia Woolf agreed that *Ulysses* was the work of genius that T. S. Eliot declared had "destroyed the whole of the 19th century," but she nonetheless sensed its "brackish" unpleasantness and the feeling that "myriads of tiny bullets pepper one and spatter one" (II, 199–200) while reading it. The broadest attack along these lines came from Wyndham Lewis, who called *Ulysses* a compendium of "stuff—unorganized brute material . . . the sewage of the Past twenty years old . . . a stupendous outpouring of matter . . . rubbish." It aspires to "an act of bringing the dead to life" but achieves only "an immense nature morte" (107–108), resembling a painterly still life in a highly negative sense of the term. Viewed generally, then, this early criticism, in its preoccupation with the unpalatable in Joyce, tended to supplant one fastidious critical extreme with another.

While recent critical work on Joyce usually moderates this judgmental impulse, it continues to focus on his subversion of essentialist standards, especially those of the Victorians. To the extent that much of this criticism tends to draw characteristically post-structuralist conclusions—about the perpetual evanescence of the subject and the radical undecidability of meaning that pervade Joyce's fiction and achieve a kind of apotheosis in *Finnegans Wake* (1939)—the Joycean text has again been subjected to extreme readings of its departures from tradition. In *Joyce's Book of the Dark: Finnegans Wake* (1986), to name one of the most exhaustive examples of this style of criticism, John Bishop argues that Joyce's main intention was to transmit the experience of dreamless sleep, a state of unconsciousness devoid not only of the images, physical sensations and language of dreams but of all forms of cognition whatever. The result is that the language of *Finnegans Wake* conveys only the radically paradoxical reality of "Real Absence" (536). "I reconstruct the nocturnal life," Joyce remarked, and in doing so he created, in Bishop's words, "a whole strange language of negation, a system of reference to no experience, whose infinitely inflected terms" endlessly subvert and postpone the reader's perception of meaning, "equally signifying the absence of perception and the perception of nothing." Expressive language thus reaches an extreme point of reduction in *Finnegans Wake*, precluding even solipsistic self-perception, which is itself precluded by "states of imperception" (48). Language, finally, is subjected to "wholesale rubbling" (19), reverting figuratively, as Bishop appears to conclude, to the state of mud, brine, rubbish and excrement that had so dismayed Joyce's contemporaries.

In its reflections of an important later direction that Joyce criticism has taken, Bishop's thesis modifies the more directly affirmative, celebratory readings of the critical tradition established by Richard Ellmann and the critics whose work he influenced. A characteristic example is Ellmann's very different analysis of the style of the "Aeolus" episode of *Ulysses*:

> Joyce seems determined to burst the confines of English by allying it with the stylized language in which Homer clothes his mythical materials, or by a linguistic innovation as radical as Dante's decision, in another *ricorso*, to use the vernacular. *Finnegans Wake* best realized the latter aspiration. (*Consciousness* 26)

Although Ellmann was almost always prepared to concede Joyce's revolutionary uses of language, he saw their potentially destructive energy as being contained by his syncretic manipulation of a broad linguistic tradition that ultimately included him among the much earlier "radical" experimenters such as Dante and Homer. This in turn enabled Ellmann to reach the kinds of interpretive syntheses toward which his generation of critics was inclined. A concluding passage in his *Ulysses on the Liffey* (1972) offers a classic instance of this manner of reading, with its redemptive emphases:

> Bloomsday becomes everymansday, and everywomansday, in that all necessary elements of desirable life have been gathered together. None of the principal figures is complete in himself, but together they sum up what is affirmable. At the end we are brought back to the earth, to spring, to vegetation, and to sexual love. (167)

Ellmann's hermeneutics derives principally from his conception of Joyce's comic sense of language as the product of the writer's reaction to an always-increasing disparity between the power of language and the power of reality. The consequent perception, in the words of Fred Miller Robinson, is that "language increasingly evokes chaos as it attempts to dispel it, and so fails as it succeeds, and vice versa" (39). To come to the realization that language probably cannot order the world, and that it certainly can not transform it, is to discover a comic truth, hence an occasion for a festive salute to the unfailing temporal cycles that console humanity in its belittlement. Elliott B. Gose, Jr., pursues this idea in his reading of *Ulysses* and places Leopold Bloom in "a general pattern of degradation" that completes itself at the end of his waking day when he is reduced to the ink forming the enigmatic dot at the conclusion of "Ithaca": "Bloom has literally been reduced to a tiny smudge of carbon. 'Here is Bloom,' says Joyce. . . . 'Ultimately he is no more than printer's ink on my page.' Thus, finally, is Flesh made Word" (180). Comic reduction, moreover, is succeeded by comic sublimation as Bloom becomes not merely an object but a celestial one, revolving in his vast orbit as a "suncompelled" comet (598). In this way, Gose argues, Joyce's narrative arrives at a characteristic climax of ludic affirmation.

The figure of the deified artist that Joyce mulled over early in his career, along with many writers of the *fin de siècle,* was at most a provocative metonymy, and at moments a mischievous posture, but it probably accounts for much of the great quantity of sympathetic writing about his works as daemonic miracles of transformation. Among the later examples of this treatment is Sheldon Brivic's *Joyce the Creator* (1985), which develops the notion that Joyce's writing was his "personal enactment of the principles of the godhead" and that accordingly "a major factor in Joyce's relationship to God was competition" (13). As creator he performs a "transcendent function" in his own work (9), enacting the role of the demiurge who as "cosmic artificer" acquires "the constructive power of God" (60). Beryl Schlossman's study published in the same year, *Joyce's Catholic Comedy of Language*, argues similarly but more soberly from a Catholic apologist position that Joyce's central subject is "the intersection of Catholic flesh and art in the Passion of the Word." She portrays Joyce's Catholic mysticism as a means of clarifying the "signification of 'unreadability'." He conveys "the mystery of the letter and its limits" as an expression of "his illicit *jouissance* at the heart of the radiant, eucharistic sublimation of writing" (ix-xv). Brivic and Schlossman extend the critical tradition that defines Joyce's writing as a collection of sacral texts whose resistance and impenetrability in effect withhold them from the worldly realm of the readable and thus preserve them from the limiting circumscriptions of critical analysis. The quasi-divine comedian who brings this about, however, for all his sublimating powers, appears to effect nothing substantially different from Ellmann's cyclical pattern of reduction and regeneration; and these critics' apparent contentment with that critical matrix suggests that assumptions about literary language as sublimation had become something of a blocking obsession in Joyce criticism by the time of the centennial publications of the 1980s. Since then, most of his readers have begun to search for a more problematic, or at any rate a less complacent, way of describing their means of access to his work.

Critical inquiry such as Bishop's accordingly takes another direction, emphasizing the concept of Joyce's verbal opacity as a more or less fixed constant that blocks interpretive attempts to adduce a clarifying subliminal radiance. Even after a half-century of effort on the part of Joyce's readers to explicate *Finnegans Wake*, it remains for Bishop a work whose "stupefying illegibility" (3) enabled Joyce to bring literary language to a paradoxical state of "rich indefinition" (4). His "systematic darkening of every term in *Finnegans Wake* was an absolute necessity" that he imposed on himself in his desire—as he phrased it—to "reconstruct the night" (3–4). In its virtual celebration of Joyce's text for its unreadability and all that this implies—subversions of linguistic hierarchies, resistance to closure, or what Margot Norris terms their "texticidal strategies" (21)—Bishop's argument reflects the post-structuralists' anti-metaphysical conception of literary language as an enclosed and coded but ultimately unexpressive system. This is the language that Roland Barthes, in an early and disarming formulation, compares to an onion: "a construction of layers (or levels, or systems) whose body contains, finally, no heart, no kernel, no secret, no irreducible principle, nothing except the infinity of its own envelopes— which envelop nothing other than the unity of its own surfaces." Literary style, he adds, "is essentially a citational process, a body of formulae, a memory (almost in the cybernetic sense of the word), a cultural and not an expressive inheritance." Its producer, the writer, only transforms prior model texts, crafting "representations, not essential elements; citations, not expressions; stereotypes, not archetypes" (Chatman 9–10).

Whether opaque or transparent, literary language tends toward the same absence of communication. The illegible "infinitely inflected terms" that Bishop reads in *Finnegans Wake* are finally indistinguishable from the innumerable "envelopes" that for Barthes refute all claims made for a text's original, essential meaning. Both, on the other hand, ironically concede a quality of expressiveness to this language simply by acknowledging its continued function *as language,* constructed on the basis of recognizable etymological principles. Bishop's book is itself a case in point—a massive display of linguistic resourcefulness which implicitly denies that any of the *Wake*'s language is nothing but noise. He in fact attributes a supreme communicative energy to Joyce's language in demonstrating its limitless capacity for expressing nothing as though that "nothing" were an object— an inverted "something" that is the object of infinite exposition. *Finnegans Wake* contains the residues of signification. With "each word that would not pass away" (186) it preserves the irreducible vocables of thought and emotion in the silence of "lextinction" (83). In the very materiality of its language, in the body of sound itself at "the deleteful hour" (118), it clusters the traces of an unrecoverable speech.

Toward the conclusion of *A Portrait of the Artist as a Young Man* (1916), Stephen Dedalus pledges himself to "silence, exile, and cunning"

(247), partly in reaction against this dysfunctional language. In his prior conversation with the English-born dean of studies at University College, Dublin, Stephen feels the hostile otherness of his speech: "His language, so familiar and so foreign, will always be for me an acquired speech. I have not made or accepted its words. My voice holds them at bay. My soul frets in the shadow of his language" (189). Significantly, in his adversarial stance toward the dean's English he tends to materialize its words: they are objects that are "made" and "accepted" or refused; they are hunted animals held "at bay"; they cast shadows. Among the most disheartening of Stephen's childhood experiences is his discovery that the instability and imprecision of language in its daily use destroy its power to penetrate the reality of the adult world. He discovers how treacherously words appear to offer radiant "glimpses of the real world about him," previewing "the great part which he felt awaited him" (62), only to reveal their actual opacity in daily use. At Clongowes Wood College, for example, the word *kiss* betrays him as he learns to his shame that there is no safe answer to the question posed by Wells about kissing one's mother. Consequently, he is denied an answer to his own question, "Why did people do that with their two faces?" (15). The supreme word *God* thwarts him similarly as it refuses to emerge from a thicket of baffling self-referential abstractions: "God remained always the same God and God's real name was God" (16).

The opening of the second chapter of *A Portrait* verbally reflects the confusion of Stephen's life away from his school at Clongowes Wood. His Uncle Charles' inappropriate use of "salubrious" and "mollifying" (60) betrays a language sunk in genteel shabbiness. By the time Stephen makes his decision to leave Ireland at the conclusion of *A Portrait,* he has developed an active distrust of this unfit and unstable language. In his diary he contemptuously records a remark made by an old Irish peasant: "Ah, there must be terrible queer creatures at the latter end of the world," and adds the comment, "I fear him. I fear his redrimmed horny eyes. It is with him I must struggle all through this night till day come, till he or I lie dead, gripping him by the sinewy throat. . . ." Such strange and uncharacteristic violence becomes intelligible when it is seen as a reaction to the old man's nonsensical language, symptomatic of the senility into which the common speech of Ireland had fallen. He withdraws this attack, however—"Till he yield to me? No. I mean him no harm" (251–52)—conceding implicitly that language like the old man's is beyond redemption. His words properly call forth not the indignation but the silence of the artist who knows he must resort to some altogether different kind of speech.

Stephen begins to discern features of this linguistic *terra incognita* in the purified sounds that remain when words have been hollowed out by the materialistic "tradition of the marketplace" (188). His initial reaction to such language is typically negative:

> he found himself glancing from one casual word to another on his right or left in stolid wonder that they had been so silently emptied of instantaneous sense until every mean shop legend bound his mind like the words of a spell and his soul shrivelled up, sighing with age as he walked on in a lane among heaps of dead language. (178–79)

In its strange liveliness Stephen's image of verbal rubbish carries him past this instinctive revulsion to an ironically constructive sense of the materiality of these denatured words. In connecting him to the previous moment when he walks in a lane toward the university, "choosing his steps amid heaps of wet rubbish . . . stumbling through the mouldering offal" (175), this "dead language" joins the profane "disorder" with its "faint sour stink of rotted cabbages" that "was to win the day in his soul" (162) over the passionless appeal of the Jesuits. Within its apparent senselessness, Stephen finds vestiges of signification:

> His own consciousness of language was ebbing from his brain and trickling into the very words themselves which set to band and disband themselves in wayward rhythms:
>
> > *The ivy whines upon the wall*
> > *And whines and twines upon the wall*
> > *The ivy whines upon the wall*
> > *The yellow ivy on the wall*
> > *Ivy, ivy up the wall.*
>
> Did any one ever hear such drivel? Lord Almighty! Who ever heard of ivy whining on a wall? Yellow ivy: that was all right. Yellow ivory also. And what about ivory ivy?
> The word now shone in his brain, clearer and brighter than any ivory sawn from the mottled tusks of elephants. (179)

Within this nonsense lies the essence of a truth that Stephen's artistic response to language seeks to affirm above all else: that words having otherwise virtually ceased to function as verbal signs can be substantially transformed, achieving an epiphanic *claritas* when they materialize in the imagination. Increasingly he depends on such moments to allay his fear that language has become hopelessly degraded, that even his alphabetic sense of language will fail him: "The letters of the name Dublin lay heavily on his mind, pushing one another surlily hither and thither with slow boorish insistence" (111). The oppressive quality of this image is far more characteristic than the "soft liquid joy" that Stephen feels flowing through the "liquid letters" of the dying speech of Yeats's Countess Cathleen as her "long soft vowels hurtled noiselessly and fell away" (226). While he seeks out the immediate relations of words and objects, at times perceiving their interchangeability—for example, he can fully conceive of the reality of women's souls and bodies "only amid softworded phrases or within rosesoft stuffs"—such sensuality of linguistic perception is often dimmed by guilt. Shame tinges his response to the kiss of a prostitute, which is like "vague speech" that "pressed upon his brain as upon his lips" (101); elsewhere his image of a woman's face is "transfigured with a lecherous cunning" as she takes her place among the "jeweleyed harlots of his imagination" (99, 116). A coarse outburst by his friend Cranly stirs Stephen's apprehension that Dublin speech has become an inert mass that seems both heavy and hollow, sounding only "an echo of the sacred eloquence of Dublin. The heavy lumpish phrase sank slowly out of hearing like a stone through a quagmire. Stephen saw it sink as he had seen many another, feeling its heaviness depress his heart" (195). The artist's material tends thus to revert to the "the sluggish matter of the earth" (169) that he began with.

Joyce's acute sense of the physical properties of language owed much to the Catholic concept of the Divine Logos, and in particular to the paradox of spiritual reality seeking to manifest itself in the very incarnation that imposes mortality. The Annunciation, the Immaculate Conception and the sacrament of the Eucharist all rest on the doctrinal principle that the Logos entered history as a man and not only as a visiting deity. The creating Word was in historical fact made flesh. According to his brother, Stanislaus, Joyce developed the collateral notion of artistic transubstantiation early in his career. In *My Brother's Keeper* he recalls that Joyce asked him whether he thought "there is a certain resemblance between the mystery of the Mass and what I am trying to do? I mean that I am trying in my poems to give people some kind of intellectual pleasure or spiritual enjoyment by converting the bread of everyday life into something that has a permanent artistic life of its own" (103–104). This was at the time when Joyce composed his collection of epiphanies, which he also called *epicleti*, from the epiclesis or invocation at the moment of transubstantiation of the Eastern Orthodox Eucharist (*Letters* 55). Conspicuously, in the concluding journal entries of *A Portrait*, Stephen arrogates the mysteries of the Eucharist and the Annunciation to the secular process of aesthetic inception in which the artist becomes "a priest of the eternal imagination, transmuting the daily bread of experience into the radiant body of everliving life. . . . In the virgin womb of the imagination the word was made flesh" (221, 217).

Joyce's notion of the artist as priestly celebrant is always undercut to some extent by his wary irony, but it would be wrong to conclude that his intention is mere reductive parody. One way of illustrating this is to note

Fr. Robert Boyle's suggestion that Stephen's use of "transmuting"—as well as Joyce's "converting," perhaps—appears to prefer a term associated with medieval alchemy and therefore avoided by theologians including Duns Scotus and Thomas Aquinas, who adopted the novel "transubstantiation" (47). Even in the euphoric mood of the *Portrait* diary, Stephen seems to acknowledge the need to severely delimit the artist's hieratic function. He accepts this constraint not out of modesty, nor glibly, but in recognition of the debasement of the language he is condemned to use. Deprived of the transubstantiating potency of the Host, the artist is denatured along with his medium. He becomes the *poète maudit* whose imaginative creations can arise only from his improvisations on the black mass. They emerge from a forensic alchemy that pores over fragments of dead language in search of traces of the original Real Presence.

A principal factor contributing to the powerlessness that Stephen feels in *Ulysses* is his conviction that language has been usurped and corrupted by the materialism represented by Buck Mulligan. Mulligan's opening mock-consecration of the Host is in effect a black mass for the Word itself, reducing it to its material or "accidental" aspects—"the genuine christine: body and soul and blood and [w]oun[d]s" (3). Sooner or later, all created things in Mulligan's world are, as he says of Stephen's mother, "beastly dead" (7). The offense this gives to Stephen stems from his perception that if his mother's death is beastly, then his own is equally so. His growing demoralization becomes a measure of Mulligan's ascendancy, and as Stephen celebrates his own black masses in the later episodes, he nearly succumbs to Mulligan's nihilism. In the "Oxen of the Sun" episode, he even coins the blasphemous term "subsubstantiation," defined by Boyle as the "bestial exclusion of the divine" (52), to register his dejection. The name of the Creator has become for Stephen no more than a "shout in the street," a heedlessly furious profanity blurted at the darkest moments of the "nightmare of history" that he is unable to stop dreaming.

The early "Proteus" episode extends this worst of dreams throughout time and space, envisioning Mulligan's version of the Creation as a ruined cosmos of objects in flux, decaying, breaking down, becoming formally indistinct, even engulfing the very words that name them: "A bloated carcass of a dog lay lolled on bladderwrack. Before him the gunwale of a boat, sunk in sand. *Un coche ensablé* Louis Veuillot called Gautier's prose. These heavy sands are language tide and wind have silted here" (37). As in *A Portrait*, Stephen observes the transformation of language to ponderous matter, but now it is associated with the decomposition of a once-living body. (One of Joyce's entries for "Proteus" in Phillip Herring's '*Ulysses*' *Notesheets* reads, "incarnation, descent of man to dog" [287], and Stephen's black mass in "Circe" inverts "God" to "dog" [489]). The Logos is thus uncreated and bestialized in Stephen's imagination as it approaches its own extinction, dwindling to a dull, lifeless mass.

Stephen's sense of linguistic dispossession becomes an impasse that leads to his effacement by Leopold Bloom in the later episodes of *Ulysses*. Bloom's earthiness offered Joyce a way out of Stephen's decadent fixation on materialized language—on old phrases of the Elizabethans, for example, "tarnished by time" and "sweet only with a disinterred sweetness" (*Portrait* 176, 233), or on the "coffined thoughts" of the library books in *Ulysses* "in mummy cases, embalmed in spice of words . . . but an itch of death is in them" (159). This is not to suggest that Bloom's character represents a wholly satisfying resolution of the crisis of language that troubles Stephen. Although he is far more comfortably at home in the physical Creation than Stephen ever can be, Bloom is burdened with lifeless linguistic matter of a different kind. His materialism nonetheless contrasts sharply with Mulligan's because, even though it is mired in banalities, it is benign and humane; at moments it is even reverent. By assigning an organ of the body to each episode following Stephen's opening three, Joyce signaled an ontological shift to Bloom's sensual, appetitive contact with experience. Although his physical vitality is in some ways limited, especially as it involves his sexual role in his marriage, he craves the natural sensuality of his wife, Molly, whom Joyce characterized as the Flesh that continually assents ("[das] Fleisch [das] stets bejaht" [*Letters* 169]). The Blooms are the artistic raw material that Stephen has not transformed, "lumps of earth" awaiting the artist's shaping hand.

In *Joyce the Creator*, Sheldon Brivic discusses the *prima materia* that Joyce indicated in the "Linati Schema" for *Ulysses* as an essential thematic concept of the "Proteus" episode. He refers to St. Augustine's discussion of a pre-Creation consisting of formless matter (39–40). The idea of a material reality without characterizing features appealed to Joyce as a means of modifying Stephen Dedalus's artistic aspiration to a perfected, god-like creation. From this revised perspective the artist creates from chaos rather than a perfect void because his linguistic material exists in an intermediary stage between inception and artistic transformation. Increasingly in Joyce's later writing, traces of this anterior formlessness persist as signs of the artist's fixed limitations. These become most evident in the opaque language of the later episodes of *Ulysses*, and they culminate in the practically unreadable passages of *Finnegans Wake*. Despite his remarks to the contrary, Joyce realized that readers of this dense writing would experience the sensation of encountering a sort of verbal anti-matter, or a wall of words erected as a virtually physical obstacle to comprehension. In some later passages Joyce produces this effect simply by typographical device, as in the absence of punctuation and indentation in

Molly Bloom's soliloquy at the conclusion of *Ulysses*, or their rarity in the
distended paragraphs and catalogs of "Ithaca" and "Oxen of the Sun."

The opening page of "Oxen of the Sun" (314) offers a dramatic
example of language that is becoming indistinguishable from primal
matter. Following three initial incantatory celebrations of childbirth, Joyce
placed a paragraph consisting of two bewildering Latinate sentences. The
first extends to 118 words that can be paraphrased without substantial loss
of meaning thus: a nation's continued prosperity depends on its citizens'
procreation. Not only does this banality fail to reward the effort of reading
it, trudgingly elaborating a point that scarcely needs to be made, but the
next sentence consumes another 168 words to reiterate the statement. This
second version takes the form of a rhetorical question asking whether it is
possible for anyone to be so ignorant as to be unaware of the verity just
asserted. A similar case is the compendium of the properties of water in
"Ithaca" (549–50). It is readily apparent that its 472 words are part of
some Rabelaisian joke, even while they may seem to place inordinate
pressure on the diligent reader's sense of the comic—as Robinson states it,
the awareness of the prodigious linguistic precision of "Ithaca" as
"hilariously unnecessary" (35). Because of such verbal superfluities, the
episode projects a kind of logomania. In Karen Lawrence's words, it
parodies the mental projects that allow anything to be compared and
classified in relation to anything else in a doomed effort to satisfy "the
desire for an intelligible pattern" (194).

There can hardly be a greater difficulty facing a writer in a time of
cultural disintegration. Joyce's accumulations of verbiage, precisely
because they issue so often in triteness and futility, exemplify the
imperfectly transformable material that becomes more and more inchoate
as a writer tries and fails repeatedly to give adequate expression to
contemporary reality. Again, the stylistic parodies of "Oxen of the Sun"
may be taken as a case in point. They are arranged in the historical order
of their models' composition, proceeding from the initial primitive
incantations to the cacophony of contemporary slang at the conclusion.
Commentaries on Joyce's use of this formal device have usually focused on
the "embryonic development" that he indicated as the main conceptual
principle of the episode's organization. A theme that seems to emerge
logically from this approach is that language, like the many children of
Mina Purefoy, who again gives birth during the episode, is constantly being
born, with an inference of evolutionary development in both processes of
generation. The principal difficulty with this reading appears in the
episode's last paragraphs, whose style Joyce characterized as a "frightful
jumble" of slang and "broken doggerel" (*Letters* 139). It comes as close to
linguistic chaos as any passage in *Ulysses,* and because of its terminal

position in the time frame of "Oxen of the Sun," it appears to suggest a much darker historical force than evolution. Language, that is, not only fails to grow and evolve historically, but it actually devolves toward exhaustion and silence. Analogously, the birth of young Purefoy is in fact a doubtful basis for historical optimism. Doady and Mina Purefoy, it is implied, despite the Dickensian heartiness of the passage celebrating their son's delivery, can ill afford this addition to their family. He is their eighth surviving child, and by naming him after a cousin in the Treasury Remembrancer's office they betray their concern that they may be unable to provide for him (343). Doady is employed far from prosperously as second accountant at the Ulster Bank, and he is getting old, his "curfew" perhaps about to "ring" (345). Mina's labor has gone on dangerously long, and it has been a "hard birth" (316), probably reflecting Joyce's belief that his mother's death was hastened by multiple pregnancies. Although it may be excessively severe to argue that the terminal farrago of slang in "Oxen of the Sun" is the verbal equivalent of a mis-birth—despite little Purefoy's doubtful future, he is born healthy—there is unmistakably something abortive about it.

The sources that Joyce drew on for the stylistic parodies in *Ulysses* have been examined carefully for historical clues to their linguistic function. What these tend to reveal, as Lawrence observes in her study of "Oxen of the Sun," is that Joyce repeatedly ignores his sources and "makes the model recede into a wash of words" (143). James Atherton reaches a similar conclusion (Hart and Hayman 313–39). Hugh Kenner seeks to account for the mass of verbal debris in "Ithaca" and the "worn fragments of acoustic junk" in the barroom songs of "Sirens" (87). He proposes that information is being "marmorealised" in "Ithaca," that Joyce performs "great feats of marmorealisation" before the reader's eyes as his words take on a quality of commemorative engravings in marble. Kenner is unclear, however, in concluding from this that the example of the water catalog "achieves in one page the improbable feat of raising to poetry all the clutter of footling information that has accumulated in schoolbooks." Nor is it certain that this lyric note is heard in the expressive "liturgical cadences" and in the "grave catechetical manner that suffuses [the meeting of Stephen and Bloom] with the calm of the paradigmatic" (135–39). In his effort to derive a redemptive theme from Joyce's parody, Kenner appears to exceed the logic of his lapidary metaphor. Rather than the serene resolution that he perceives, the marmoreal/memorial language present in *Ulysses* becomes progressively rigid—petrified—as it transforms the memory of verbal signification into the equivalent of inscribed funerary stone.

The conclusion that the language of *Finnegans Wake* extends this process of materialization further but stops short of terminal illegibility becomes finally, perhaps, a question of trust on the part of Joyce's sympathetic reader. With few exceptions, Joyce probably did not allow purely aleatory or other irrational elements to remain in the published texts. Deliberate obfuscation was not part of his method. Even when the reading process slows down to gazing and frowning at resistant alphabetical characters and at the sigla, hieroglyphs, geometric drawings and doodles that Joyce scattered throughout, they remain superficially recognizable and resolve themselves into dimly familiar symbols. The attentive reader can usually detect at least a faint resonance of meaning, or a sensation of some signification having been muted but not lost entirely.

At every point in his career, there is evidence of Joyce's conviction that literary language can never be wholly free of obscurity. His epiphanies, among his earliest compositions, may be read as literary attempts to acknowledge inexpressible states of consciousness. The modernity of the stories in *Dubliners* (1914) can be succinctly demonstrated by Joyce's selection of the three words—*paralysis, gnomon, simony*— that bemuse the narrator of the opening story, "The Sisters." They appear initially to detach themselves from its verbal structure, and they never enter into a fully rationalizing context. Notwithstanding extensive critical efforts to place them in a supposedly implicit syntax, these words retain their opacity. They form a resistant but not altogether incomprehensible set of signifiers. While Colin MacCabe asserts persuasively that they finally yield "no interpretation except strangeness and an undefined evil" (*Revolution* 34), it may be noted further that the three words are nouns and that they become paradoxically less comprehensible as their substantive quality is fully apprehended. *Simony* and *paralysis* supply an ecclesiastic and physiological matrix for the degeneration that has befallen the boy's mentor, Father Flynn, albeit obscurely. *Gnomon*, on the other hand, naming irreducible geometric objects—the style of a sundial or a Euclidean polygon—remains contextually so obscure that the readings it elicits must all seem forced. Anticipating the darkened language of *Finnegans Wake*, the inexpressive, object-like impenetrability of *gnomon* opposes its materiality to efforts of interpretation. MacCabe's work on Joyce's material language goes further than any other criticism in its attempt to account for this intractable element. He traces its development in Joyce's later works, noting moments in *Ulysses*, beginning with the eleventh episode, "Sirens," when the letters that form the words are "no longer an evident source of meaning" (81). *Finnegans Wake* continues this withdrawal from signification with its full demonstration of the ways that "Joyce's texts grant a primacy to the material of language over the fugitive meanings that attach to it," thereby dispelling the illusion of window-like transparency in the "classic realist texts which they displace" (133).

MacCabe's approach, like Bishop's, owes much to the central formulations of French post-structuralist theory. This is particularly evident in its embrace of the notion of writing as the playful activity that engages various discourses but reaches no interpretive closure and neither attaches to nor proceeds from an external historical reality. Leopold Bloom, viewed in this light, becomes interesting as a character principally for his "joyful entering into the various ways of signifying world and self" (*Revolution* 101). Although such a reading runs counter to the humanist essentialism that characterizes the criticism fostered by Ellmann and his adherents, it appears otherwise to depart in no essential way from the conventions of "festive comedy" that intertwine interpretation and celebration in observance of a principle of critical decorum from the 1950s and early 1960s. In MacCabe's attack on the criticism that approaches Joyce's works as "complicated crossword puzzles whose solution is the banal liberal humanism of the critic" (*Revolution* 2), he is mainly intent on excluding the idea of the verbal riddle and all other notions anticipating closure from the critical enterprise.

As a consequence of MacCabe's postmodern hermeneutics, he passes over Joyce's use of the insoluble linguistic puzzle as a reflection of the reduced but at some point irreducible human personality itself, the ineluctable characterization that he sought from the beginning in the epiphanies and stories. Joyce's opening portrait of the paralyzed priest in *Dubliners* introduces a gallery of minimized beings. They represent a materialized and hollowed-out Dublin whose citizens are nearly bereft of a story to tell: Maria, in "Clay," reduced in her prim and trite virginity to the inanimate matter of the title; or Corley in "Two Gallants," whose mechanical sexuality is expressed by the image of his head as a rotating oily knob; or the insane mother of "Eveline," ending her days in inarticulate raving, "Derevaun Seraun! Derevaun Seraun!" The condition of these characters became for Joyce, in the long run, an unsolvable mystery. "*Jouissance*" and the other playful echoes of Joyce's name that his critics have so often invoked to characterize his antic levity in *Ulysses* and *Finnegans Wake* are really apt only if they acknowledge its disturbing historical dimensions. Joyce addresses these directly in only a few instances—the grim humor of Stephen Dedalus's nightmare of history in *Ulysses* (28), for example, or the "ecstasy catastrophe" (565) that conveys Leopold Bloom's racial memory of disastrous and uncompensated loss.

Finnegans Wake, then, may be read as Joyce's meditation on the enigma of the word that becomes only flesh. He regarded the artist's revelation of this descendental process as the work of an outlaw who not only exposes a forbidden truth but who is also guiltily implicated in it. *Finnegans Wake* often represents itself reflexively in the letter that the hen, one of *Anna*

Livia Plurabelle's myriad emanations, scratches up from a domestic rubbish heap—the "heaps of dead language" of *A Portrait* given a rather more specific form. The letter is "darkumound numbur wan" (386), primal matter originally taking verbal form but obscured and faded by years of subterranean decay. Its news, reported obscurely and with weary redundancy throughout the *Wake*, consists mainly of variations on the main narratives of the Freudian "family romance." Its actors include the patriarchal HCE and the maternal/filial/feminine ALP, who both chides his backsliding and defends him from charges of murky sexual offenses. These are adumbrated in an episode in Phoenix Park involving two girls and three young male soldiers. Incestuous overtones are heard repeatedly in the many voices that puzzle over the letter's contents. The anguished generational strife they entail is accented by the recurrent Oedipal encounter between HCE and the "cad," a cheeky youth smoking an impudently phallic pipe who asks him seemingly innocent but nonetheless guilt-arousing questions and riddles about time. To the many inquiring voices—a babel of local gossips, family tattletales, inquisitors on various tribunals, self-important chroniclers, children avid for bedtime stories—who try to decipher its scant narrative, the letter is always for the most part illegible. It appears as a bewilderingly multi-faceted "proteiform graph . . . a polyhedron of scripture" supposedly written by "a purely deliquescent recidivist," Shem the Penman, a chronically delinquent, dissolute, criminal personality (107). Querulous voices delving into the letter's origins insinuate that these "shemletters" betray his shame: it has been degraded to "litter" (93 and *passim*) and debased to "low"-relief "strangewrote anaglyptics" (419). Even the separate characters forming its words appear obscurely as chaotic symbols on an unreadable map with "cardinal points":

> These ruled barriers along which the traced words, run, march, halt, walk, stumble at doubtful points, stumble up again in comparative safety. . . . It is seriously believed by some that the intention may have been geodetic. . . . But by writing thithaways end to end and turning, turning and end to end hithaways writing and with lines of litters slittering up and louds of latters slettering down . . . where in the waste is the wisdom?" (114)

The interchangeable obscured document and blank page—that familiar trope of modernism—form a central motif of *Finnegans Wake*. They occur dramatically in one of HCE's most menacing encounters with the cad, whose pipe becomes a weapon wielded by a "starving gunman." He is nonetheless recognizable "in or out of the lextinction of life and who the hell else, by your blanche patch on the boney part" (here and elsewhere the cad figures as the upstart Napoleon who shoots Wellington off his "wide harse" [10]). The cad's language is decipherable with a "Nichtian glossery" (both darkened night-words and page-blanking nothing-words) that "is nat language at any sinse of the world" (83). Generational conflict thus erupts as a war of words whose fury abates periodically through the mediation of ALP; but the bellicose "Quarrellary" is this: "The logos . . . comes to nullum in the endth" (298). The illegibility of *Finnegans Wake* is revealed at the "deleteful hour" when words are erased from memory. When they are inscribed on the blank sheet, they are tinged with guilt, as one of Shem's alter egos, the outcast Glugg, reveals: "He would jused sit it all write down just as he would jused set it up all writhefully rate in blotch and void, yielding to no man in hymns ignorance, seeing how heartsilly sorey he was, owning to the condrition of his bikestool [German *Beichstuhl*, confessional]" (229).

The source of this language-effacing guilt is first exposed in one of Shem's early historical identities, the disreputable Roman poet Caddy who, in contrast to his brother Primus and the "decent people" he associates with, "wrote o peace a farce. Blotty words for Dublin" (14). Glugg, that is, tries to pass off his piece of verse as a pacifier in the "Bloody wars" he wages with Primus over their sister, but it is exposed as a piece of arse because of his transparently prurient interest in her. This scandalous revelation renders his words null and void—or so boast Primus and Caddy's other detractors. Their attack on Glugg blots his words from their formal historical record of Dublin-Rome. His writing is nullified as expunged ink, reduced to the equivalent of excrement.

Joyce's language of the outlaw emerges from a larger conception of speech as a product of the Fall. Indeed, the idea of verbal utterance as an act of theological transgression was a key to his artistic identity. Earlier writers who fell foul of ecclesiastical dogma and were accused of heresy often figure in the intellectual background of his work. Giambattista Vico, who along with Giordano Bruno plays this role most prominently in *Finnegans Wake*, conjectures in *The New Science* that the genesis of language came about as man's startled reaction to the sound of divine thunder. His fear carried him beyond infantile onomatopoeia to articulate speech in the naming of the Father:

> Human words were formed next from interjections, which are sounds articulated under the impetus of violent passions. In all languages these are monosyllables. Thus it is not beyond likelihood that, when wonder had been awakened in men by the first thunderbolts, these interjections of Jove should give birth to one produced by the human voice: "*pa!*" (107)

Vico's etymologies for words that connote *father* trace them to the exclamations of children "dazed with fear" (108). Joyce, from his vantage in the evolution of psychoanalytic theory, recognized in Vico's idea something more complex and more troubling even than abject terror in the presence of divine authority; for him, these fearful outcries represented the consciousness of transgression in the voice of the thunder itself, which in *Finnegans Wake* is always characterized by guilty stammering. Further adapting Vico, Joyce imagined that Viconian man cries out the name of the Father when his angry thunder interrupts his copulation and other guilty acts that are sexual in nature from a pathological or sado-masochistic perspective. Joyce's ten hundred-letter thunderclaps, even as they announce the *ricorso* that heralds the new theocratic age, are counterpointed not only by stutters but also by the audible traces of defecation, further embroiling creation and degradation. From its beginnings, then, language is appropriated by the criminal creator of words, the "outlex" whose "back life will not stand being written about in black and white" (169).

Drawing on the early Gnostic heresy that equated the Creation and the Fall, Joyce implicates the Creator in the crime of artistic inception. Thus he places the work of art in a radically paradoxical context that both exalts and degrades it. The extreme tensions that result work toward its incoherence and disintegration. This subversion of conventional aesthetic values at times virtually consumes the work of art and even becomes its principal subject. Aesthetic instability takes on the aspect of a permanent condition, and negation acquires the creative status of affirmation. The daemonic artist, seeking a principle of subversive form, is like a hell-bound Dante without Virgil as guide, describing circles of ruin that finally close concentrically on himself as the object of his own corrosive imagination. Such a figure of the *poète maudit* shaped Joyce's image of the artist early in his career, beginning with his satirical broadside of 1904, "The Holy Office" (*Critical Writings* 149–52). He castigates his fellow Irish poets for their hypocritical delusions:

> But all these men of whom I speak
> Make me the sewer of their clique.
> That they may dream their dreamy dreams
> I carry off their filthy streams
> For I can do those things for them
> Through which I lost my diadem,
> Those things for which Grandmother Church
> Left me severely in the lurch.
> Thus I relieve their timid arses,
> Perform my office of Katharsis.

Here is the self-portrait of the formerly honored teller of truth in whose rejection all aesthetic value is overturned. The poet's language becomes flowing sewage and malodorous refuse (Joyce wrote of *Dubliners* that "it is not my fault that the odour of ashpits and old weeds and offal hangs round my stories" [*Letters* 63–64]); the historical bearer of the sacred Word becomes a chamber servant; and Aristotle's purgative *katharsis* functions as an enema. His abysmal debasement, however, is finally affirmed as the heroic stance of the outcast poet, assumed autonomously as his powers of imaginative inversion prevail over those of his craven rivals:

> Where they have crouched and crawled and prayed
> I stand the self-doomed, unafraid,
> Unfellowed, friendless and alone,
> Indifferent as the herring-bone,
> Firm as the mountain-ridges where
> I flash my antlers in the air.

Such lofty and grandiloquent disdain soon became an unsustainable—and undesirable—posture for Joyce. He went on to portray the artist in *Ulysses* as a chastened and even a failed, self-contradicting figure. Stephen Dedalus appears in the opening pages as Icarus, drowning in material reality; later, anticipating the scapegrace Shem the Penman, he returns as a priest *manqué* who is present at the black masses that deny the Easter resurrection in the act of celebrating it amid the brothels of Dublin.

Once he had abandoned the heroic pose of "The Holy Office" and *A Portrait*, Joyce encountered the difficulty of characterizing the artist and his work as more that the sum of their failures. In "Shem the Penman" (169–95), the last of his self-portraits, Joyce emphasizes the regressiveness of the artist's personality as Shem withers in the face of his inquisitorial examiners. While these adversaries tend to coalesce in the voice of his brother Shaun, who addresses his indictment of Shem to "your honour" (181), they modulate eventually to Shem's attack on himself: "me, branded sheep, pick of the wasterpaperbaskel" and the "unseen blusher in an obscene coalhole . . . dweller in the downandoutermost where voice only of the dead may come" (194). Like the guilt-ridden transgressions of HCE that he attempts to describe, Shem's lapses, while they take an outwardly verbal form, are presented as being vaguely sexual. His retreat into his "Haunted Inkbottle" (182) is a form of regression to the Freudian developmental stage of pre-genital infancy, in which sexual acts have not yet been distinguished from the ingestion of food, and procreation is associate with and explained by excretion. Shaun details his decrepit "bodily get-up" (169) and the physical "shame" through which his "lowness creeped out first via foodstuffs" (170) when he "kuskykorked himself up tight in his inkbattle house" (176).

Thus incarcerated, as "pious Eneas" he writes with his excreted ink on the parchment of his own skin—"the only foolscap available"—in a scene rendered as a travesty of the Virgilian epic. In this autobiographical passage (185–86) Joyce concedes the literary artist's inessential nature. Once perceived as heroic and godly—a pious Aeneas—he has dwindled to a corporeality ("unheavenly . . . human only, mortal") that betrays the greyness of age despite his art, like Oscar Wilde's Dorian Gray and his "chagreenold" model, Balzac's *Le peau de chagrin*. In his degeneration he approaches the sub- or extra-human ("his own individual person life unlivable"). He is a cephalopod squirting ink on his low-grade paper skin, obscenely producing his no longer ingestible excremental matter ("not protected by copriright"). He is the "first till last alshemist," powerless to transubstantiate this material. He can create nothing but an exchange of "transaccidentated" accidentals—the abjectly literal bread and wine of an unsanctified Eucharist—since his imagination is powered only by the "slow fires of consciousness" (like Shelley's "fading coal" in *A Portrait*). Lost to him are the volcanic refiners' fires of Heraclitis and the Old Testament (Malachi 3:2) that manifest the immaterial origin of all things.

Shem's engendering process leaves a "corrosive sublimation" (mercuric chloride), both poison and preservative, a chemical solid transmuted to gas without attaining a vital fluidity. As his individual presence fades, he leaves his litter/letters with their ever-recurrent "cyclewheeling history" whose eternal words "would not pass away." The words are deathless not because of any redeeming sublimation but because they have already reached a nadir of materiality "through the bowels of his misery" and can pass no further. The once-transparent "crystalline" transparency of the writer's world, his Holy Office, has become an opaque bottle of fecal ink, and as its inhabitant he has become his own Katharsis-Purgative. Excrement becomes the terminal point of correspondence between language and physical experience.

Sigmund Freud's theoretical writing on art and sexuality dwells on the unconventionality and social isolation of the artistic personality. This is particularly apparent in "Leonardo da Vinci and a Memory of His Childhood" (1910) (XI, 63–137), with *Psychopathology of Everyday Life* (1904) one of two works by Freud in Joyce's Trieste library (Ellmann, *Consciousness* 109). Freud examines evidence of Leonardo's "cool repudiation of sexuality" (69) and his consequent substitution of an all-consuming inquisitiveness in which "investigation becomes a sexual activity" (80). By sublimating this knowledge so as to develop emotionally "beyond love and hatred," Leonardo "investigated instead of loving" (75). In doing so he exemplified the burgeoning of creative sexual repression in the Renaissance, and he accordingly gained a reputation among the pubic as a "great and pure man" (70n, 86). At the same time, the repressed energies of his passion for knowledge led him into the intellectual demimonde that sheltered "the despised alchemists, in whose laboratories experimental research had found some refuge at least in those unfavourable times" (66). A secret sense of alienation is manifested in such grotesqueries in Leonardo's notebooks as the clinical illustration of sexual intercourse, replete with ignorant errors and distortions that suggest the artist's troubled sexuality. Whereas primitive societies had openly worshipped genitalia, portraying them and their functions with great accuracy and sublimating them into attributes of divinity, Freud observes contrary tendencies in Leonardo's time: "In the course of cultural development so much of the divine and sacred was ultimately extracted from sexuality that the exhausted remnant fell into contempt" (97). Freud accordingly draws on the familiar notion of "how frequently great artists take pleasure in giving vent to their phantasies in erotic and even crudely obscene pictures" (70). Leonardo's copulating pair appears at first glance to be one of many striking examples of his alert and incisive observation and surpassing draftsmanship; but Freud identifies it as an imperfect sublimation of the infantile "intense desire to look, as an erotic instinctual activity" centered on the primitive desire "to see other people's genitals" (96).

Freud's essay on Leonardo fills in much of the background for the opposing personalities of Shem and Shaun, especially as it reflects on their voyeuristic obsessions. Shaun enacts the public display of Leonardo's form of repressed sexuality, popularly perceived as moral purity; it is a pose that constantly disfigures but fails to conceal his Shem aspect, with its crude, obscene, disaffected fixations. Shaun upbraids Shem for describing the parents' genitalia, but he does so in a way that unconsciously implicates himself: "he bares sobsconcious inklings shadowed on soulskin" (377). Juxtaposed dualistically, the two brothers perform the central historical dramas of *Finnegans Wake,* all referring back to its main cyclical structures. Joyce derived these principally from Vico and Giordano Bruno. Vico perceives a recurrent process of universal disintegration followed by theocratic re-integration. Bruno's doctrine of reconciled opposites causes the warring brothers to assume the contrary but potentially integrated emotional identities of Tristopher and Hilary, from Bruno's motto, *"In tristitia hilaris hilaritate tristis"* (Atherton 37).

Other male pairs analogous to Shem and Shaun appear throughout *Finnegans Wake,* generally to re-enact scenes from this regenerative comedy. Their divisiveness at times reaches such extremes of polarity that it invokes the specter of a cataclysmic breakdown of the historical cycle. A case in point is Joyce's principal fable of generational conflict, "Buckley and the Russian General" (337–54). The tale of Irish Private Buckley's assassination of the Russian general at the Battle of Sevastopol is told by the rival siblings Butt and Taff, who render the moment of patricide as an assault on the Thunderer's authority by the "abnihilisation of the etym" (353). In this striking instance of black humor Joyce alludes to the new theories of nuclear physics demonstrating that matter can indeed be destroyed. By the punning analogy of "etym" and *atom*, he implies that the materialization of language could conceivably extend equally to the point of annihilation. In that drastic eventuality, even the miserable plight of the "alshemist" would seem bearable in contemplation of the loss of the material basis on which his despair—and whatever hope he may cling to—rests. The prospect of this ultimate deletion occasionally raises a note of relieved gratitude in the voices of the *Wake* that brood on the uncertain survival of the letter:

> we ought really to rest thankful that at this deleteful hour of dungflies dawning we have even a written on with dried ink scrap of paper at all to show for ourselves, tare it or leaf it . . . after all that we lost and plundered of it even to the hidmost coignings of the earth and all it has gone through . . . cling to it as with drowning hands, hoping against hope all the while that . . . things will begin to clear up . . . as, strictly between ourselves, there is a limit to all things so this will never do. (118–19)

This timorous passage is characteristic of the moments of near-awakening that occur in the latter phases of the book; it is detectable even in the most rhapsodic passages of the concluding *ricorso*, as though the end of the nightmare of history were scarcely to be hoped for. The "hour of risings" is greeted all the more gladly for the possibility that it may never have arrived: "It was a long, very long, a dark, very dark, an allburt unend, scarce endurable, and we could add mostly quite various and somewhat stumbletumbling night." The ceaselessness of universal birth conveyed by "allburt unend"—German *all[e] [Ge]burt[en]*, all births—counters the sense of near-termination—all but an end—and takes up the similarly ambiguous reference to Lake Albert, formally Albert Nyanza, as a life-giving source of the Nile, but spelled "Allberths neantas" to supply the undertone of annihilation from the French *néant*. Even more ominously than the late passages of the "Oxen of the Sun" episode of *Ulysses*, distinctions between birth and abortion tend to become blurred in *Finnegans Wake* (598). It tells of a "dromo of todos," at once a cycling race course for everyone (Spanish *todos*) and a drama of death (German *Tod*).

In *Creativity and Perversion*, Janine Chasseguet-Smirgel sees in the works of the Marquis de Sade an extreme expression of the artistic materialization of language. Among De Sade's anticipations of modernism is his despair of aesthetic sublimation and his consequent efforts to challenge nature by outrageously violating its "stubborn reality" (9). Sensing that the conventional means of differentiating genders and generations had been lost in a massive erosion of the principles of division and separation, he takes the next step and imaginatively abolishes them, jettisoning distinctions between male and female, between parent and child, indeed, between virtually all conceptions of the "high" and the "low," in his quest for the chaos of indifferentiation (4). He finds that the potential of his perversion is limited only by the irreducibility of matter itself, which the science of his day regarded as indestructible. Nature therefore becomes the inversion of the divine refiner's fire—a cauldron in which Sade ultimately reduces the highest and most highly formed reality, God, to the lowest and most formless, excrement (4).

Chasseguet-Smirgel builds on Freud's conception of the artistic personality as a mixture of "efficiency, perversion, and neurosis" (90). This antithetical structure replaces the orthodox sublimating impulse with a reversed idealism. The effect is de Sade's exaltation of his own infantile Ego in its pre-genital non-differentiation and its worship of the excremental products of the body. He achieves a "neo-creation" composed of "new forms" and "hybrid beings" (19). The new reality of infantile regression ultimately reduces both body and language to playthings; in the words of Hans Belmer, quoted by Chasseguet-Smirgel, "The body can be compared to a sentence inviting one to disarticulate it for its true elements to be recombined in a series of endless anagrams" (21). Clinically, she concludes, this perversion expresses the over-estimation of objects that results from the inverted religiosity of self-adoration (94). She notes the conspicuous case of Oscar Wilde's aestheticism, in which "art is reduced to its decorative function" so that the Ego may be "transfigured" by the idealized objects and settings surrounding it. It is a state the artist arrives at by means of a ceaseless effort of creation to preserve the illusion that the idealized aesthetic object is not merely "a means of masking sadism and anality" (98). Failing such transfiguration, art approaches the terminal condition of the word made flesh.

Of the many manifestations of Shem's artistic personality in *Finnegans Wake*, none departs substantially from this model of sadomasochistic regression. "Shem the Penman" opens with a view of "what this hybrid actually was like to look at" (169) and goes on to develop his deeply regressive nature. Even in his final appearance as the Archdruid, figured in the *Ricorso* on a triptych of Irish saints, his verbal defeat at the hands of a Shaun-like St. Patrick (612) is still suffered in the mortifying context of defecation, repeating a key element in the archetypal clash of Buckley and the Russian General. It acts as a pervasive impasse in *Finnegans Wake*, and it provides what is perhaps the most accurate measure of the price Joyce paid for renouncing the subliminal function of literary language. His tendency, moreover, to seek compensation in the palliative role of the maternal ALP is unsatisfactory on several grounds, not the least being its recapitulation of a pattern of infantile sexual organization. Her role as HCE's partner is for the most part stereotypically maternal. It casts her as the apologist for her man in the midst of calumny, buttressing his tottering ego, and supplying other kinds of emotional prosthesis. As sexual partner, by the same token, she variously plays the scold, the whore, and the victim of his incestuous proclivities. In her maternal relationship with Shem she is indicted as co-author of the letter and, as the scavenging hen, she is credited with retrieving it from history's rubbish heap. She thus plays the paradoxical role of the guilt-inducing seductress who authorizes the creation of the word but is herself exempted from judgment by virtue of her extraverbal female nature. Shaun characteristically exposes his hypocritical piety in stressing this in the pseudo-homiletic manner of the second part of Book 3: "In the beginning was the gest he jousstly says, for the end is with woman, flesh-without-word, while the man to be is in a worse case after than before since she on the supine satisfies the verg [French *verge*, rod, wand, penis] to him" (468).

The notion of the feminine "flesh-without-word" actually exempts ALP from bestial subsubstantiation by locating her in the pre-verbal context of the language of gesture. This idea was made current in the 1930s by the Abbé Jousse, the linguistic experimenter whose work interested Joyce (Ellmann, *James Joyce* 634). Jousse held that all verbal expression was originally an act of gesticulation that was replaced by the empty, passive conventions of alphabetic writing. He attributed to woman an innately wordless nature that enables her to retain traces of this gestural utterance, while men fall obsessionally into the realm of logo-erotic creation. Men enter the female body as an arena of creativity, but this is an illusion that is shattered in the inevitable dissolution of meaning. The sad plight of the male creator is that he "wanamade singsigns to soundsense and yit he wanna git all his flesch nuemaid motts [newly-made/cloud-heaven-originated words/girls] truly prural and plusible [his procreativity nullified by his concupiscence]" (138). He begins with words-as-voids, combines them in expressively musical forms, then recedes with them into pre-human, insect-like unconsciousness: "In the buginning is the woid, in the muddle is the sounddance and thereinofter you're in the unbewised [German *unbewusst*, unconscious, *unbewiesen*, unproved] again" (378). The female observes this recurrence in moods ranging from compassion to contempt, with the latter sounding bitterly in ALP's dying speech near the *Wake*'s conclusion:

> All me life I have been lived among them but now they are becoming lothed to me. And I am lothing their little warm tricks. . . . How small it's all! And me letting on to meself always. And lilting on all the time. I thought you were all glittering with the

noblest of carriage. You're only a bumpkin. I thought you the great in all things, in guilt and in glory. You're but a puny. Home! (627)

The central artistic themes that Joyce developed in *Finnegans Wake* involve the writer's preoccupation with verbalized beginnings. Although a portrayal of the gestation of humanity and its languages was clearly one of his large-scale objectives, he was left in the end mainly with the story of their dissipation. The cyclical patterns of sacred and secular history described in prior narratives retain their redemptive potential in *Finnegans Wake* only to the very small extent that a return to an original innocence can be conceived of in terms of an imaginative escape from the trap of sadomasochistic perversion. Joyce envisions a number of paradisal scenes suggesting this possibility in *Finnegans Wake*, and it is perhaps not always necessary to see them as negated entirely by the scenes of the Fall that invariably follow them. One such scene, to cite only the simplest, occurs just prior to the Oedipal debacle of "Buckley and the Russian General": "We are once amore as babes awondering in a wold made fresh where with the hen in the storyaboot we start from scratch" (336). Given that the tumultuous cycles of time will not pause, they may appear to do so as the Viconian *ricorso* posits a moment when origins may be imagined as realities before the confused disorder of origination sets in. It is the fresh world of the "storyaboot," the children's nourishing porridge, in the story ever about to begin, once upon a time prior to the Word's incarnation. Joyce leaves "amore" unqualified in this scene: the logos is not yet corrupted, and although the Fall is inevitably at hand—"it was of him . . . to feel to every of the youngling fruits"—the hen-scratched, pen-scratched letter can be its own beginning, written in a gesture of origins without origin and accordingly innocent, even though what appear to be its decomposed traces bear the marks of the Fall: "Leave the letter that never begins to go find the latter that ever comes to end, written in smoke and blurred by mist and signed of solitude, sealed at night" (337). Never beginning and ever ending are the same; *fin negans* means asserting in a continuous present that the end of the wake-vigil has always occurred "not yet," an expression that echoes from the *Wake*'s opening page.

The modern critical tradition that has sought to distinguish between Joyce's aesthetic and reductive materialism has done so mainly by reading his later works insistently as comedies. This effort has resulted both in the spirit of humanistic affirmation of Richard Ellmann's work and in the application of various postmodern concepts of discursive play or, for the Bakhtinian revival, "carnivality." In their very different ways these main branches of the tradition have produced an image of the Joycean *corpus* that is richly innocent of dogma and free of authoritarian closure. Their readings of the "joyicity" of *Ulysses* and *Finnegans Wake* remain convincing to a certain extent, but they tend to ignore the limiting regressiveness that it entails. In Joyce's later vision of the devolution of literary language, he withdraws from it into an infantile incapacity for articulated speech. Childhood innocence being a state of sweet vulnerability, it is just as well that Joyce meant quite another thing; he meant the child's nightmare of "catastrophic cataclysms which make terror the basis of human mentality" (*Ulysses* 572). This is the "ecstasy of catastrophe" that cannot hope to verbalize the enormity of its sense of waste and loss and is "innocent" only as it is pre-verbal.

CHAPTER THREE

F. Scott Fitzgerald's New World:
Transfiguring America

The preceding chapters examine some of the most conspicuous works of fiction by early modernist writers for various kinds of circumscription. Joseph Conrad and James Joyce both betray an increasingly acute sense of the debility of the language and the literary conventions that they were required to adapt to their purposes; and their work at times displays—more or less consciously—evidence of some personally limiting artistic vision. It becomes clear that the aesthetic vitality of their writing does not entirely escape the deleterious effects of the subversive energies that they direct toward antithetical historical realities. Other readers, including Harold Bloom, Ihab Hassan and Hugh Kenner, have commented at length on the self-subverting impulses of modernism, but they have regarded it almost exclusively as the constructive power of those master craftsmen whose handiwork emerges intact from the hostile environment in which it was created. Images of the canonical figures of modernism rising superbly above the cultural ruins of their time have accordingly been, in a word, overdrawn. In the chapters that follow, further manifestations of the paradoxical subversiveness of modern fiction will be studied in three writers whose first important work was published in the 1920s. As a result of a continuing conflict between the literary imagination and historical actuality, distortion and error sometimes mar their work, but sometimes they also serve to accomplish these writers' artistic ends.

Among the American novelists of the modern period, F. Scott Fitzgerald is an extreme case of the literary imagination caught in conflict between its transfiguring vision and the consciousness of unyielding fact. No successful writer of fiction in his time, unless it be Thomas Wolfe, abandoned himself more fully to the expression of romantic desire while at the same time laying claim to a plausible reflection of an actual world. Luckily, he was well aware of this proclivity, and in the most successful work he produced in the 1920s—pre-eminently *The Great Gatsby* (1925)— he was determined to convert it to a strength. He searched for a means of preserving what his biographer Andrew Turnbull calls "a taut realism but also a gossamer romance" (*Scott Fitzgerald* 151), relaxing the powerfully destructive tensions between them by means of rigorously disciplined form, restrained style, and extensive revision. At its worst, Fitzgerald's writing prior to *Gatsby* tends to force his concessions to actuality, causing the collapse of his "gossamer romance" into the effusion and bathos that flaw *This Side of Paradise* (1920) and *The Beautiful and the Damned* (1922). With *The Great Gatsby*, however, he set out to create a narrative that would be both romantic and skillfully crafted. With a more rigorous aesthetic discipline, the world as it was given to him—the New York and Long Island settings, the practical sense of time passing, the transplanted Midwestern characters—could be faithfully preserved but transfigured nonetheless. Jay Gatsby's tragic assertion of "the unreality of reality" (105) could be presented convincingly, as he expressed it to his editor, Maxwell Perkins, as an "intricately patterned" and "consciously artistic" achievement reached "through the sustained imagination of a sincere yet radiant world" (Turnbull, *Scott Fitzgerald* 146–67).

The resulting novel that he published in April 1925 has been accorded a unique position among Fitzgerald's works, not only for its nearly flawless form but also for its fully realized settings. H. L. Mencken was among the first to note these apparent strengths, judging that the new novel showed hard work on every page, greatly improving on the "extraordinarily slipshod—at times almost illiterate" writing that had marred his previous works. Conrad Aiken similarly applauded Fitzgerald's movement away from "the sham romanticism . . . which the magazines demand of him." Mencken also liked the settings, commenting that the "Long Island he sets before us is no fanciful Alsatia; it actually exists" (Bryer 212–13, 244); but privately, some of Fitzgerald's correspondents were hardly enthusiastic about the quality of this realism. The criticism of his old Princeton friend, John Peale Bishop, was the most apt; he complained about Fitzgerald's factual inaccuracies and advised him to strive for James Joyce's precise use of detail. Bishop cited the early scene in Daisy Buchanan's living room (12–15) as an example of *Gatsby's* lack of "clear visualization" and its tendency to depict "things . . . which could not . . . have been seen . . . details . . . which could not have been as you describe them. . . . Your own experience of things outside yourself still seems to me a bit blurred, whether considering a thing felt or a thing seen" (*Correspondence* 168). Fitzgerald's friend and Long Island neighbor, Ring Lardner, had sounded an earlier warning of this kind in his comments on the proofs Fitzgerald sent him. "There ain't any lower level at that station," he observed in his mock-prole epistolary manner, referring to Nick Carraway's non-existent "lower-level" waiting area at the Manhattan terminus of the Long Island Railroad in Penn Station (42), "and I suggest substitute terms for the same." There was more: "On Page 82, you had the guy [Gatsby] driving under the elevated at Astoria, which ain't Astoria, but Long Island City." Fitzgerald never corrected these mistakes, even though there could have been no arguing with Lardner's dogged factuality; but in the second printing he did include two other corrections proposed by his friend. "Union Station" (183) in Chicago replaced the misnamed "Union Street Station" of the proofs; and the "ebb-tide" that threatens to ground Dan Cody's yacht on Lake Superior (104) was suppressed in response to Lardner's observation that there are no tides on the Great Lakes (*Correspondence* 154).

The reasons why Fitzgerald corrected some of these errors, either at the suggestion of others or independently, but allowed others to stand are unclear. He claimed that he and Zelda devoted six weeks to revision of the galleys during a working holiday in Italy in the winter of 1924; and he reported with apparent satisfaction to Perkins and to Ernest Hemingway that they had corrected "thousands" of errors. That he was being fastidious in matters of historical fact as well as the minutiae of style and grammar is evident, for example, in his request to Perkins for information on the medal of the Montenegran Order of Danilo, which Gatsby shows to Nick Carraway as they drive through "Astoria" (71). Fitzgerald wanted to know "whether a courtesy decoration given to an American would bear an English inscription" (*Letters* 165–77). This kind of diligence makes his concern for the demands of "taut realism" quite clear, but in many other instances the competing claims of a "gossamer romance" seem to have tempered Fitzgerald's devotion to the world of "sincere" factuality. His failure to act on some of Lardner's suggestions bear this out. "Astoria," after all, has an appreciably greater allure than "Long Island City"; and, conversely, the invented lower level of Penn Station supplies an appropriately depressed setting for Nick's retreat from Tom Buchanan's and Myrtle Wilson's sordid love nest. On the other hand, the relatively inexpressive tides of Lake Superior or the mistaken name of the Chicago train station could give way to the truth without loss of the kinds of resonance that Fitzgerald strove after. The main thing, as he later stated in his Preface to the Modern Library edition of *Gatsby* (1934), was to mediate the claims of contending realities through his fidelity to "truth or the *equivalent* of the truth, the attempt at honesty of imagination."

Factual errors of the kind spotted by Lardner, Bishop, and later readers are part of a pattern of skewed settings in *The Great Gatsby*; and, as we shall see, the temporal settings are often similarly awry. Fitzgerald's intention to correct mistakes of this kind is evidence of his determination to get the intricate chronology and settings of his novel as close to the actual calendar and map as he could. For example, he accurately shifted the location of St. Olaf College, which Gatsby attended for two weeks, from northern to southern Minnesota (105). Elsewhere he tried but somehow failed to change "Muhlbach Hotel" (correctly spelled Muehlbach)—where he has Tom Buchanan rent rooms when he marries Daisy—to "Sealbach Hotel" (properly Seelbach) because the former is in Kansas City and the latter is in Louisville, the scene of the wedding (80, Cambridge Edition 148). Occasionally, too, there are deliberate errors. When Tom refers to "'The Rise of the Colored Empires' by this man Goddard" (17), for example, it is clear that the mangling of Lothrop Stoddard's *The Rising Tide of Color* (1920) was intended as an accent on his heedless stupidity. Nonetheless, despite the handful of revisions that Fitzgerald actually made after the first printing of *Gatsby*, he left numerous mistakes untouched and apparently did not even notice many others. These oversights are puzzling when placed in view of his clear intention elsewhere to render his settings by means of authentic detail. (Another case in point is the painstaking guest list of plausible Euro-American surnames that Nick jots down on a train timetable "in effect July 5th, 1922" [65].) It may be supposed that Fitzgerald simply lacked sufficient time for the attentive work such a revision would require. Just four months passed between the two printings of *The Great Gatsby* (there were no others during his lifetime), and his and Zelda's lives were characteristically disordered during this period. The inaccuracies that remain in the text no doubt result in part from a combination of haste, distraction, inebriation, ignorance, faulty memory and neglectful editing by Perkins; some, on the other hand, may be read as examples of Fitzgerald's deliberate undermining of Nick Carraway's narration, whose reliability is open to question in any event. Be these circumstances as they may, they do not preclude the possibility that these slips of Fitzgerald's pencil were also to some extent guided and patterned by his imaginative transfiguration of a palpable historical world.

The alterations of Penn Station and other New York settings that Lardner spotted are part of a series of errors and distorted perceptions that disfigure Fitzgerald's Manhattan. A prime example is the setting of Tom and Myrtle's Sunday party at their apartment on West 158th Street in chapter 5 (27–42). Nick grows weary of the revelers' behavior and thinks, "I wanted to get out and walk eastward toward the park through the soft twilight." By "the park" he clearly means Central Park, through which he, Tom and Myrtle have traveled by taxi earlier in the day. Since its northern end at West 110th Street now lies forty-eight blocks south of him, he does just as well to stay on at the apartment, for his project of approaching Central Park by walking eastward is doomed. Nick is momentarily lost, suddenly incompetent as a guide through his story of New York. By way of explaining his mistake, it could be pointed out that Tom's whiskey has altered his perceptions; indeed, as he recalls two years later, "everything that happened" at the party "has a dim, hazy cast over it." It is perhaps a matter of opinion whether Nick could be drunk enough to obliterate so much of upper Manhattan from his memory and still be sober enough to make his way back downtown some seven hours later to wait in Penn Station's "lower level" for the four o'clock train to West Egg. If, on the other hand, Nick is to be excused for making the mistake of a recently arrived easterner, it should be recalled that he has spent four years at Yale and, as fictional Yale characters regularly do, would have made numerous excursions to New York. These would have made him familiar with at least the general situation of Central Park, through which he has in any case traveled earlier the same day, sober and in June sunlight.

It may therefore be appropriate to ask why he did not wonder about the route their taxi takes, heading incomprehensibly eastward from Penn Station across mid-Manhattan to Fifth Avenue, then "back again over the Park" toward their destination to the northwest. Such a detour is quite unlikely for the principal reason that Tom, whose "peremptory heart" is set on fornication at the earliest possible moment—he and Myrtle disappear into the bedroom soon after their arrival at their apartment—would surely not be expected to tolerate such an indirect route. As with his other disfigurations of the city's layout, Nick's sense of location cannot be relied on for such critical alertness. The imagined romance of the setting itself blinds him to such pedestrian realities and offers him a fantasy instead— "Fifth Avenue, so warm and soft, almost pastoral, on the summer Sunday afternoon that I wouldn't have been surprised to see a great flock of white sheep turn the corner." Nick finds this vision of Fifth Avenue so appealing that he says to Tom and Myrtle, "I have to leave you here," but they insist that he ride on with them. Later, in the Manhattan evening, it is the similarly alluring "soft twilight" that would entice Nick away not only from Tom and Myrtle's awful party and toward the pastoral park but also away from other unromantic realities of New York.

Nick's forgotten Upper West Side of 1922 Manhattan, lying above midtown and west of Central Park and Harlem, provides some of the least hospitable settings in Fitzgerald's fiction. From February to July 1919 Fitzgerald lived there, alone and unhappy, on Claremont Avenue, which lies between Broadway and Riverside Drive and extends eleven blocks northward from 116th Street to Tiemann Place. An apartment in the building at the northeast corner of Claremont Avenue and Tiemann Place was his first New York home, and its small, shabby rooms seemed all the more dreary because he published only one story while he lived in them. His frustration was compounded by Zelda Sayre's refusal to marry him while his prospects for making a good living remained so poor. When Prohibition arrived in July, Fitzgerald retreated to his parents' house in Minneapolis, but he later used "the hundreds" of Manhattan repeatedly as a fictional setting for his characters' suffering. In *The Beautiful and the Damned* the tormented marriage of Anthony and Gloria Patch reaches its lowest point when money trouble drives them to an apartment "on Claremont Avenue, which is two blocks from the Hudson in the dim hundreds" (405). Earlier, in an episode that anticipates this miserable setting—and Nick Carraway's ride with Tom and Myrtle as well—Anthony carries on a demeaning affair with a theatre usher named Geraldine whom he accompanies in "a taxi through the Park" to her "apartment in the labyrinthine hundreds" (47); and in a story from *All the Sad Young Men* (1926), "The Sensible Thing," the young engineer George O'Kelly, struggling against poverty in New York, 700 miles from his girlfriend in Tennessee, glumly rides the subway from Times Square to 137th Street on the way "to his home—one room in a high, horrible apartment-house in the middle of nowhere" (217). Fitzgerald's aversion to this section of Manhattan produces a full-blown vision of evil in *This Side of Paradise* when Amory Blaine and a friend accompany two women to an apartment "out over the hundreds" where he has a terrifying encounter with a devilish character with pointed feet who pursues him through the moonlit streets of a vague and sinister neighborhood (109, 119).

Like a predisposed tourist, Fitzgerald could seldom get his imagination to encompass any part of Manhattan that lacked the midtown glamor centering on the Plaza Hotel. The stretch of Fifth Avenue between 42nd Street and 59th Street, the parallel avenues with other posh hotels lying just to the east, and the lower end of Central Park were the virtual extent of the gossamer realm that held out the promise of satisfying his desire for a vividly romantic landscape. The greatness of that desire is stated vigorously in his undergraduate story, "The Spire and the Gargoyle" (1917, Kuehl 217–38), in which Amory Blaine tries to ennoble his truant excursions to New York by supposing that Fifth Avenue could "stand for what religions and families and philosophies of life had stood for."

The romance of monied New York offers Amory's imagination "relief from the painted, pagan crowds of Broadway." The theatres, restaurants and saloons of the district west of Fifth Avenue drew a crowd that Fitzgerald usually describes with revulsion. Amory Blaine watches the "squalid phantasmagoria" of an audience leaving a Broadway matinée and descending into the hellish subway (255). In the next scene he flees this grotesque humanity and enters the sanctuary of Fifth Avenue, projecting himself into his memory of "a well-dressed young man gazing from a club window on Fifth Avenue and saying something to his companion with a look of utter disgust. Probably, thought Amory, what he said was: 'My god! Aren't people horrible!'" (256). In *The Beautiful and the Damned*, Anthony Patch views these crowds with even greater loathing; and in *Gatsby,* Nick Carraway, watching the taxis crowd the West Forties on their way to the theatre district, prefers to "walk up Fifth Avenue and pick out romantic women from the crowd and imagine that in a few minutes I was going to enter into their lives" (57–58).

The Fifth Avenue of Fitzgerald's fiction is a privileged arena where dreams seem to be fully realizable. It either obliterates ordinary reality or forms a barrier between it and a desired world. This is true, for example, of the early story "May Day" (1920) in which Fifth Avenue isolates a world of opulence and success from the encroachments of squalor, drunken despair and mob violence. To the east lie the elegant repose of the Biltmore and the champagne breakfasts of the Commodore. To the west, a crowd of mutinous soldiers clamors past the cheap restaurants under the elevated railway of Sixth Avenue, briefly invading Fifth Avenue, then lurching eastward along 43rd Street to attack the offices of a socialist newspaper, where the police drive them back. In a parallel action, Gordon Sterrett, the failed artist who has tried with only modest success to enter this world, renting rooms on East 27th Street, is finally repelled back across Fifth Avenue to "a small hotel just off Sixth Avenue" where he commits suicide. By sectioning mid-Manhattan off as a shining citadel in his early New York stories, Fitzgerald anticipated the incompatible worlds of West Egg and East Egg in *The Great Gatsby*. These Long Island settings, like those in Manhattan, take part in his larger theme of conflict between eastern and western American experience.

Fitzgerald's urban preserve with its restricted access is to some extent the creation of an impressionable and insecure newcomer, and his descriptions of it are not essentially different from others of its kind. A conspicuous instance is *Manhattan Transfer*, published in the same year as *Gatsby*, in which John Dos Passos conveys a glamor-struck visitor's first impressions: the Plaza, for example, "gleamed white as mother-of-pearl" (109). What makes Fitzgerald's imaginative rendering an original of its kind is the way it tends to distort the physical realities of the setting to make them conform to his transfiguring vision. A closer look at the settings on the Upper West Side of Manhattan, that region of tawdry exile, is a particularly revealing case of this sort of reconfiguration. Just as Nick Carraway re-positions Tom and Myrtle's apartment in order to retain imaginative contact with the pastoral milieu of Central Park, so the Claremont Avenue apartment of the Patches is momentarily wrenched free of its depressing location. As Anthony lounges there in the evening gloom, he distracts himself with the narrow view from his windows:

> looking up One Hundred and Twenty-seventh Street toward the river . . . he could just see a single patch of vivid green trees, that guaranteed the brummagem umbrageousness of Riverside Drive. Across the water were the Palisades, crowned by the ugly framework of the amusement park—yet soon it would be dusk and those same iron cobwebs would be a glory against the heavens, an enchanted palace set over the smooth radiance of a tropical canal. (405)

This standard piece of early-Fitzgerald fantasia glosses over a mistake in the setting: the corner apartments at 200 Claremont Avenue have a view to the west along Tiemann Place, not 127th Street, which is cut off at its western end by the diagonals of Lawrence Street and 125th Street. Fitzgerald later makes another puzzling reference to his first New York neighborhood in the autobiographical "My Lost City" (1932), where he gives unintended resonance to his title by recalling that he "wandered through the town of 127th Street, resenting its vibrant life." This is in fact 125th Street, as Gloria notes in *The Beautiful and the Damned* when she observes the lively street scene more accurately but not without some of Anthony's sense of psychic dislocation:

> She had been pleased for a part of the day—the early afternoon—in walking along that Broadway of Harlem, One Hundred and Twenty-fifth Street, with her nostrils alert to many odors, and her mind excited by the extraordinary beauty of some Italian children. It affected her curiously—as Fifth Avenue had affected her once, in the days when, with the placid confidence of beauty, she had known that it was all hers, every shop and all it held, every adult toy glittering in a window, all hers for the asking. Here on One Hundred and Twenty-fifth Street [all was] very rich and racy and savory, like a dish by a provident French chef that one could not help enjoying, even though one knew that the ingredients were probably left-overs. . . . (412–13)

Emotionally Gloria never leaves her parents' tenth-floor suite at the Plaza. Whatever vitality she senses in the Italian immigrant community of this section of Harlem is transposed to the Fifth Avenue touchstone of the imagination, and the actual setting becomes no more than a stale, dispiriting simulacrum. Equally, when a fit of depression drives Amory Blaine uptown from his cherished haunts, the anonymous streets lead him into an alien world. He boards a bus in front of Delmonico's restaurant on Fifth Avenue at 44th Street, musing that he may "leave New York for good," and rides up Riverside Drive, past the undistinguishable crossing streets: "One Hundred and Twenty-seventh Street—or One Hundred and Thirty-seventh Street. . . . One Hundred and Twentieth Street? That must have been One Hundred and Twelfth back there. One O Two instead of One Two Seven." In his demoralized state he deliberately becomes quite lost—willfully disorienting himself in order to annihilate the abject surrounding reality. He leaves the bus at the (non-existent) intersection of Riverside Drive and 127th Street and wanders further uptown, picturing himself as a mad phantom prowling on a "dark continent upon the moon" (257–61).

For Fitzgerald's characters it is usually the case, as Amory's friend Monsignor Darcy tells him, that "our home is where we are not" (27). Where he *is*, accordingly, is a paradoxical state of homelessness, where even the irreducible identifying symbols of street names fade from memory. As he was working on the scene of the party on West 158th Street in *The Great Gatsby*, Fitzgerald noted, with the same apparent disorientation, "Memory of 125th" as a "source" (Bruccoli, *Some Sort* 184). No doubt an element of this acute feeling of dispossession entered into his portrait of Nick Carraway and all his other characters who at times don't know—perhaps they can't know—exactly where they are.

Fitzgerald's imaginative obliterations of Manhattan's Upper West Side reached a sort of comic apotheosis in his evident success in persuading himself that it was located in the Bronx. In "My Lost City" he characterizes his Claremont Avenue residence in 1919 as "my drab room in the Bronx" (*The Crack-Up* 23); and in "The Spire and the Gargoyle," Amory Blaine, exiled from a school much like Fitzgerald's Princeton to a stultifying job in New York, broods on the "skeptical office philosophy of his associates"; he fears that its arid tenets may draw him into their materialistic dream of "a girl, a ten thousand dollar position, and a Utopian flat in some transfigured Bronx." At no time did Fitzgerald live in any part of New York City except Manhattan. Other boroughs tended to figure as a places haunted by dreamless ghosts like George Wilson of the fictional Valley of Ashes, based on dumping grounds in the Borough of Queens. These outposts of Fitzgerald's imagination seemed incapable of transfiguration, but they could be dislodged, replaced and otherwise made malleable by the sovereign power of romantic desire. Only settings like Fifth Avenue, with their subliminal radiance, remain fixed by their promise to respond fully to each of his succeeding imaginative overtures.

Nick Carraway's sense of location in other parts of Manhattan is just as uncertain. In the fourth chapter (65–85) he meets Jordan Baker at the Plaza on a late July afternoon and, as dusk approaches, they take the carriage ride into the park. Nick observes that "we had left the Plaza for half an hour and were driving in a victoria through Central Park. The sun had gone down behind the tall apartments of the movie stars in the West Fifties. . . ." A clear-eyed observer who passes a half-hour being drawn northward in the park in mid-summer would actually observe the sunset farther to the north, behind the apartments in the West Sixties or even farther uptown. Movie stars of the 1920s not being so readily associated with this area due west of Central Park, however, Nick's romanticizing vision refracts his image in their direction toward mid-town and away from the dark encroachment of the uptown neighborhoods.

Nick appears similarly to misperceive the rising sun of Manhattan on his way to work: "In the early morning the sun threw my shadow westward as I hurried down the white chasms of lower new York to the Probity Trust." Because the buildings along the avenues of lower Manhattan had already formed the bulk of its characteristic "canyons" by 1922, they would accordingly have given morning commuters the sensation of moving through a rayless gloom, relieved only fleetingly by sunlight glimpsed at intersections. (Fitzgerald noted this effect accurately in *The Beautiful and the Damned*, describing October sunlight "loitering in the cross-streets" where, as the evening falls, "the stray beams fled the westward streets" [13, 135–36].) But the enticing image of "white chasms" as well as Nick's growing sense of the clinging past represented by the West, toward which he imagines his shadow extending, again causes him to position the sun awkwardly.

A further problem arises if it is asked why he is out in the sunshine as he travels from Penn Station to Wall Street. He customarily boards the Long Island Railroad train from West Egg at 9:15, "half an hour from Broadway" (Turnbull, *Scott Fitzgerald* 135), and arrives at Probity Trust at approximately ten o'clock after a rapid ride of some three miles downtown from Penn Station. This would have been possible only by subway. Although some of the tracks of the New York commmuter trains were elevated—the Sixth Avenue line noted in "May Day," for example— Fitzgerald himself first made his way around New York mainly underground, as do the less prosperous characters in his fiction. In "My Lost City," he remembers the "square foot of the subway" (*The Crack-Up* 25) that he occupied on his way to work at an advertising firm in 1919; Amory Blaine recalls "the ghastly, stinking crush of the subway" (255); and Anthony Patch refers to "the crowded horror of the morning subway" (231) that carries him from his mid-Manhattan apartment to Wall Street, where he works for six weeks in 1916, like Nick Carraway six years later, as a bond salesman.

Nick's luncheon with Gatsby and Meyer Wolfsheim (73–79) on the day of his meeting with Jordan Baker at the Plaza provides a final Manhattan setting in *The Great Gatsby* that is distorted by a series of errors. Some of these are intentional; others extend imaginative patterns that have already been noted. At noon Nick goes from Wall Street to the restaurant located in a "well-fanned Forty-second Street cellar" in the midtown theatre district.

There he joins Gatsby and Wolfsheim, a gambler and a principal denizen of Fitzgerald's debased world of Broadway. He mentions to Nick that they have just been conferring "across the street" at the Metropole Hotel, which was in fact located one block north on Forty-Third Street near Broadway. The common sense conclusion that Fitzgerald merely made an inconsequential mistake in his numbered streets is forestalled by a further mistake: if the three men are in fact having lunch across from the Metropole, then they would have to be sitting not in a restaurant but in George M. Cohan's Theatre, whose main entrance was on Forty-Third Street near Broadway. The "Presbyterian nymphs" that float incongruously on the restaurant's ceiling may derive from Fitzgerald's recollection of the theatre, built in 1911 when the interiors of New York's playhouses were decorated with this style of kitsch. It is likely also that Fitzgerald was thinking of Gatsby's first encounter with Wolfsheim in "Winebrenner's poolroom at Forty-third Street" three years earlier; Wolfsheim claims that he took the famished Gatsby to lunch and bought him "four dollars' worth" of food on that memorable day (179). Perhaps Fitzgerald conflated the two Forty-Third Street luncheons, distorting the temporal as well as the spatial setting of Nick's narrative. At the conclusion of the Wolfsheim luncheon, a fortuitous note of irony sounds when Tom Buchanan runs into Nick in the restaurant and asks, "How'd you happen to come up this far to eat?" Because of the blurred setting, it is impossible to determine precisely how far "this far" is; all that is clear is that Nick has been drawn further into Jay Gatsby's un-placeable dream, somewhere west of Fifth Avenue.

The distortions in Nick's account of this episode may also be seen as projections of Meyer Wolfsheim's radical disfiguring of reality. His sentimental lunch-time evocation of his assassinated fellow-gambler Rosy Rosenthal is a congeries of historical fact, flawed memory and lies; as such, it provides a kind of hazy nucleus for this radically disoriented scene. According to contemporary reports in the *New York Times*, the gambler Herman Rosenthal was shot to death a little before two o'clock in the morning on July 16, 1912. Four gunmen lured him out of the café in the Metropole Hotel, where he was dining alone, by sending in an unidentified young man to tell him he was wanted outside. As he left the hotel he was shot repeatedly in the head and fell dying to the sidewalk as his killers escaped in an automobile. Witnesses described that block of Forty-Third Street as brightly lit and cleared of people by policemen just before the shooting. It was proven eventually that New York City Police Lieutenant Charles Becker had hired the gunmen to take revenge against Rosenthal for informing the District Attorney that he and Becker were partners in a Manhattan gambling house, for which Becker had arranged protection by the police. Becker believed he could get away with Rosenthal's murder because he assumed—correctly at first—that the police would naturally suspect members of the fraternity of professional gamblers whose operations were clustered in the area. Rosenthal had recently transferred his activities from lower Manhattan to his home on Fifty-Second Street and was resented as a interloper. In a series of trials, despite his cunning, Becker and his accomplices were all convicted and electrocuted in Sing Sing prison in 1915.

Ten years after Rosenthal's death, Wolfsheim gets only two essential facts right: Rosenthal left the Metropole café against advice, walking into the gunmen's trap; and five men were executed as murderers (Wolfsheim alertly corrects Nick's mistaken recollection of four). Otherwise, his account is spurious. He boasts that he and four others were with Rosenthal in the Metropole and that he had cagily warned him against leaving. He adds, "It was four o'clock in the morning then, and if we'd of raised the blinds we'd of seen daylight." The actual time was two hours earlier and the "daylight" was supplied artificially by Becker's henchmen. Wolfsheim details the attack on Rosenthal as three shots in the stomach rather than the reported indeterminate number of head wounds. He is clearly fond of the story of his fast friendship with the tragic Rosenthal. He has told it often over the decade, embellishing it for listeners such as his protégé, Gatsby, whose capacity for grand invention has surpassed even that of his mentor. To the extent that he is consciously lying—or has lied so often in succeeding versions that he has gradually come to believe them himself— his self-serving motive is apparent. Gamblers such as Arnold Rothstein, a model for Wolfsheim, were actually delighted with the assassination and the resulting sentences. An upstart competitor had been eliminated, Becker's scandal would force the police temporarily to suspend their interference in the gambling business, and the gamblers themselves could effortlessly consolidate their power. Wolfsheim still secretly gloats over this windfall and basks also in the glow of later triumphs, most notably fixing the 1919 World Series (evidently with the help of his apprentice, Gatsby), then avoiding prosecution. He has become an *éminence grise* in the world of Broadway graft, wistfully reminiscing about his great days and benevolently proffering "gonnegtions" to the rising generation of crooks.

Fitzgerald's intention to portray Meyer Wolfsheim as a liar and a fabulist is clear. The old rascal's depiction of his world, prudently fantasized from the beginning, has been elaborated over the years. He defers, like Gatsby, only to the most elemental actualities of time and space. Fitzgerald subtly places his character within the larger pattern of Gatsby's gigantic delusion that he is something radically unlike a criminal. Nick takes on the impossible task of detecting the reality within their masterly inventions. He is repeatedly absorbed into the highly energized vortices of their self-creation, sure of his bearings only at moments when their stories collide violently with fact or likelihood—as, for example, when Gatsby alludes mawkishly to "something very sad" that happened to him "long ago" and then names San Francisco as his parents' home in the "middle-west" (69–70). Nick tries to penetrate illusions such as these, partly in order to put his own dislocated world back in place, and his uncertain success in doing so is a measure of Fitzgerald's struggle to mediate the romantic and the mundane. Readers who note these factual contradictions may shift their attention from the central illusionist characters such as Gatsby and Wolfsheim, and from the incompletely authoritative command of their reality achieved by Nick, to the author's process of crafting the narrative. These are moments when *The Great Gatsby*'s reflection of ordinary empirical reality can be seen to falter and even fail, leaving a sense of the obliteration of such reality—what Nick refers to as Gatsby's insistence on "the unreality of reality." Gatsby and Wolfsheim had to be portrayed by Nick as characters who are so wholly intent on their emotional transfigurations of experience that they tend to expose the distorting imagination of the author himself. In order for their romantic visions to achieve reality, the world of daily experience must be disassembled and reconstructed in an enabling shape. The actual world is, in this respect, essentially nullified, "material without being real" (169).

Although the convincing Long Island settings in *The Great Gatsby* surely merited Mencken's praise, in some of their minute detail they actually betray the most elaborate distorting patterns in the novel. The very moon that regularly illuminates them appears repeatedly in the wrong position and phase, so that hardly a night goes by without moonbeams to brighten the characters' lush illusions. When Nick arrives in chapter 3 (43–64) at his first party in Gatsby's garden "a little after seven," he soon notices "the premature moon, produced like the supper, no doubt, out of a caterer's basket." "By midnight" he observes that the moon "had risen higher"; and when he leaves the party well after three o'clock a "wafer of a moon was shining over Gatsby's house, making the night fine as before, and surviving the laughter and the sound of his still glowing garden." Continuous, intense lunation over eight hours is a notable feat of survival, and the moon's later appearances are no less exceptional. Gatsby's party in August (110–18) is again moonlit, as Nick observes while he watches a movie director and his famous star: "their faces were touching except for a pale, thin ray of moonlight between." On this night, however, it is suddenly "dark" when the party breaks up. In front of Gatsby's house "only the bright door sent ten square feet of light volleying out into the soft black morning." The moon next appears in chapter 7 (119–53) in an early phase—a "silver curve"—beyond the Buchanans' house after lunch on the day of Tom's confrontation with Gatsby at the Plaza Hotel. Nick notices the early moon "already in the western sky," resuming the theme of fragile illusions as well as the ominous motif of the inescapable West. As before, his weakness for romantic coloring leads him to ignore intractable fact: this western moon must shortly sink below the horizon. It does not. At 9:30 that night Nick remarks "the luminosity of [Gatsby's] pink suit under the moon" as he keeps his vigil below Daisy's bedroom window. As Nick leaves him "standing there in the moonlight—watching over nothing," his rendering of Gatsby's tragic emotion not only reverses the moon's orbit but promotes it to a fuller phase.

During Fitzgerald's stay in France in 1925 after *The Great Gatsby* had been published, he wrote to his friend Marya Mannes, who had recently moved to Manhattan:

> You are thrilled by New York—I doubt you will be after five more years when you are more fully nourished from within. I carry the place around the world in my heart but sometimes I try to shake it off in my dreams. America's greatest promise is that something is going to happen, and after a while you get tired of waiting because nothing happens to people except that they grow old, and nothing happens to American art because America is the story of the moon that never rose. (*Letters* 488)

The particular work of American art that he had lately published, to the contrary, is virtually the story of the moon that rises and sets freely—the story of the sun that shines implausibly and the park that moves uptown. The five years forecast by Fitzgerald as the period of his correspondent's inevitable disenchantment with New York resonate, perhaps, with the five years between Gatsby's first love for Daisy Fay in Louisville and his death in West Egg; but the "inner nourishment" that he projects as recompense for his friend's lost illusions is something that neither his characters nor he can ever receive in the disenchanting East. As the moon of American art fails to rise on New York, the city must be periodically exorcised and dreamt away in the ceaseless substitution of new dreams for dead ones. For Fitzgerald it seemed an activity of persistently, irresistibly projecting a glamorous world to nullify the moonless wastes of George Wilson's Valley of Ashes. It is the world transfigured into ever more radiant states—Jay Gatsby's "orgastic future" (189) that appears to be just beyond his grasp because it seems infinitely removed from George Wilson's nothingness.

The peculiar impossibility of the American dream lies in its darkness, as Fitzgerald's letter implies. Because the moon refuses to rise on the American artistic landscape, and because American dreams lie, if anywhere at all, "somewhere back in that vast obscurity beyond the city, where the dark fields of the republic [roll] on under the night," Fitzgerald rejected the naturalistic settings of this dreamless American art—the art of Theodore Dreiser and Sinclair Lewis—for its material unreality. He sought refuge from it finally in the synthetic America of the Hollywood movie sets of *The Last Tycoon* (posth. 1941). There he could place his moons, suns, parks and avenues anywhere he cared to, believing, like his early dreaming character Anthony Patch in *The Beautiful and the Damned*, in the essentially dramaturgical nature of a life lived imaginatively: "Life, it seemed, must be a setting up of props around one—otherwise it was a disaster. There was no rest, no quiet" (282). Hollywood promised a final means of achieving what the young James Gatz of North Dakota achieved, "an outlet for his imagination . . . a promise that the rock of the world was founded securely on a fairy's wing" (105).

Reduced to a rock, the phenomenal world is absolutely unsatisfactory, but it is by the same token endlessly redeemable by the transfiguring power of the imagination. This points to a central paradox in Fitzgerald's fiction: the creative vision of the artist and often of his central characters simultaneously destroys and creates, dismantling the world in the act of shaping its radiant forms. Formless and sterile, the North Dakota of James Gatz ironically supplies his imagination with the most fertile of all possible fields because there is nothing there to resist it, no prior creation with which it must contend. Its emptiness is really another manifestation of the virginity of the forests that Nick imagines as greeting the first Dutch settlers of Long Island (289). This is the main reason why a tangible foundation in actuality was so essential to Fitzgerald's creativity. The "gorgeous concreteness" (393) of Gloria Gilbert's beauty, for example, is proof that the rock-like world and the unearthly fairy's wing of imaginative desire are contingent after all, finally of one substance. Even though this beauty is transient, its material basis keeps it always within reach, sustaining the hope that its elusiveness may be compensated endlessly by the imagination in its tireless assertion that reality is unreal. Accordingly, the settings of Fitzgerald's novels may be seen as more than mere assemblages of stage props, with paper moons and portable walls. They are collateral worlds with arenas for the enactment of liberated desire.

As with the physical settings of *The Great Gatsby*, the chronology has been overestimated as part of one of the high formal achievements in modern American fiction—a point developed at length by Thomas Pendleton in *I'm Sorry about the Clock: Chronology, Composition, and Narrative Technique in* The Great Gatsby (1993). Adapting a conventional seasonal pattern with its attendant emotional rhythms to his contemporary settings, Fitzgerald has generally been credited with skillfully shaping the four-month period in 1922 into a masterly structure of tragic inevitability.

His prophecy that the critics would acknowledge his novel as a consciously artistic achievement proved largely correct in this respect, owing in part to the reviewers' lack of time and patience to note the numerous flaws in Nick's narrative of the summer's events. Like the physical settings of *The Great Gatsby*, the time structure is subjected to a series of distortions. They appear equally to be unintentional errors, but their more positive interest lies in the patterns they form as Fitzgerald reshapes the temporality from which they are drawn.

Nick's dependence on Jordan Baker for most of the story of Daisy Fay Buchanan's life since the autumn of 1917, when she meets Lieutenant Jay Gatsby in Louisville, causes no great problems of factuality. Even though he perceives the dishonesty of her character when her own interests are at stake, Jordan's account of Daisy's past may be taken as reliable on three counts: she has no personal reason to invent or misrepresent any of the background she gives Nick; she is on friendly and increasingly intimate terms with him when she tells him Daisy's story; and her version of the past five years contains no discrediting contradictions. It is mainly from her that Nick learns of Gatsby's departure from Louisville for the war in France in November 1917, followed by Daisy's brief engagement ending in February 1919. She then meets Tom Buchanan "in the middle of the spring" (151) of 1919 and marries him hastily in June, taking time, however, to send a parting letter to Gatsby at Oxford. After a long honeymoon in Hawaii and a brief residence in Santa Barbara, Tom and Daisy move on to Chicago where their daughter Pammy is born in April 1920.

To this point Nick's chronology is consistent, but it begins to unravel when he enters on his own account of the summer of 1922. In June of that year, says Nick, two years and two months after the birth of Daisy's daughter, she tells him that Pammy is "three years old." Two months later (a week after Nick mentions the "August foliage" in Gatsby's gardens) this little girl of indeterminate age also acquires an indefinite appearance, suggesting that Fitzgerald's distortions of time and space are coterminous. Daisy teases her about her "old yellowy hair" and observes to Nick, "She's got my hair," leaving no means of accounting for the scene in which Gatsby kisses Daisy's "dark shining hair." A later scene further confuses the image as she appears at Nick's house with a strand of rain-soaked hair resembling "a dash of blue paint" on her face. When Gatsby first sees Pammy on this day, she seems "unreal" to him because she cannot fit into his plan to erase the five years (or precisely four years and nine months) of his separation from Daisy. Trying to clarify this history, Nick is again so strongly caught up in the whirlwind of Gatsby's desire that his own sense of time is impaired. Consistently in error, he imagines that Gatsby believes that Daisy could have "obliterated four years" by telling Tom she has never loved him during the three years and two months of their marriage. Gatsby's dominating presence distorts the reality of the scene, leading Nick to subvert his own chronology unknowingly and involving the author and even the unwary reader in a concentrated, passionate effort to abolish time.

Nick's sometimes insufficiently skeptical reaction to Gatsby's stories of his past leads to further contortions of the time structure. When Gatsby gives him and Daisy a tour of his mansion, he tells them, "It took me just three years to earn the money that bought it"; Nick swiftly objects, "I thought you inherited your money" (65), recalling the time he caught Gatsby in the fib about the fortune bequeathed to him by the parental Midwesterners of San Francisco. Gatsby tries to shore up the story of his wealth with another lie about losing his inheritance during the war, but Nick, seizing an evident advantage, presses Gatsby further on the source of his money. Gatsby turns at bay and retorts rudely, "That's my affair," then changes the subject. Nick appears nevertheless to sense that he is for once master of the situation, confident of his power of penetrating Gatsby's illusions: "I think he hardly knew what he was saying" (95); but in a later scene he fails to register further data he might have used to cast doubt on Gatsby's rapid rise to great wealth.

It appears certain that Gatsby returned penniless from Europe in the summer of 1919, soon after Daisy's marriage (he speaks of the three years between that time and the spring of 1922, when he bought his house, shortly after the Buchanans' arrival in East Egg). As startling as Gatsby's three-year rise to wealth may be, there is reason to believe that he made his fortune even more rapidly than he claims. Before his funeral Gatsby's father gives the clearest hint of this, telling Nick that his son bought a house for him "two years ago," that is, around September 1920. The narrowest conclusion to which this revelation might have led Nick but did not is that Gatsby prospered rapidly enough during the year after his return from the war to be able to buy a house for Henry Gatz. In his confused grappling with Gatsby's past it does not occur to him to consider seriously that he shared Meyer Wolfsheim's huge winnings from the fixed World Series of October 1919. Nick does in fact pause briefly to wonder whether this might be part of the truth behind Gatsby's confidential association with the gambler, but he fails to interpret evidence that would have given a solid base to his suspicions. Once more, Nick is too much engrossed in Gatsby's and Daisy's romance to be consistently adept at rooting out the truth.

As though it were inevitable, then, as a stormy twilight ends the day when Nick brings about the reunion of the two lovers, he looks out of Gatsby's window and senses a reality that in fact cannot be: "the hour of profound human change" when "the electric trains, men-carrying, were plunging home through the rain from New York" (101). Nick forgets that it is not a work day, and that the men he imagines as returning from their work in Manhattan don't exist. He has been given a free hand in setting up Gatsby's meeting with Daisy, and he surely would not have chosen a day that would require him to miss work at Probity Trust (he has a daily railroad pass and uses it conscientiously). The scene closes as the three rapt characters gaze westward at the dramatic sunset, and Nick watches "a pink and golden billow of foamy clouds above the sea" where there is no sea, only Long Island Sound, characterized by him earlier in a more sober moment as a "domesticated . . . wet barnyard" (9).

Try as he will to piece together a coherent chronology, Nick eventually confuses the calendar so badly that dates become chaotic. Although he appears to have a clear sense of other characters' ages, for example, he somehow forgets his own thirtieth birthday, recalling it only after Tom's exposure of Gatsby at the Plaza puts him in an introspective mood. Even if it is granted that a man of Nick's sensibility and circumstances may plausibly fail to take note of the day he leaves his twenties, it must be added that he doesn't appear to know what the day of the week it is, birthday or not. On the previous Saturday night, Nick looks at Gatsby's house and misses seeing the bright lights of his weekly parties (119). On the "next day," Sunday, Gatsby telephones Nick to extend Daisy's invitation to lunch at her house "tomorrow," Monday (120). Consequently, on this weekday (helplessly obeying the summons, Nick leaves work before noon to catch the train to East Egg) the five characters eventually make their way to the Plaza where they hear "the portentous chords of Mendelssohn's Wedding March from the ballroom below" (134). It is highly unlikely, even in Fitzgerald's improvisatory "jazz age," that a wedding would take place on a Monday afternoon, but he and his narrator have imaginatively re-entered the immune precincts of Fifth Avenue. On the way there, Nick hears Jordan Baker exclaim, "I love New York on summer afternoons when everyone's away. There's something very sensuous about it—overripe, as if all sorts of funny fruits were going to fall into your hands" (125). Her city is transformed into a hilarious, pre-lapsarian orchard, just before the fall into time, where the only people present are the dreamers.

The most massive breakdown in Nick's chronology occurs in his account of Gatsby's affair with Daisy. "For several weeks," he recalls, remembering the period just after Gatsby's reunion with Daisy, "I didn't see him . . . but finally I went over to his house one Sunday afternoon" (107). Tom Buchanan arrives and Gatsby mentions meeting him "about two weeks ago" (108) at the luncheon with Meyer Wolfsheim and Nick, even though this happens two days before Nick's last view of Gatsby "several weeks" before. Then, on "the following Saturday night," i.e., after Nick's "several weeks" plus six days since that sighting, Nick attends another party and falls in with the tipsy people he had met there along with Gatsby himself. This, he recalls, was "two weeks before" (110). So roughly a month passes during which it is wholly uncertain when, or if, Nick "saw" Gatsby. His twisted order of events is really a symptom of the persistent difficulty he has in "seeing" Gatsby and the lives he influences clearly enough to fix them in time. At the party that he dates so doubtfully, he senses "the dim, incalculable hours" of early morning when all "romantic possibilities" (115) seem to be present. Nick's warping of time continues to the conclusion of the main narrative as he reconstructs George Wilson's movements on the afternoon when he murders Gatsby. He reports Wilson's appearance at Gad's Hill by noon, his disappearance for three hours, and then his arrival, the clock notwithstanding, at West Egg by two-thirty (168). Finally, in his valedictory chapter, Nick makes it plain that he is writing Gatsby's story two years after his death (171), even though he had opened his narration by referring to the events of "last autumn" (6).

As he completed work on *The Great Gatsby*, Fitzgerald wrote that its "whole burden" was "the loss of those illusions that give such color to the world so that you don't care whether things are true or false as long as they partake of the magical glory" (*Correspondence* 145). His irony is quite characteristic in that it actually renounces romantic transcendence while at the same time sacrificing everything to it. Illusions will surely be lost, he agrees, the truth and falsehood of "things" will not be compromised, and yet he must infuse them with a radiance—"the magical glory"—that transfigures what it can not transcend. His particular sense of entering into this exalted state of being is perhaps best understood as a modern instance of Catholic sacramentalism locked in its struggle with material necessity. It is of a kind—perhaps an Irish kind—with James Joyce's attempt to uncover the sacred in the secular, but its expression is more overtly affective. Fitzgerald's early religious experiences in the Catholic churches of St. Paul and Buffalo included spells of intense piety, and he even seriously considered the possibility of entering the priesthood. This was an idea that he took up intermittently until it was dispelled by his love for Zelda Sayre. In those early devout days, he gazed at the popular depictions of Jesus that he eventually used as models for some of his central characters, whom he tended to think of as spoiled priests. He was no doubt deeply impressed by accounts and illustrations of the transfiguration of Jesus recorded by the New Testament apostles (Matthew 17:1–8, Mark 9:2–8 and Luke 9:28–36). Matthew relates the events that occurred when Jesus had led Peter, John and Thomas to the summit of a mountain: "He was transfigured before them, and his face shone like the sun, but his garments became white as light. . . ." Moses and Elijah appear and talk to Jesus, and the disciples hear "a voice from the cloud . . . saying, 'This is my Son, the Beloved [in Luke, 'the Chosen'], with whom I am well pleased. Listen to him.'" Partly because of its earth-bound concreteness, the exact theological significance of the transfiguration of Jesus is uncertain. It is not, that is, an apotheosis; nor is it properly a metamorphosis, since it results in a change of none of Jesus' physical traits or circumstances. He becomes for a time a miracle of light, then resumes his daily aspect.

In her study of the Catholic element in Fitzgerald's writing, Joan M. Allen argues that he conceived of Jay Gatsby—as well as the later central characters, Dick Diver and Monroe Stahr—as a personality who radiates secular forms of this divine emanation. Commenting on the vagueness of his physical descriptions of Gatsby, she notes, "As if his brilliance would blind the reader . . . Gatsby's person is never described" (105). In her discussion of Nick Carraway's designation of Gatsby as "one of the Sons of God," Allen further suggests that "Gatsby, with the religious conviction peculiar to saints, pursues an ideal, a mystical union, not with God, but with the life embodied in Daisy Fay. . . . God sent his son to die for a dream" (104, 109). Before this drama climaxes in Gatsby's death, he achieves his brief moment as a transfigured Son of God when his reunion with Daisy seems complete: "He literally glowed; without a word or a gesture of exultation a new well-being radiated from him and filled the little room" (90).

Fitzgerald's clerical friend, Monsignor Cyril Sigourney Webster Fay, whom he met while he was at a preparatory school in New Jersey, exerted a strong religious influence on him at the beginning of his writing career. Fay presented an image of the Roman Catholic Church that was both more palatable and more exciting than its rather sober manifestations back in the Midwest. As Fitzgerald phrased it in his 1922 memorial to Fay for the *New York Tribune*, titled "Homage to the Victorians," he "made of that Church a dazzling, golden thing" and infused it with "the romantic glamour of an adolescent dream." He had nonetheless warned Fitzgerald that it was a mistake to believe that "you can be romantic without religion. None of us can. . . . I discover that if I did not have a good hold on the mystical side of religion the romance would have died down considerably" (Allen 50). Fitzgerald reflected his struggle against the clergyman's insistence on transcendental mysticism in his portrayal of Fay as Monsignor Darcy in *This Side of Paradise*. He tells Amory Blaine that the sole spiritual reality that is accessible through his romantic imagination lies in the choice between "an out-and-out materialistic world—and the Catholic Church" (147). Typical of Fitzgerald's main characters, Amory Blaine challenges the assumptions of Darcy's extreme antithesis in his search for a mediating reality that is both material and spiritual. In the long run, the romantic imagination discovers that secular romanticism is, as Darcy insists, impossible; but its failure confirms the reality of secular pathos rather than a truth of sacred theology.

This tragic realization is particularly forceful in Fitzgerald's later work. Significantly, the Christ-like martyrdoms of Jay Gatsby, Dick Diver and Monroe Stahr result from conceivably avoidable circumstances or accidents rather than any force that might be attributed to some implacable force of sacred or profane history. In the case of Gatsby, Nick can even assert that he "turned out all right at the end" (2), still committed, like a faithful pilgrim, to the "dead dream" in which he "fought on as the afternoon slipped away, trying to touch what was no longer tangible, struggling unhappily, undespairingly, toward that lost voice across the room" (137). These paradoxes—a dead man who is "all right," a dead dream still vital, a voice that is both touchable and intangible, present and lost—resolve themselves in a spiritual extension of the romantic dream that the experiences of actuality at times reveal. This is the radiance that emanates from his most fully romanticized characters. It is heard in the "deathless song" of Daisy's voice (97); it is manifested in the beauty of Gloria Gilbert in *The Beautiful and the Damned*, "a gossamer projection of a land of delicate and undiscovered shades" (71) which is nonetheless madeutterly real by virtue of her "gorgeous concreteness"; in the St. Cecilia-like Clara Page of *This Side of Paradise*, it emits a "golden radiance" that "metamorphosed" her ordinary self without substantial change; and it is revealed by Monroe Stahr who, with the note of mortality that sounds throughout *The Last Tycoon*, rules his Hollywood realm "with a radiance that is almost moribund in its phosphorescence" (163). In spite of the unyielding contingencies that gradually diminish and dissipate this glow, Fitzgerald imagines it as an elusive but permanent spiritual reality always about to be seized.

The principal male figures in Fitzgerald's later novels conform increasingly to the type of the self-sacrificing martyr whose ceaseless efforts of creation supply the world with realized romances, but in doing so they sap his vitality. These characters are able to produce the illusion of a divine power of creation *ex nihilo*, but in their sub-divinity they may never rest from the generation and replenishment of their perishable dreams. Jay Gatsby established this type firmly in Fitzgerald's imagination, and he is followed by Dick Diver and Monroe Stahr, both re-projecting Gatsby's image of the impresario of a benevolent, limitlessly diverting spectacle. They see themselves as the philanthropists the world truly needs and desires most, and in performing this role they escape the confining self-absorption of the earlier characters, Amory Blaine and Anthony Patch.

In *Tender Is the Night* the love-struck Rosemary Hoyt regards Dick Diver as the incomparable "organizer of private gaiety, curator of a richly incrusted happiness" (88). She sees in him the promise that "he would open up new worlds for her, unroll an endless succession of magnificent possibilities"; and it is characteristic of Fitzgerald's conception of these possibilities that Dick confirms Rosemary's belief in him by transforming the definite, concrete world they inhabit. He literally invents the setting on the French Riviera at Gausse's hotel—"the beach," as Nicole Diver explains, "that Dick made out of a pebble pile" (28). As a reveler in their "carnivals of affection" (36), Rosemary senses in Dick and Nicole the capacity for "an act of creation different from any she had known." Dick reveals his quasi-divine potency in the dinner party scene of chapters 6 and 7—a combined Last Supper (eleven people are present with Dick) and Transfiguration. Rosemary appears "dewy with belief," and the Divers' guests have "the faces of poor children at a Christmas tree."

> The table seemed to have risen a little toward the sky like a mechanical dancing platform, giving the people around it a sense of being alone with each other in the dark universe, nourished by its only food, warmed by its only lights. And, as if a curious hushed laugh from Mrs. McKisco were a signal that such a detachment from the world had been attained, the two Divers began suddenly to warm and glow and expand. . . . Just for a moment they seemed to speak to everyone at the table, singly and together, assuring them of their friendliness, their affection. (43)

This scene even conveys a sensation of heavenly arrival, expressed as Rosemary's "conviction of homecoming, of a return from the derisive and salacious improvisations of the frontier." Americans abroad, the guests feel compensated "for anything they might still miss from that country well left behind." They "had been daringly lifted above conviviality into the rarer atmosphere of sentiment" in a moment of "diffused magic" that "was over before it could be irreverently breathed" (43).

Dick's slow decline ensues as Nicole's mental crises and his obsession with Rosemary poison his creativity. Nicole remarks that he "used to want to create things" but he gives way increasingly to an impulse to "smash them," betraying the destructiveness that lies within the power of the creator. ("I was never disposed to accept the present," Fitzgerald wrote in a letter of April 1938, "but always striving to change it, better it, or even sometimes destroy it" [*Correspondence* 494].) He begins to sense that the continued existence of his vastly diverting world depends on his friends' faith in it, "but at the first flicker of doubt as to its all-inclusiveness he evaporated before their eyes, leaving little communicable memory of what he had said and done" (36). The reality of reality eventually defeats him. When he tells Mary North, bitterly, "You're all so dull," her retort spells the ruin of his romantic world: "But we're all there is!" (348).

It was perhaps inevitable that Hollywood should have provided the characteristic settings for Fitzgerald's last works. There he could continue to elaborate the "story of the West" begun in Gatsby's New York. The possibility of selling his writing to the movie-makers had long been on his mind, and it is clear that their work shaped his imagination powerfully. It is a mistake, however, to conclude that his later fiction was simply overwhelmed by the wholly synthetic realities of the motion pictures. For all its absorption in Hollywood glamor, *The Last Tycoon* is an autonomous creation that develops powerfully out of the work he achieved before Hollywood came to dominate his writing. This is especially evident in his characterization of Monroe Stahr, whose experience extends the secular exaltation of the Christ-like martyr beyond the point where he left off with Dick Diver; and yet he emerges as one of Fitzgerald's most convincingly human creations.

The aura that Stahr emits originates at least as much in Fitzgerald's religious sense of his character as it does in the shining images of the silver screen, which seem to highlight the phosphorescent quality he develops during his reign over his Hollywood empire. Indeed, a hazy cinematic glow pervades the characterization of *The Last Tycoon* like a kind of aether. In Stahr's image of his deceased wife, Minna, for example, he remembers her flesh as giving off a "peculiar radiance as if phosphorous had touched it" (79); but she and the other characters who move in this ambient light are always rendered as they actually appear. There really is a marked radiant quality about Stahr as he circulates among the lights and reflecting surfaces of his studios; and his image of Minna is actually evoked by his first sight of his lover Kathleen as she appears at night at the door of her house with its lights behind her. For Fitzgerald's imaginative purposes, the light of the cinema was an imitation—often a highly convincing one—of the world's own radiance. Stahr's particular glow has a "moribund" quality because of the menace of death that his failing health projects upon his creations (in the conclusion that Fitzgerald planned he dies at an early age—a virtually Christ-like 34 years). What Fitzgerald seeks to convey finally in these visions of light and warmth is his most intense expression of the transfiguring human reality that had always been the greatest object of his writing. His conception of Stahr is that of a modern heaven-sent redeemer who first appears thousands of feet aloft in an airplane about to land in Los Angeles. Fitzgerald's adoring narrator Cecilia Brady views his arrival as a kind of divine visitation, carrying him from his obscure origins in the Bronx "through trackless wastes of perception where very few men were able to follow him" (26):

He had flown up very high to see, on strong wings, when he was young. And while he was up there he had looked on all the kingdoms, with the kind of eyes that can stare straight into the sun. Beating his wings tenaciously—finally frantically—and keeping on beating them, he had stayed up there longer than most of us, and then, remembering all he had seen from his great height of how things were, he had settled gradually to earth. (28)

Cecilia's mythological Stahr descends to earth as a fully human, benevolent presence, sent by no supernatural power other than his own great desire: "he came here from choice to be with us to the end" (29). His motive is a boundless philanthropy, seeking "to care, for all of them" (55).

Monroe Stahr is Fitzgerald's most thoroughgoing maker of this transfigured reality because he acts with the fewest limits on his power and his means. He has "inherited the world" in Hollywood "full of confidence and joy" (148). Through repeated feats of invention he realizes the ambition that Jay Gatsby fails to achieve—"passionately to repeat yet not to recapitulate the past" (106); and "if there is no present" sufficiently opulent, then he need only "invent one" (131). He sustains this ever-present reality in the film sets that he constructs endlessly, with their artificiality transformed by moonlight so that "in an enchanted distorted sort of way, it all comes true." The "new music" of Hollywood is composed by musicians who themselves are "always new" (113), providing perpetually fresh accompaniment to Stahr's acts of creation. An actress he photographs is presented "so slowly, so close, so real that you believe in her" (186); and the woman he loves is not only a resurrection of the deceased Minna but is herself transformed by his passionate vision. He sees Kathleen sitting alone at a long white table:

Immediately things changed. As he walked toward her, the people shrank back against the walls till they were only murals; the white table lengthened and became an altar where the priestess sat alone. Vitality welled up in him, and he could have stood a long time across the table from her, looking and smiling. . . . When she came close, his several visions of her blurred; she was momentarily unreal. . . . they danced out along the floor—to the last edge, where they stepped through a mirror into another dance with new dancers whose faces were familiar but nothing more. In this new region he talked, fast and urgently. . . . Her eyes invited him to a romantic communion of unbelievable intensity. (89)

These are the achieved illusions of Stahr's youth. "That was one thing about Stahr—the literal sky was the limit" (54). Although they fade as his health declines and he loses Kathleen (he believes that she "promises to give life back to him" [177]) and he becomes embroiled in Hollywood rivalries, the end that Fitzgerald projected for him comes about not as an ultimate limitation on his illusions but rather as the result of an airplane accident. None of his adverse mortal circumstances were to lead to his death, and it is as though Fitzgerald intended to finish his portrait of the last tycoon by giving him a kind of omnipotence within his created Hollywood world. His death even seems a part of the limitless powers of creation and destruction that he wields. Los Angeles, for example, is seen as "a desolation he helped to create" (185); and the house he builds for himself gives off a "hard glitter" like "the shiny surface of a moon" (101)—a "Hint of Waste Land," as Fitzgerald noted in his last outline (following p. 165). He shapes and controls "the new Hollywood; but occasionally he liked to tear it apart just to see if it was there"; and yet this destructive energy does not arise from the sort of demoralization that defeats Dick Diver. "Unlike *Tender Is the Night*," Fitzgerald observes in his notes, *The Last Tycoon* "is not the story of deterioration—it is not depressing and not morbid in spite of the tragic ending" (168). Monroe Stahr retains his greatness, immeasurably removed from the confining unreality of his origins in the Bronx.

The notes for the completion of *The Last Tycoon* show that Fitzgerald intended—as he always did in his best work—to retain an essentially realistic concreteness as he shaped the settings. For reasons of plotting, he even planned to recast the entire chronology in order to allow the airplane to crash in the Rocky Mountains during the snow season (181). The finished parts of the novel rarely betray the sorts of distortions of space and time that abound in *The Great Gatsby*, and this is so mainly because Hollywood presented Fitzgerald with a setting that was either already transformed or rich in transforming potential.

Of all Fitzgerald's works, the story "Absolution" (1924) makes the most specific statement of his attitude toward Roman Catholic spirituality. It centers on the conflict between an anguished priest, the Rev. Adolphus Schwartz, and Rudolph Miller, his adolescent parishioner. Rudolph is Fitzgerald's closest approximation of a portrait of Gatsby as a boy. The story is set in Gatsby's native "Minnesota-Dakota country," and the characterization focuses on Rudolph's Gatsby-like romanticism: "There was something ineffably gorgeous somewhere," he imagines, "that had nothing to do with God" and that reveals a "finer" human reality, "brightening up the dinginess" and making life "radiant and proud." Rudolph pursues this vision in his reaction against the agonized spiritual struggles that leave Father Schwartz "unable to attain a complete mystical union with our Lord." Father Schwartz's mysticism is not vital enough to contain his sensuality: he is obsessed with the Swedish girls of the town, and even the drugstore there, with its aromas that "drifted, rather like incense, toward the moon" as he walks by it, arouses in him the pain of an overwhelming earthly reproach to the chaste ceremonies of the Church. In its horribly irresistible appeal, this concrete "open world of wheat and sky" is, like the face of God, "terrible to look upon," and it drives him to insanity. Because his visions of a greater reality are always tainted by carnality, which both appeals to and repels him, there can be no absolution for Father Schwartz.

In the last stages of mental dissolution, Father Schwartz gives Rudolph some bizarre advice: "When a lot of people get together in the best places things go glimmering," he exclaims, urging the boy to visit an amusement park at night, and adding strangely, "it won't remind you of anything." He concludes with the warning, "But don't get up close . . . because if you do you'll only feel the heat and the sweat and the life." His revulsion may be taken in part as Fitzgerald's reflection on his own difficulty in including ordinary characters' lives sympathetically in his imagined transfigurations of American reality. That swarming, perspiring world is almost invariably an ugly presence in his fiction; the Broadway theatre crowds, for example, or the European immigrants and laborers noticed briefly in his early fiction are for the most part merely loathsome or abject—omens of "the world's preposterous barrenness," as he expresses it in *The Beautiful and the Damned* (360). In young Rudolph Miller, on the other hand, Fitzgerald appears to envision an alternative, collateral world apart from the polarized conflict between Father Schwartz's surrogate heaven of the night carnival and his hell of salaciousness. Rudolph glimpses it when he escapes from the priest's confessional and returns to the sensually transfigured Dakota fields where "the blue sirocco trembled over the wheat" and the "blond Northern girls" are luminous in the moonlight. By blending the Mediterranean sirocco with the warm chinook winds of the Great Plains, by allowing a hardy intensity of the North to radiate sensuously from the ordinary Swedish girls, Fitzgerald achieves a rare affirmation of this unglamorous life. "Absolution" stands out among Fitzgerald's works as a story about being gladly at home in exurban America by virtue of the earthly but exquisite vitality that frees the imagination from a tormenting sense of its exclusion from divinity.

As a portrait of Rudolph Miller in adulthood, Gatsby represents a rejection of that Western world as a place of "dark fields" inhabited by dreamless, hopeless ghosts like his parents, "shiftless and unsuccessful farm people—his imagination had never really accepted them as his parents at all" (99). Their antagonistic world, centrally symbolized by Wilson's dismal garage in the Valley of Ashes, stands in radical opposition to Gatsby's image of Daisy Fay in Louisville, "gleaming like silver, safe and proud above the hot struggles of the poor" (150). Fitzgerald's principal characters commonly begin the invention of a superior identity by pretending to annul their Western past. A character such as Rudolph Miller who is emotionally attached to it must nevertheless supplement that attachment through imaginative creations such as the flamboyant, British-sounding name, "Blatchford Sarnemington," that he contrives to replace his plain Midwestern one. In this he anticipates James Gatz, requiring an idea of himself as one who "lived in great sweeping triumphs."

Fitzgerald's deference to the verisimilitude of place in his best fiction allowed him the greatest imaginative freedom when he used American settings with the fewest encrustations of Old World culture. Manhattan and the north shore of Long Island were, in a sense, too fully pre-shaped to escape contortion by the pressures of his transfiguring vision. As a Westerner who tried and failed to merge with the East, Nick Carraway speaks for Fitzgerald when he concedes that the East "had always for me a quality of distortion. . . . After Gatsby's death the East was . . . distorted beyond my eyes' power of correction. . . . perhaps we possessed some deficiency in common which made us subtly unadaptable to Eastern life" (177–78). By admitting this as a shortcoming only speculatively, Nick may be asserting a positive aspect of the Westerner's sense of identity with the frontier—a sense of self that is expressed through what are perceived as original acts of creation. The East is blurred because it tends to reflect the Old World sense of self that emerges from a series of adjustments to a cultural *fait accompli*. Fixed, pre-formed psychological realities are alien and even incomprehensible to Nick the Westerner, and so his eyes will inevitably distort them. When Fitzgerald places his characters in Europe, as he does in *Tender Is the Night*, the settings come alive most fully when he rids them of Europeans, placing his group of American expatriates in a cultural void to be filled by his Western imagination. The Hollywood of *The Last Tycoon* accordingly becomes the supreme American setting, malleable to a virtually infinite degree, literally a place of daily changing forms that evolve from Monroe Stahr's sense of creative limitlessness.

This essentially Western quality of Fitzgerald's imagination appears in his tendency to seek a totality of creative vision by distorting, evading or obliterating whatever resists it. His objects of desire approach a totality of glamor and desirability as the obstinately unredeemable, disfigured world of the ordinary dwindles to non-existence. Everything except the concreteness of objects themselves is expendable in his effort to spare a part of the world from imaginative sterility. The uncluttered and inchoate western American landscape thus becomes the setting with the fullest potential for this vision, as is perhaps best exemplified by "The Diamond as Big as the Ritz" (1922). This story epitomizes Fitzgerald's penchant for American settings that are opulent but hollow, containing a central personality or object that is in some way refulgent, and promising a compensatory totality of well-being. It opens with the formulaic departure of a young Westerner for the East. He bears the conventionally plain, plausible Euro-American name, John T. Unger, and his home is located unpromisingly in "Hades—a small town on the Mississippi River." Hades is one of Fitzgerald's ambiguous evocations of the West; it is hellish in its remoteness from his centers of glamor, but, like the grain fields of "Absolution," it is also a place of strong sensual appeal. As he sets out on his journey to a school in New England, John senses that "the lights of Hades against the sky seemed full of a warm and passionate beauty." At the school he befriends Percy Washington and goes home with him on holiday to his father's diamond domain in Montana. At "Fish, Montana," a prefiguration of the Valley of Ashes in *Gatsby*, John and Percy leave their train and see spectral figures of a de-vitalized Hades that has been transposed westward. These wraiths appear as "twelve sombre and inexplicable souls who sucked a lean milk from the almost literally bare rocks upon which a mysterious populatory force had begotten them [but then] abandoned [them] to struggle and extermination." They represent the appalling triumph of realism:

> To observe, that was all: there remained in them none of the vital quality of illusion which would make them wonder or speculate, else a religion might have grown up around these mysterious visitations. But the men of Fish were beyond all religion— the barest and most savage tenets of even Christianity could gain no foothold on that barren rock—so there was no altar, no priest, no sacrifice; only each night at seven [when the train passed through, the twelve men appeared as] a congregation who lifted up a prayer of dim, anaemic wonder. (93)

These are George Wilson's fellow ghosts and Father Adolphus Schwartz's companions in despair. Their existence is a dreamless, enervated stupor. They are the twelve Fish apostles of no redeemer, and as sentient creatures they are reduced to the function of mere observation, with its incapacity for illusion, wonder or worship. They image a "Godforsaken" American nightmare, as Percy calls them, in an illusionless wasteland.

Fish, Montana and its hollow men stand in antithetical relation to the astonishing splendor of Braddock Washington's estate, reached by John and Percy by means of a vertical ascent out of a rocky gulch. As they approach this marvel of light and luxury, they enter Fitzgerald's most luminous fictive setting. In order to shield his domain from the destructive incursions of the men of Fish and, by extension, the America they represent, Percy's father has literally "changed nature to separate it" from them. He has caused official maps of the region to be altered, set up a powerful magnetic field to distort surveyors' compasses and substituted defective surveying instruments "that would allow for this territory not to appear." He has even had a river deflected from its bed to complete his concealment. As a result, the location of his glowing world can be indicated only negatively as lying "where the United States ends." The imperceptive dwellers in the surrounding wasteland can achieve no conception of it; for them it is an inconceivable Nowhere, and yet it is itself a palpable reality, a collateral New America discovered and transformed by the latter-day founding father, Braddock Washington. The chateau he has built is a "floating fairyland" with a room constructed entirely of diamonds that "dazzled the eyes with a whiteness that could be compared only with itself, beyond human wish or dream." The means of this supreme transfiguration is the diamond mountain itself, the barren rock of the world made ultimately resplendent as a consummate, tangible assurance of the unreality of reality. Inescapably, this concrete illusion is shattered before long by an incursion of destructive forces from "the United States," but despite its disintegration it remains for John Unger an image of his own "radiantly imagined future—flowers and gold, girls and stars, they are only prefigurations and prophecies of that incomparable, unattainable young dream." He understands that the diamond mountain was made possible by a reduction of the antithetical world to a set of inferior illusions that present reality only through its deficient instrument of observation, the merely recording eye.

Braddock Washington chooses a designer from Hollywood to build his jeweled paradise because he is the only one to be found who is accustomed to working with unrestricted sums of money. Like George O'Kelly in "The Sensible Thing," he implies Fitzgerald's metaphor of the artist as an architect of privileged illusions. O'Kelly rises above the nullities of Tennessee and Manhattan's 137th Street to achieve a "position of unlimited opportunity," and his means of doing so is a career in the material-bound world of construction engineering:

> All his life he had thought in terms of tunnels and skyscrapers and great squat dams and tall, three-towered bridges, that were like dancers holding hands in a row, with heads as tall as cities and skirts of cable strand. It had seemed romantic to George O'Kelly to change the sweep of rivers and the shape of mountains so that life could flourish in the old bad lands of the world where it had never taken root before. He loved steel, and there was always steel near him in his dreams, liquid steel, steel in bars, and blocks and beams and formless plastic masses, waiting for him, as paint and canvas to his hand. Steel inexhaustible, to be made lovely and austere in his imaginative fire. (218)

Here are the essential elements of Fitzgerald's artistic vision—wonder-conceived structures erected and shaped by the infusion of human form and beauty. Their fictive setting is an altered and vivified landscape of the mind whose profuse and malleable materials are sublimated by the refining fire of the imagination that creates as it attacks their formlessness and inertia. Their perishable images are products of the continuously creative acts of an artistry that emerges from the formless immensity of America. Fitzgerald perceived this essential feature of the American arts through the eyes of the inspired New Yorker of "My Lost City" who stands near the top of the newly opened Empire State Building and views the contingent realities of the ephemeral city and the land: "from the tallest structure he saw for the first time that it faded out into the country on all sides, into an expanse of green and blue that alone was limitless."

The inaccurate, distorted spatial and temporal settings that are discussed in this chapter are significant for what they show of the points of strain and fissure that appear as Fitzgerald's fictions transform a given world. Viewed as a group, they may appear to expose Fitzgerald's willfully romantic imagination as it soars out of control; but they also represent his lashing out at the resistant order of time and space that obscures the truth of Monsignor Darcy's apothegm, "our home is where we are not." If they are unintended, they are also idiosyncratic, revealing the ways a particular writer applies stress to his material, but offering scant support to general theoretical statements about the decentering of narrative authority. They may also be thought of as part of the disorder of subversion, or perhaps the overflow of material that literary form cannot envelope. The secularity of Fitzgerald's dismantling and transfiguring art demanded such a powerful and persistent outpouring of imaginative energy that it was bound, perhaps, to leave some disorder. The following discussions of different sorts of error in William Faulkner and Ernest Hemingway are intended to expand the view of modernist writing as an art of spirited mistakes.

CHAPTER FOUR

William Faulkner's Civil War:
Transposed History

"A writer is a liar, ma'am," William Faulkner declared memorably at the University of Virginia, adding, "That's why they call it fiction" (Coy Ferrer and Gresset 38). Despite such statements of disdain for factuality that Faulkner made occasionally when he discussed his writing, he has drawn as much attention from critics who read fiction as social history as any writer of the modern period. This being so, it may be asked what complicating implications his attitude toward facts might have for social historians, for whom the concept of the writer as a liar is clearly problematic. How are they to take his remark to Malcolm Cowley in 1946, "I don't care much for facts and am not much interested in them" (Cowley 89)? Or later to Jean Stein: "ideas and facts have very little connection with truth" (Merriwether and Millgate 252)? If these are to be dismissed as examples of the glib sallies that Faulkner liked to share with his correspondents and questioners, then what of similar disavowals he makes more soberly in his fiction—in *Requiem for a Nun* (1951), for example, when his narrator-historian affirms the "limitless . . . capacity [of] man's imagination to disperse and burn away the rubble-dross of fact and probability, leaving only truth and dream" (225)?

The romanticist's claim to a higher truth of the artist's autonomous vision, countering the fact-ridden photographic naturalism of the later nineteenth century, had become an imposture by Faulkner's time. William Blake's road of excess could no longer be relied upon to lead to the palace of wisdom; and there was an unmistakable archness in Stephen Dedalus's boast in *Ulysses*, "A man of genius makes no mistakes. His errors are volitional and are the portals of discovery" (156). Perhaps with a more becoming modesty, the modern writer might plausibly re-invoke the venerable concept of the sovereign imagination that transforms empirical reality as it is sensed and remembered, earning him an occasional exemption from common standards of factuality whenever they stood in his way. As a question of aesthetics, the matter would appear to be resolved thus simply, were it not for Faulkner's painstaking efforts to locate his imaginative history of Yoknapatawpha County securely in that same disobligingly factual world. Indeed, his geography of the South reflects historical actuality even more literally than its principal literary paradigm, the Wessex of Thomas Hardy's novels. While Jefferson is to Oxford, Mississippi, as Hardy's Christminster is to Oxford of Oxfordshire, Faulkner's settings tend to retain their historical names, as Hardy's do not. His Memphis remains Memphis, Jackson is always called Jackson and New Orleans bears no other name in his works. With nearly the degree of particularity that Joyce attained in his portrait of Dublin, Faulkner's town and county and outlying destinations are imaginary places that nonetheless have exact and plausible historical settings; and the intricacay of their chronologies produces an illusion of historical density and continuity. Clearly, Faulkner cared a great deal for facts, and his statements to the contrary may be taken as expressions of his uneasy sense that he sometimes got the facts of his world wrong. Committed as he was to a rendering of the past that would coincide with a consensus view of recorded history, his errors of fact cannot be explained away simply by appealing to the radical freedom of the writer's imagination. As with Scott Fitzgerald's mistaken settings, they may be identified and their patterns read as though they were structural motifs.

Questions of accuracy that arise from the many instances of Faulkner's uncertain command of the history of the South have usually been laid to rest with remarkably ready forbearance by his sympathetic readers. No doubt correctly preoccupied with their central inquiry into the results of his search for a redemptive tragic vision of the Confederacy in ruins, they have generally overlooked or dismissed the errors and inconsistencies that occasionally disturb his fictive ordering of the past. In his groundbreaking examination of Faulkner's South, *William Faulkner: The Yoknapatawpha Country*, Cleanth Brooks characterizes his historical material as "a kind of imaginative construct" that justifies the critic's indulgence of standards of accuracy less severe than the historian's (211). In a similar vein, Hyatt Waggoner proposes the expression "creative remembering" (162) to characterize the hypothetical versions of the past proposed by the narrators of *Absalom, Absalom!* (1936). Papers read at the 1984 Salamanca conference on "Faulkner and History" extend this critical tradition by further exempting the Yoknapatawpha legend from scholarly criteria of accuracy. In "William Faulkner: Fiction as Historiography" (Coy Ferrer and Gresset 39–50), François Pitavy concedes characteristically that Faulkner was "admittedly no historian" (49), but he echoes earlier apologists by asserting an "ordering vision" (47) that enabled Faulkner to transcend his deficiencies as a chronicler of the South. Pitavy also displays a later tendency among historical critics, including a number of those at the Salamanca conference, to grant a great deal of authority to Faulkner's impromptu remarks on the subject of "facts" in his interviews and letters. These have become an important part of the tradition that has created an image of Faulkner as the downright teller of truths higher than those of the mere chronicler of events.

Brooks encounters some of the difficulties caused by this view when he attempts to construct genealogies for the principal families of the novels and stories. Noting the various dates given for the birth of "old Bayard" Sartoris and for the death of his father, Colonel John Sartoris, in *Sartoris* (1929), *The Unvanquished* (1938) and *Requiem for a Nun*, Brooks speculates first that "Faulkner was careless or perhaps simply did not attach very much importance to exact dates." He adds quickly that he "*was* carefully exact" (his emphasis) in indicating dates for other members of the Sartoris family. Brooks evidently finds little interest in the flat contradiction he uncovers, concluding that it is "not really of great consequence whether the climactic event in *The Unvanquished* [the murder of John Sartoris] took place in 1873, 1874, or, as *Sartoris* has it, 1876, or even, as in *Requiem for a Nun*, 1878" (451). Because Faulkner clearly worked hard—though in some instances not hard enough—to create his lifelike family trees, it is not altogether logical to cite conflicting dates as evidence of his indifference toward their internal consistency. Viewed only as incidental blemishes on a grand canvas, such flaws would indeed appear to be insignificant; but the readiness with which Brooks and later students of Faulkner's "creative remembering" have passed over them has missed an opportunity to identify an important pattern of transposed historical settings that pervades his fiction and is particularly evident in his work set during the Civil War. Brooks, of course, is right to conclude that few, if any, of these miscalculated dates are of any great significance individually; but together they display a basic design that formed in Faulkner's historical imagination over a quarter-century as he constructed his story of the secessionist South. The overall result is an affirmative conception of a history translated from "facts" to "truth," embodied in a metaphorical April day that condenses many events of the Civil War into a collateral moment of violent action containing all warfare. This imagined instant out of time occurs repeatedly in his fiction, and its tragic intensity is almost always vitiated by the paralyzing obsessions that threaten to trap his characters as they try to recollect and reconstruct the war. With the artist's conditional exemption from ordinary rules of truth-telling, Faulkner escapes this trap, continuously purging his narrative of a fixed chronology. Through this process he achieves the interpretive fluidity of the Joycean epiphany.

Faulkner's fiction provides a composite sketch of the principal land campaigns of the Civil War, principally in *Sartoris* (titled "Flags in the Dust" in an early version), *Absalom, The Unvanquished* and *Requiem for a Nun*. In nearly every instance this cumulative portrait appears to blend fiction with reliable historical accounts of the war. His great-grandfather, William Clark Falkner, who served in both theatres, was the principal model for Colonel Sartoris. Like Faulkner's ancestor, Sartoris recruits a regiment in northern Mississippi soon after General P.G.T. Beauregard's capture of Fort Sumter in Charleston harbor on April 13, 1861. With his second in command, Colonel Thomas Sutpen, the plantation builder of *Absalom*, Sartoris leads his men to northwestern Virginia where they take part in the two battles at Manassas/Bull Run (July 1861 and August 1862). The historical "Mississippi Two" regiment formed part of General T.J. Jackson's left flank in his defense of Henry House Hill at First Manassas. (This was the action that earned Jackson the moniker "Stonewall.") Faulkner describes their role at Second Manassas in scant detail, partly, no doubt, because his great-grandfather had previously lost his command and resigned from the regiment. He focuses instead on the death of Sartoris's younger brother Bayard, killed in a raid led by Jackson's cavalry commander, J.E.B. Stuart, a few days prior to the main battle.

Following the Confederate victories at Manassas, disaffection among Sartoris's troops lead to his defeat in an election for the colonelcy held in the fall of 1862 (Colonel Falkner was ousted in this manner the previous April). Replaced by Thomas Sutpen, he returns bitterly to Jefferson. Sutpen commands the regiment in Robert E. Lee's campaign in Virginia and is involved in the Confederate disaster at Gettysburg in July 1863. Faulkner glimpses their long, dejected retreat through the Shenandoah Valley in *Absalom*. Sutpen and his men march slowly southward, hauling the Italian marble gravestones he has bought for himself and his wife, Ellen Coldfield Sutpen, who has died at their home, Sutpen's Hundred, in the same year. He reaches Jefferson in the late autumn of 1864, presumably having participated in the terrible campaign against Ulysses Grant's Union armies that drove Lee's forces back on Richmond during the previous spring. After only twenty-four hours in Jefferson, Sutpen returns to the war, joining James Longstreet's corps in the doomed defense of the capital.

Faulkner outlines the wartime experiences of Sutpen's sons Henry and Charles Bon in the speculative monologues of *Absalom*. These provide his fullest portraits of the war in the West as well as the final campaign in

Georgia and the Carolinas. The brothers join the "University Greys" (426), a unit their classmates at the University of Mississippi have formed. In early April 1862 they join their first battle as part of the Confederate counterattack on Grant's advancing armies at Shiloh and Pittsburgh Landing in Tennessee. Henry Sutpen is wounded in this grim two-day engagement, and other casualties among Faulkner's characters include General Jason Lycurgus Compson, who loses an arm, Gavin Breckbridge (the fiancé of Drusilla Hawk, who later marries John Sartoris in *The Unvanquished*), who is killed, and Colonel Gavin Blount ("A Return"), also killed. Shiloh is the costliest battle of the war for Faulkner's characters, perhaps reflecting his sense of the severe consequences of this defeat for northern Mississippi (Oxford lies ninety miles southeast of the battlefield). In the long Confederate retreat from Shiloh, Henry and Charles march with the armies of Joseph Johnston and John Hood along the three-year road to their surrender in April 1865. Toward the conclusion of *Absalom*, Quentin Compson imagines their ordeal:

> the starved and ragged remnant of an army having retreated across Alabama and Georgia and into Carolina, swept onward not by a victorious army behind it but rather by a mounting tide of the names of lost battles from either side—Chickamauga and Franklin, Vicksburg and Corinth and Atlanta. (431)

The Battle of Chickamauga (September 19–20, 1863), fought on the outskirts of Chattanooga, Tennessee, stands among the few important Confederate victories in the West; the other battles Quentin mentions were losses, the most fateful being the fall of Vicksburg, Mississippi, to Grant's siege on July 4, 1863 (the day of Lee's defeat at Gettysburg). Vicksburg was the last Confederate stronghold on the Mississippi river (Memphis and New Orleans fell earlier); its loss isolated the southern secessionist states from vital resources west of the river in Louisiana, Arkansas and Texas, effectively ending whatever chances of winning the war they may still have had. Grant's victory concluded his second campaign against Vicksburg; in the previous year, following Shiloh, he had tried to attack it from the east by moving overland through northern Mississippi. His advance on Corinth, Mississippi resulted in its evacuation on May 30, 1862, but his further progress southward bogged down by the end of the year, forcing him to withdraw to Tennessee. There he devised the successful "river strategy" for capturing Vicksburg. The late Battle of Franklin, waged south of Nashville on November 30, 1864, was fought desperately, and at huge cost, by the Confederates under John Hood in an effort to distract the Federal armies of William Tecumseh Sherman from their march across Georgia; but Sherman, who had taken Atlanta on September 2, advanced nonetheless, weakly resisted by Johnston's ragged force. Charles Bon records the despairing sense of "walking backward for almost a year now" (434) as he and Henry and their comrades retreat almost constantly in front of Sherman, driven relentlessly toward surrender in North Carolina.

Bon sees his personal fate reflected in this calamity, supposing (as Quentin Compson conjectures) that "the whole purpose of the retreat seemed to him to be that of bringing him within reach of his father, to give his father one more chance" (433) to acknowledge him as his son. This is the condition Bon has set for renouncing his engagement to his half-sister, Judith Sutpen. Neither the meeting nor the reconciliation takes place, however, because Thomas Sutpen refuses an opportunity to embrace Bon when the final days of the war bring them into the same camp. Sutpen is detached from Longstreet's corps at Richmond and sent with his unit to reinforce Johnston in North Carolina; finding that his sons are stationed nearby, Sutpen arranges a reunion with Henry but ignores Bon, who decides consequently to carry out his suicidal plan to force the issue of marriage to Judith. Bon returns with Henry to Jefferson, "dodging Yankee patrols" (447)—implying that they have deserted prior to Johnston's surrender to Sherman on April 18—and Henry kills him in front of the house at Sutpen's Hundred on a day that Faulkner apparently intended to coincide with the South's capitulation. Thomas Sutpen finally manages to return to Jefferson in January 1866. He learns of Bon's death and Henry's disappearance and begins his futile effort to restore his patriarchal domain, Faulkner's central symbol of the South in defeat.

Lafayette County, Mississippi—Faulkner's Yoknapatawpha—became directly involved in the war after Shiloh. It was the scene of a series of minor battles that concluded in August 1864 when the Union army burned the center of Oxford and withdrew to the east to support Sherman. Since the greater part of Faulkner's historical transpositions involve the fate of Jefferson/Oxford and its citizens, it would be well to develop this history in some detail. The large-scale views of the war in given in *Absalom* do not depart from the historical record; but as the war encroaches on Yoknapatawpha, transposed history begins to supplant it.

One of the greatest obstacles encountered by Grant and Sherman in their decisive campaigns against Vicksburg and Atlanta was the cavalry led by General Nathan Bedford Forrest. This remarkably capable officer figured more prominently in Faulkner's imagination than any other Southern military leader. His career was a model for the exploits, both audacious and foolhardy, of the mounted warrior who appears repeatedly in Faulkner's war fiction. Because he was regularly overmatched by the Union forces he engaged, and because the technology of warfare was rapidly making the cavalry unit obsolete, Forrest's strategy was often based on theatrical deception and terrorism. Sherman became so exasperated by the repeated failures to remove this menace to his supply lines that his orders to his subordinates in Tennessee and Mississippi became increasingly pointed in their insistence that Forrest's death was to be a principal objective of their operations in Mississippi. Naturally, he became, and continued in Faulkner's time to be, a legendary figure.

In Sherman's final attempt to eliminate the Confederates in Mississippi, Forrest again escaped, but Oxford was nearly destroyed. Faulkner gives his version of the battle that preceded this disaster in the story, "My Grandmother Millard and General Forrest and the Battle of Harrykin Creek" (1942). Historically, in August 1864 Sherman ordered General A.C. Smith to advance from Tennessee along Grant's railroad route through Holly Springs, Mississippi, and across the Tallahatchie River, eleven miles north of Oxford. Forrest, who was to the east at Harrisburg, believed at first that Smith's movement was a feint to cover the major thrust he expected closer to his position; he concluded otherwise when Smith achieved his crossing by replacing a destroyed bridge. "Fortunately for Forrest," writes his biographer, Robert Selph Henry, "Smith's movements, even after he was across the Tallahatchie, continued to be supercautious. . . . On August tenth his advance pushed the Confederates back across Hurricane Creek, and six miles beyond to the little university town of Oxford" (332). James R. Chalmers, leader of the small force opposing Smith, evacuated Oxford and fell back on the heights above the Yocohan River south of the town. Smith then entered Oxford, but, learning of Forrest's approach from the east, unaccountably withdrew to his Tallahatchie crossing. Forrest accordingly entered Oxford—the third occupation of the day—and waited for Smith's next move. Heavy rains through the following week prevented any further action other than light skirmishes and a failed attempt by Forrest's cavalry to cut the railroad line north of Smith's positions.

While Smith awaited supplies for his more than 20,000 troops, Forrest did what he could to strengthen his poorly equipped 4,000. Then on August 17, with the rain still falling, Smith ordered another march on Oxford; Forrest responded with a bold raid on Memphis. In the rain and growing darkness of August 18, he spirited half his men out of Oxford on the road east toward Panola (now Batesville), leaving Chalmers with orders to demonstrate in the vicinity of Smith's positions and otherwise stall him for at least two days. Forrest's cavalry stormed into panic-stricken Memphis on Sunday morning, August 21. The surprise was such that the Union commander, Cadwallader Washburn, narrowly escaped capture in his bedroom and had to flee to the city's fort without his clothing. Reporting only thirty-five casualties in the day's action, Forrest claimed four hundred

Union troops killed or captured and three hundred horses and mules taken. He eluded Union pursuers and headed back toward Oxford.

Chalmers met with some success in delaying Smith's attack by concealing his own weaknesses. His most effective stratagem took the form of a remarkably noisy advance against Federal pickets at Hurricane Creek, following which a Union officer reported fending off an attack by the rebels "in force" (341). Smith eventually saw through Chalmers's theatrics and, on August 22, drove him back, seizing Oxford again while Forrest was still west of the town. He immediately set fire to the courthouse and most of the other buildings on the central square, then withdrew rapidly to Holly Springs. His haste was prompted by a message from Washburn reporting the havoc Forrest had raised in Memphis while he was assumed to be defying the Union threat to Oxford. This message also carried Washburn's order to intercept Forrest's retreat, but Smith had already pressed his evacuation too far ahead to make this possible. When Forrest learned of Chalmers's retreat and the fires in the town, he decided to return instead to his old base to the south in Grenada. For Oxford the war was over.

Faulkner represents the "Battle of Jefferson," so called in *Requiem for a Nun* (233), more fully than any other military action of the war. In "My Grandmother Millard and General Forrest and the Battle of Harrykin Creek" he recreates its early phases. Written in the lighthearted manner of much of Faulkner's later work, the story reshapes historical material in order to focus the narrative on a love affair involving the gallant cavalier, Lieutenant Philip St.-Just Backhouse, who serves in one of Forrest's brigades. The narrating character, "old Bayard" Sartoris, remembers his boyhood experience at the time of the clash at Hurricane Creek, where Chalmers formed his defensive line to resist the Union advance on Jefferson. Forrest himself appears, summoned by Bayard's maternal grandmother, Rosa ("Granny") Millard, who knew him in Memphis before the war. Forrest grumbles about the insubordination of young. Backhouse, who has ignored his orders to proceed no farther than "to make contact and then fall back" from Smith's advance guard:

> I spent four days getting Smith just where I wanted him. He [Backhouse] divided his men and sent half of them into the bushes to make a noise and took the other half who were the nearest to complete fools and led a sabre charge on that outpost. He didn't fire a shot. He drove it clean back with sabres onto Smith's main body and scared Smith so that he threw out all his cavalry and pulled out behind it and now I don't know whether I'm about to catch him or he's about to catch me. (693)

This fanciful account of Forrest's strategy being foiled by the excessive valor of his men replaces the dismal reality of the clash at Hurricane Creek with a series of saving illusions. The demonstration that Chalmers actually made is accurately reflected in the "noise" made by the men Backhouse leaves behind; so is the resulting confusion in the Federal ranks. It is patently not true, however, that Smith "pulled out" with his 20,000 men because he was "scared" by a sabre charge. Forrest's account, moreover, is made exponentially still less real by his historical absence at Hurricane Creek, owing to the raid on Memphis. Faulkner fictively transposes both Forrest and his rebel-yelling cavalry back to Jefferson by means of the imaginary Backhouse. This is an example of Faulkner's tendency to condense similar actions of the war into one imagined event dominated by the extravagant improvisations of a soldier on horseback.

The parallel love story in "My Grandmother" involves the mutual infatuation of Lieutenant Backhouse and Bayard's cousin Melisandre, who has been living with the Sartoris family since her flight from Memphis after its fall in June 1862. In another farcically gallant solo charge, Backhouse drives off a group of Union soldiers who have just battered the Sartoris privy to pieces, discovering the terrified Melisandre, who has hidden there with the family silver. She is love-struck by her savior, but the trauma of her experience in the outhouse drives her to distraction whenever she hears his surname. Granny solves this problem by browbeating Forrest until he agrees to issue an order changing his problematic lieutenant's name to Backus. All is well then, and the bewildered and resigned Forrest is free to withdraw from his second defeat at Hurricane Creek, a victim of his own cavalryman's indomitable spirit in love and in war.

The presence of Nathan Bedford Forrest as a character in "My Grandmother" lends it a genial, buoyant mood. Its deliberately relaxed standards of historical accuracy are no doubt appropriate and perhaps obligatory for material published in *Story* in the patriotic wartime atmosphere of 1943. The portrait accents the agreeable traits of Forrest's personality—his plain-spoken courtly manner, his controlled indignation, his even-handed indulgence of his young riders ("You can't punish a man for routing an enemy four times his weight" [692]). It bears no traces of the ferocity that horrified the people of Oxford during his presence in February 1863 when he ordered the trial and execution of would-be deserters in a field outside the town. Although Forrest's commander issued a pardon that prevented this gruesome spectacle from taking place, the town was not entirely reassured, and his return in the summer of 1864 was regarded with misgivings that were all the greater for his most recent notoriety. His attack on the Federal garrison at Fort Pillow on the Mississippi River north of Memphis in April 1864 had resulted in the massacre of hundreds of Union soldiers, many of them black; and it was widely believed in Oxford that Smith had ordered the burning of the town in August as retaliation for that atrocity. Despite his helpless position at Hurricane Creek and in the few battles that remained in the war, and Sherman's attempts to kill him notwithstanding, Forrest not only survived the fighting but continued to wage virtual war as the first Grand Wizard of the Tennessee Ku Klux Klan. In Faulkner's portrait, however, he appears to be quite another sort of man.

It is likely that Faulkner intended "My Grandmother" as a parody of the popular historical romances that he appears to have despised. The tale, after all, is told by "old Bayard" Sartoris, whose library includes the collected works of the elder Alexandre Dumas, classified snidely in *Sartoris* as "fiction of the historical-romantic school" (34). Because Bayard's reading is mainly confined to this type of fiction, it may be inferred that Faulkner presents him ironically as the historical romancer who whitewashes Forrest's character, departing necessarily but harmlessly from historical truth. In any case, the patterned inaccuracies that riddle the portrait reflect Faulkner's own tendency to rewrite history in a way that focuses the image of the Confederate cavalry officer as an avatar of the war's unavailing heroics. In addition to Forrest's impossible presence and command at Hurricane Creek, and apart from his distorted account of the battle, the general also claims obscurely that he has "spent four days getting Smith just where [he] wanted him." Robert Selph Henry demonstrates that, during the seven days that Forrest actually spent in Oxford before his departure for Memphis, there was no military action of any consequence; none, in fact, was possible, given the incessant rain and the weakness of his force. Smith, additionally, was exactly where Forrest did not want him, well-positioned with a secure bridgehead on the Tallahatchie, and adequately supplied by rail (332–33). When Forrest's single attempt to disrupt the line to the rear of Smith failed, he could only conclude that his position was untenable. The last-ditch raid on Memphis was a dramatic but minimally effective gambit, serving little real purpose except to heighten his personal reputation for audacity.

The story of the "Battle of Jefferson" is more strangely skewed in *Requiem for a Nun*. In the last of a series of historical prologues, Faulkner's narrator evokes "a sudden battle centering around Colonel Sartoris' plantation house four miles to the north [of Jefferson], the main line of a creek held long enough for the main Confederate body to pass through Jefferson to a stronger line on the river heights south of the town, a rear-guard action of cavalry in the streets of the town itself" (231–32). The cavalry join their infantry at this new line, and "that night the town was occupied by Federal troops, two nights later, it was on fire" (232). The flames destroy buildings on the town square and gut the courthouse.

During the next day "the distant uproar of battle" is heard in Jefferson "fading on to the east" as the Yankees press their attack, leaving Jefferson devastated and eliminated from the war "a whole year in advance of Appomattox" (233). This version of the battle has it that the Union army occupying Jefferson remained for two days before burning it, then continued to engage the retreating but unvanquished Confederates in further battles to the east. In historical fact, Smith's occupation of Oxford lasted no more than eight hours on August 22—time enough to set the fires and otherwise render the town useless as a military headquarters or depot. Learning at this point of Forrest's disturbance in Memphis, Smith evidently reasoned that there was no military advantage to be gained by sending his large army after Chalmers and his puny band farther to the south or east. This was especially apparent when it became known that pursuing Chalmers would provide no opportunity to satisfy Sherman's craving for Forrest's death. His work in Oxford was done, and it was time to return to his base at Holly Springs and to the defense of the long rail lines that would fuel Sherman in Georgia. In this respect, the historical aftermath of the fighting at Oxford was quite the opposite of Faulkner's version in *Requiem*. Instead of Smith's continued assaults on Chalmers, the reverse was the case, with Chalmers pestering Smith's army as it lumbered northward across the Tallahatchie. During this final action, which concluded when Smith had crossed the river on August 25, the Confederates could do little more than commit inglorious nuisances; and they were certainly in no position to send out daredevil raids of the sort celebrated in "My Grandmother." In truth, the action petered out in a way that scarcely supports Bayard's recollection in *The Unvanquished* that Smith and Forrest "were fighting every day up and down the road to Memphis" (145). Soon after the battle is over, Ab Snopes offers the virtually correct observation that there "ain't a Yankee regiment left in Mississippi. You might say that this here war has turned around at last and went back north" (158). Bayard remarks bleakly that "there wasn't much anybody could say about the Confederate armies now" (155).

Bayard Sartoris's mixed time references, including those first noted by Cleanth Brooks, may be said to show the strain of his effort to recall experiences from as early as the age of fifteen or fourteen from many years later, possibly as late as 1919, the year of his death. By that time all but the most intransigent historians had concluded that there hadn't been much anybody could say about the Confederate armies for months, perhaps a year, before the clashes around Oxford in the summer of 1864. Furthermore, the "battle" at Hurricane Creek was hardly a battle at all in the sense of a sustained engagement with significant tactical consequences. From a dispassionate overview of the history of the Civil War in the West, the August incidents at Oxford are surely overshadowed by the personality of Forrest and his exploit in Memphis; but Faulkner presents them as considerably more distinctive and momentous affairs than they actually were by clustering disparate events and settings around the creek flowing near the Sartoris domain, and by highlighting the largely imaginary figure of the intrepid young cavalry officer.

Transpositions such as these help to explain why an attempt to construct a consistent chronology for Yoknapatawpha County during the Civil War rests on a false assumption about Faulkner's historical method. His conflicting dates and conflated settings tend to form a pattern of events repositioned toward the earlier, more hopeful phases of the war, finally clustering them around the time of the battle at Shiloh and Pittsburgh Landing in April 1862. Critics and biographers who play down Faulkner's distortions of history are probably right to make allowances for his variable powers of recall, his autodidactic eccentricities as a historian, and even the symptoms of alcoholism evident in his unsteady grasp on information derived from his reading. By ignoring his lapses, or by explaining them away, these sympathetic readers have tended to obscure the pattern of transposed settings that provides an intimate view of his characteristically modernist shaping of time.

A closer look at historical material in "My Grandmother Millard and General Forrest and the Battle of Harrykin Creek" reveals further instances of Faulkner's inclination to predate events of the war. Even though there can be no doubt that, as a matter of historical record, the Union expedition that resulted in the capture and burning of Oxford lasted from August 10 to August 22, 1864, Bayard Sartoris says, with an air of precision, that Forrest dated his report on the Battle of Hurricane Creek "28th ult. April 1862." This inaccuracy appears in another form in *Requiem*, which places the battle first in 1863 (40), then in the "spring of 1864" (64), and finally in the "summer of 1864" (214). Faulkner's inability to allow the battle to settle into its actual historical position is also evident when Forrest addresses his report to "General [Joseph E.] Johnston at Jackson." This is impossible, whether in April 1862 or in August 1864, because Johnston was headquartered in the state capital only during the spring of 1863, preparing for the defense of Vicksburg. At the time of the date on Forrest's report, Johnston was still in the East commanding the defense of Richmond; by the actual time of the Battle of Hurricane Creek, he had long since departed from Jackson to bolster the defense of Atlanta.

It is fairly clear that Faulkner gave "My Grandmother" an April setting in order to place it prior to the loss of Vicksburg. This is indicated when Forrest makes a half-hearted attempt to cow Lieutenant Backhouse/Backus into docility by declaring, "I'll send you down to Johnston at Jackson. . . .

He'll put you inside Vicksburg, where you can lead private charges day and night if you want" (693). Even if the question of Johnston's presence in Jackson is set aside for the moment, Forrest's threat seems absurd from the standpoint of the actual military situation in the Spring of 1862; and it becomes even more irrational if it is placed at a later, more accurate date. There is little likelihood that the historical General Forrest, even with his remarkable inventiveness, would have imagined cavalry charges of any kind as part of the Confederate effort to save Vicksburg. The city had been heavily fortified during the war with Mexico, and by May 1863, when Grant laid his siege, its miles of improved trenches, traps and satellite redoubts had made it one of the most secure fortresses in North America. Accordingly, if Backhouse had been stationed "inside Vicksburg" when Johnston was at Jackson, he would have been caught in a purely defensive state of siege that offered little or no role for cavalry. In Faulkner's imagined April, however, impossible things are conceivable; and this is particularly the case when the figure of the solo mounted charger enters his imagination.

Trying to derive the birth date of Bayard Sartoris from his narrative in *The Unvanquished*, Cleanth Brooks asks, "Had Faulkner forgotten that Vicksburg fell in 1863?" (450). The opening pages of that novel set the action unambiguously on the summer day when news of the disaster reaches Jefferson. Because Bayard says he was twelve then, and since most of his references to his age elsewhere imply that he was born in September 1849, the year appears to be 1862. Again, the effect is to transpose Vicksburg to a virtual prelapsarian time when its fall was only a rumor, a nearly unthinkable possibility, as it appears to be on the date of Forrest's report to Johnston. Within the imaginary time frame created by Bayard's accounts of the spring and summer of 1862, the war resembles an early act of a tragic drama in which the omen of Shiloh has been read, but Vicksburg still appears to be safe, and the second delusive Confederate triumph at Manassas in August is yet to come.

Faulkner's war stories related to Second Manassas center anecdotally on the ignoble death of the first Bayard Sartoris in a cavalry raid before the battle. The note of fatality that Faulkner sounds in his approach to one of the most inspiring victories for the South is in keeping with his general view of the war as a tragic illusion; it also appears to relate to the family story of his great-grandfather's analogous fall from the military glory he had won at First Manassas—another tragic story of April. In February 1862 William Clark Falkner was furloughed from his regiment at its winter quarters near Harper's Ferry and returned to his home in Ripley on a thirty-day recruiting leave. According to Joseph Blotner, when he rejoined Mississippi Two at Yorktown, Virginia, many of his men had joined in opposing his leadership because of his "ruthless disciplinary methods" and the "recklessness rather than courage" they thought he had displayed at Manassas (24). They consequently ousted him from his colonelcy in a regimental election held on April 21 and 22. He resigned and returned to Mississippi, where he nursed his anger and eventually set about raising another regiment. Thus rehabilitated, he led his men on a few successful expeditions against Union patrols near the Tennessee line, but other set-backs led him to resign his commission in October 1863. The fictional career of Colonel John Sartoris is roughly parallel, but unlike his model he is actively involved in the war to its conclusion, with intervals in Jefferson. Although his men reject him also, he retains command until he has led the regiment at Second Manassas. Since the actual Colonel Falkner was no more than an unpleasant memory for many of his former troops at that battle, it may be that Faulkner decided on personal grounds to treat it only indirectly through the story of Bayard's fatal raid. What is unmistakable is that he dates this quasi-historical event incorrectly by placing it in his imaginary month of April 1862, resonating as the historical setting of his great-grandfather's downfall.

Virginia ("Jenny") DuPre, the sister of Colonel Sartoris, recites the story in *Sartoris*, preserving the encrustations of more than a half-century of retellings that "grew richer and richer, taking on a mellow splendor like wine." Bayard's terminal exploit in the war had been, to be sure, a "hairbrained prank," but for Jenny it had also "become a gallant and finely tragical focal point to which the history of the race had been raised from out the old miasmic swamps of spiritual sloth by two angels valiantly fallen and strayed, altering the course of human events and purging the souls of men" (9). These two cherished objects of Jenny's ancestral memory, evoked alternately as juvenile pranksters and valiant angels, are Bayard and the cavalry commander, J.E.B. Stuart. Their story "had to do with an April evening, and coffee. Or the lack of it, rather . . . and Stuart's military family sat in the scented darkness beneath a new moon, talking of ladies and dead pleasures and thinking of home. . . . Thus they sat in the poignance of spring and youth's immemorial sadness" (11). Stuart decides that they should treat themselves to coffee; because the only way to get it is to take it from the stores amassed in the area by the Union army, he leads a daring raid on its headquarters. They burst in upon the commander, General John Pope himself, and snatch a pot of hot coffee from his breakfast table; then "they toasted one another in sugarless and creamless scalding coffee" (12). Pope narrowly escapes, but the raiders capture one of his officers, with whom Stuart exchanges civilities while the spreading reports of his raid bring Federal troops to the camp. They shoot the coffee pot out of Bayard's hand, and he and the others flee "with the thunderous coordination of a single centaur" (13) to safety in the dense woods. In further colloquy with the captured Union major, Stuart offers him a horse to ride back to his unit, declaring, "No gentleman would do less for a fellow officer." The major retorts, "No gentleman has any business in this war. . . . There is no place for him here. He is an anachronism, like anchovies. At least General Stuart did not capture our anchovies" (16). Hearing this, Bayard gallops back to Pope's depot for the anchovies, "jumped his horse over the breakfast table and rode into the wrecked commissary tent, and a cook who was hidden under the mess stuck his arm out and shot Bayard in the back with a derringer" (17). Stuart then retires to his camp, having lost only one man besides Bayard, whom he calls "a good officer and a fine cavalryman, but . . . he was too reckless" (18).

Jeb Stuart's April eulogy for young Bayard Sartoris echoes the divided opinion of William Clark Falkner that his men expressed in the regimental election of April 1862; but the downfall of the historical Confederate colonel and his fictional counterpart seems merely abject in comparison to the valorous demise of the figure evoked by Jenny DuPre. In her rapt commemoration, his "brief career swept like a shooting star across the dark plain of their mutual remembering and suffering, lighting it with a transient glare like a soundless thunder-clap, leaving a sort of radiance when it dies" (18). As an instance of historical romance, Jenny's fable exceeds even the historical revisions in Faulkner's portrait of Forrest in "My Grandmother"; and the heavily ironic tone of the narrative makes it plain that there is little in her account of the death of her brother that could be accepted as historical fact. Although the detached manner of the narrative seems to imply Faulkner's grasp of the more sober historical truth, his own distorting imagination is evident in the recurrent motifs of the errant one-man raid and the imposed April setting.

Stuart's raid on the Union headquarters at Catlett's Station, Virginia, took place in August 1862, a week before the massive battle broke out around Manassas Junction. Neither did Jenny's crescent moon appear above Stuart's coffee-less camp, nor did a "mounting golden day" (15) light his way back from the raid. Instead, heavy rain fell throughout, making for what Stuart called "the darkest night I ever knew" (Thomas 146). Indeed, a thunderstorm helped to conceal his troops' movements as they approached Pope's bivouac. The coffee and the fatal anchovies, on the other hand, are not inventions but actual items of the provisions that Pope had assembled. Allan Nevins describes these as "the richest body of stores ever brought into the field, a prodigal variety of materials to feed, clothe, and arm the Union troops. . . . [Confederate] officers threw open these treasures . . . toothbrushes, candles, coffee, tea . . . lobster salad, potted game, jellies. . ." (II, 177). Similarly, Thomas states that Stuart's officers came back from the raid with scarce supplies such as canteens, field glasses and pocket watches; and when Stuart's commander, Stonewall Jackson, sent in a large force four days later to capture or destroy the rest of this hoard, they returned laden with such improbable rations as pickled oysters, potted lobster and French champagne. They even captured Pope's uniform and sent it to Richmond, where it was exhibited to enthusiastic crowds at the State Library (147, 149).

The ensuing battle was one of Lee's masterpieces. After Stuart and Jackson had plundered and burnt Pope's depot, they hid in the woods in order to avoid engagement with the Union forces until they could join the main corps of Lee and Longstreet as they moved forward from the Shenandoah Valley (Nevins II, 177). As the battle lines formed on August 29, a massive Confederate flanking movement caught Pope's badly coordinated units by surprise and succeeded so well by the end of the second day that the entire Union army retreated chaotically to Washington. In its execution and outcome, Second Manassas might be seen, as Faulkner appears to have seen it, as a large-scale recapitulation of the preliminary maneuvers by Stuart and Jackson; and Jenny DuPre's story of Bayard's raid can equally be read as an apt metaphor for the battle itself—an illusion of final victory in the war which is dispelled tragically in a Confederate cavalryman's dying moment. By her compulsive recital of Bayard's heroic tale, however, Jenny continually denies this tragic reality. Her Civil War is no more than a facile coalescence of romance and history, sustained by an obsessional character who is caught up in an endless action. Young Bayard Sartoris never finishes dying; he is always *going* to his death in a permanent postponement of the war's catastrophe. Faulkner himself, despite his posture of ironic distance from Jenny's romance, also falls into her kind of wishful memorializing through his invention of the unvanquished characters and the transposed events that blur the image of his disgraced great-grandfather in April 1862. In the writing that followed *Sartoris*, however, he achieved a measure of freedom from this compulsive romanticization of the war.

The remoteness of the war in Virginia is another factor in the tendency of Faulkner's Jefferson characters to transform it into fiction. Generally, they share a sense of the distant unreality of the battles fought far beyond their corner of Mississippi. Lee's later campaigns and Johnston's desperate resistance to Sherman in Georgia and the Carolinas are therefore only sketched in *Absalom* and *The Unvanquished* as acts in a remote drama that seems nonetheless to follow much the same course as the war known more intimately to Jefferson and Yoknapatawpha County. In *Sartoris,* Virginius MacCallum, aged either seventy-four (321) or seventy-seven (334), likes to tell people that "in 1861 he was sixteen and he had walked to Lexington,

Virginia and enlisted, served four years in the Stonewall brigade and walked back to Mississippi" (310). He appears to be equally proud of making this journey on foot in order to serve under the great Jackson, as well he might be, since his round trip covers some 1400 miles. Old MacCallum's Faulknerian memory, like that of his contemporary, Virginia DuPre, and like Quentin Compson's in *Absalom*, gravitates back to Yoknapatawpha as the principal point of reference for a general grasp of Southern history. It is therefore probable that Jenny's story of young Bayard Sartoris and General Pope's gourmet provisions, while it conforms to the spirit and even to some of the historical facts of Jeb Stuart's career, is based more directly on an outstanding exploit of a similar kind in Mississippi—Van Dorn's destruction of Grant's stores in Holly Springs in late 1862.

Apart from Forrest's spectacular feats, no incident in the Civil War made a greater impression on Faulkner than the raid by General Earl Van Dorn, the cavalry commander of Braxton Bragg's right wing. He evokes it repeatedly, first in *Sartoris* and again in three works of the 1930s: "A Return" (1930), *Light in August* (1932) and *Absalom*. Old Bayard's ancient crony Will Falls enjoys diverting him with doubtful tales of his service under Colonel Sartoris in the "summer" of "sixty-three and -fo' . . . dodgin' around Grant's army" as the Yankees advanced south from Jefferson to Graneda. Will claims that the Sartoris regiment briefly joined forces with Van Dorn but returned to Jefferson for the harvest. On their way back to their homes they are supposed to have surprised a Union army camp, taken the soldiers' clothing and coffee, then allowed them to escape in the night—Jenny's pre-Manassas story transported in its essentials to Mississippi. Finally, back in Jefferson, Will hears the news of "Van Dorn ridin' into Holly Springs and burnin' Grant's sto's" (*Sartoris* 223–24). In "A Return" the familiar cavalryman riding to his valiant but at the same time disgraceful death enters the story of Van Dorn's raid. Another of Faulkner's aged female survivors of the war, Lewis Randolph Gordon, narrates the story, telling of her husband, Charles, who courts her at Christmas balls in Memphis and marries her impetuously when his unit is mobilized late in 1861. Having survived the fighting and wounds in some of the war's worst battles, including Shiloh, where his commander, Colonel Gavin Blount, dies, he takes up his final assignment in Van Dorn's cavalry corps in Mississippi. "One night he rode howling into Holly Springs behind Van Dorn's long floating hair" and is killed by an "old man who had shot him from his kitchen door, apparently in the act of breaking into the chicken-roost" (*Collected Stories* 555).

This figure reappears as the Reverend Gail Hightower's grandfather in *Light in August*. He meets his end in the same raid, but Faulkner shifts the setting from Holly Springs to Jefferson. Hightower's emotional life has always been caught up in his obsession with this character. "I am my dead grandfather on the instant of his death" (465), he believes, and he relives his dying moments each night in a ritual of ecstatic and morbid reveries. From his earliest days as a clergyman in Jefferson, Hightower dismays his congregation by "talking about the Civil War and his grandfather, a cavalryman, who was killed, and about General Grant's stores burning in Jefferson . . . all mixed up with absolution and choirs of martial seraphim." He finally awakens from this sterile dream when he is able to admit to himself that he has been cut off from his own life and the life of the town he was sent to serve through his confusion of visionary religiosity with the wholly imaginary glory of his grandfather's death. He accepts the reality of the judgment pronounced by Cinthy, the family's cook: "stealin' chickens. A man growed, wid a married son, gone to war whar his business was killin' Yankees, killed in somebody else's henhouse wid a han'ful of feathers." Hightower speculates—necessarily, since he has never heard the story from witnesses—that the killer "may have been a woman, likely enough the wife of a Confederate soldier"; and he tries half-heartedly to believe that such an end might be thought finer than being shot on a battlefield "or by a woman in a bedroom" (459). In the end, though, he concedes the reality of "the crucified shape of pity and love, a swaggering and unchastened bravo killed with a shotgun in a peaceful henhouse, in a temporary hiatus of his own avocation of killing" (462). Hightower is at last freed, albeit momentarily, of his insistent, paralyzing vision of "the wild bugles and the clashing sabres and the dying thunder of hooves" (467).

Gail Hightower's version of Van Dorn's raider introduces an insinuation of sexual misconduct, suggested by his speculation on the bedroom behavior of the implicated Confederate soldier's wife. Quentin Compson is more blunt in *Absalom*, charging that sexual indiscretions hastened the demise of the quintessential Confederate calvalryman "who on one night and with a handful of men would gallantly set fire to and destroy a million dollar garrison of enemy supplies and on the next night be discovered by a neighbor in bed with his wife and be shot to death" (432). Through Hightower's and Quentin's allegations, Faulkner alludes to the scandalous circumstances of General Van Dorn's death. In the spring of 1863 (not the "next night" after the raid on December 20, 1862) he was shot dead by Dr. George B. Peters of Holly Springs. Although he was not in any meaningful sense "a neighbor," Peters did open his house occasionally for the entertainment of cavalry officers with headquarters in the town. Van Dorn, an inveterate womanizer, pressed his attentions on the doctor's wife, Jessie, to the point of gaining access to her bedroom, where the doctor surprised them in the middle of the night of May 7. When he went to Van Dorn's billet on the next day to receive the written apology they had agreed to, Van Dorn insulted him. Peters killed him on the spot and was acquitted of murder charges after the war (Hartje 309, 313).

Quentin Compson broods on the anachronistic and self-contradicting notions of warfare that led the South to defeat:

> battles lost not alone because of superior numbers and failing ammunition and stores, but because of generals who should not have been generals, who were generals not through training in contemporary methods or aptitude for learning them, but by the divine right to say "Go there" conferred upon them by an absolute caste system; or because the generals of it never lived long enough to learn how to fight massed cautious accretionary battles, since they were already as obsolete as Richard or Roland or du Guesclin, who wore plumes and cloaks lined with scarlet at twenty-eight and thirty and thirty-two and captured warships with cavalry charges but no grain nor meat nor bullets, who would whip three separate armies in as many days and then tear down their own fences to cook meat robbed from their own smokehouses. (431–32)

Nowhere in his fiction of the Civil War does Faulkner give voice to a more sweeping condemnation of Southern military leadership, and of the cavalry in particular. Although it is surely colored by Quentin's anguished consciousness of the destruction of his family as a historical consequence of the Confederate generals' failings (and by the tormented virginity that causes him to loathe their bedroom scenes), his contemptuous tone reflects Faulkner's own disenchantment. Quentin renounces the romantic "glamorous fatality" associated in *Sartoris* with the title's family name—an *idée fixe* of the post-war Southern mind "like silver pennons downrushing at sunset, or a dying fall of horns along the road to Roncevaux" (380). Gail Hightower partly exorcises this haunting image by acknowledging its imposture; Quentin Compson goes further by relegating it to the remote, semi-legendary past of Charlemagne's warrior Roland and his defeat in the Pyrenees at Roncevaux. He understands that the tradition of military command that led to the collapse of the Southern war effort arose as a pale imitation of such historical figures such as Bertrand du Guesclin, the French commander of the Hundred Years' War (or the Bayards' namesake, Pierre de Terrail, Seigneur de Bayard, whose hugely outnumbered army saved France by raising the siege of Mézières in 1515). He demystifies the swaggering, dandified cavalry commander by seeing him as an adolescent fop who exploits his aristocratic privilege in a callow, absurd parody of the warlords of medieval Europe. The actual cavalry attacks on warships that he alludes to were acts of desperation and self-aggrandizement carried out by Nathan Bedford Forrest on the Tennessee River in the autumn of 1864 (Henry 366); and the raiders who robbed and assaulted Confederate citizens were not only Union soldiers but increasingly their own defenders, whom they sometimes killed while trying to save their property or, as in Van Dorn's case, their marriages.

Van Dorn the hapless fornicator and the thieves who served under him form Faulkner's most reductive image of the South's leaders as victims of their own vainglorious illusions and the bravado soldiering they led to. Quentin's attitude, to be sure, is characteristically exacerbated in its indiscriminate scorn, and it does not preclude Faulkner's balanced, ironic image of the Confederate cavalryman's character as a mixture of the palpably heroic and the merely puerile. In their jarring contrast, Van Dorn's brilliant leadership at Holly Springs and his ignominious end— along with the bathetic parallel stories about his chicken-stealing subordinates—contributed greatly to the paradoxical quality of Faulkner's history of the war. Indeed, as conspicuous examples of the South turning on itself in wartime, Van Dorn's story may have contributed to Faulkner's decision to treat incest and fratricide as central themes in *Absalom*, exceeding the more conventional perceptions of the war as a conflict over slavery and states' rights. By conflating the incidents involving Van Dorn at Holly Springs in order to create a sense of immediate connection between his victory and his death, and by reducing his raid to little more than a misadventure in petty theft, Faulkner's historical vision achieves a sustained ironic tension that eludes the authors of popular romances and scholarly history.

This deflated cavalryman appears also, in a final reduction, as a horse thief. In the section of *The Unvanquished* titled "Retreat," for example, a captain of the Union forces occupying Jefferson repeats his recent conversation with a rebel prisoner: "He said that Colonel Sartoris didn't fight; he just stole horses." Uncle Buck McCaslin replies to this with broad sarcasm: "That's John Sartoris! He gets horses; any fool can step out and get a Yankee." McCaslin's derision is not only temperamental but also stems from his disappointment as a supporter of Sartoris as commander of the Jefferson regiment. He splutters furiously at Bayard, "when you see him, tell him I said to leave the horses go for a while and kill the blue-bellied sons of bitches. Kill them!" (60–61). His speech recalls Cinthy's denunciation of Hightower's grandfather for similar derelictions. "Raid," the following section of *The Unvanquished*, describes Granny Millard's shenanigans with young Bayard and Ringo as they trick the compliant Union Colonel Dick out of 122 mules and horses. They set out to steal more horses with forged Federal orders, encircling Union positions as they do so in a parody of the foraging maneuvers for which the Confederate cavalry leaders were noted.

The comedy of Granny Millard's traffic in livestock is based in part on Faulkner's awareness that the Confederate cavalry gave the South many of its most heartening moments in the war. As a tactical maneuver, the surprise raid by mounted troops proved at times to be the only means of stopping the larger and better equipped Union infantry. The Southerners were, on the whole, better horsemen than those trained by the Union; they usually had superior knowledge of the terrain where they operated; and, as Forrest's operations in Mississippi and Tennessee demonstrate, their sudden forays on the flanks and to the rear of Union positions could produce enough terror and chaos to wreck their adversaries' most carefully conceived plans. In his fascination with characters like Forrest, Van Dorn and Stuart, and the hope of victory that their egocentric vitality kept alive, Faulkner was not unlike other Southerners who have sought to commemorate the redeeming aspects of a mainly unredeemable experience.

The cavalryman thus supplied Faulkner with his core metaphor for the entire Southern prosecution of the Civil War. The risks he took were to some extent justified by the growing scarcity of supplies caused by the Federal blockade of the few ports remaining in Confederate control; and his daring surely inspired courageous conduct despite the encompassing demoralization of the Confederate infantry. Nevertheless, raids on Union corrals and depots were carried out increasingly for their propaganda value as the obsolescence of the mounted soldier became more and more apparent to the military command. Incapable of recharging his antiquated muzzle-loading rifles without dismounting, rarely supplied with the new breech-loading semi-automatic weapons with rifled barrels that would have made him more effective in offensive actions, and presenting himself in any event as a large target to Union sharpshooters, the Confederate cavalryman was widely perceived as the anachronistic figure depicted by Quentin Compson. As the fighting raged on, infantry soldiers were known to jeer at the mounted regiments as they made their way, plumed, caped and caparisoned, to the rear or to a distant flank—always a sure sign that an attack was in preparation. Increasingly, in order to bolster their remaining military credibility, cavalry commanders were forced to carry out the kinds of sensational and highly risky raids made famous by Stuart, Forrest and Van Dorn.

Of these three leaders, only Forrest suffered no disastrous setbacks, military or personal, and his post-war success was assured. The achievements and eventually the failures of Stuart became the most famous of all, giving Faulkner his best example of the deeply paradoxical southern war hero. In the maneuvering prior to First Manassas, Stuart's regiments circled McClellan's enormous army and returned to Jackson's position with 1200 captured horses. As with most cavalry leaders, Stuart was often allowed to extemporize his mission in the general battle strategy, and he usually did so effectively. Inevitably, as the Southern cause grew desperate, his actions near the rear lines of the Union armies became more valuable as morale-boosting displays of youthful bravery than as maneuvers with clear tactical aims. Retribution for Stuart's flamboyance came disastrously at Gettysburg. His cavalry arrived with the usual large number of captured wagons and animals, but not until the first day of fighting had finished badly for the Confederate army. Contemporary accounts of the battle in newspapers and among Lee's officers generally place the responsibility for their crippling losses on Stuart, declaring that not even Lee's genius could have contrived effective flanking maneuvers of a major battle without cavalry. A minority, on the other hand, short of exonerating Stuart, reasoned that the outcome of the first day's engagement could hardly have been different had Stuart been present, and that Lee knew that cavalry could have had little impact on the Union army entrenched in the wooded hills above him. Nevertheless, the stigma of blame for the manner of the defeat became part of Stuart's legend; and his reputation for brilliant tactics has always been darkened by a view of his career as a series of wild pranks played by a glorified cattle rustler.

A final example of Jenny DuPre's war stories shows Faulkner's technique of historical transposition approaching a breaking point. Among the characters who serve to recite the history of Yoknapatawpha County and the Confederacy, she extends the narrative back to wartime Charleston, South Carolina, where the war began and where the Sartoris family had lived before John moved to Jefferson in the 1830s. Because she remembers seeing "a lot of blockade runners" in Charleston (*The Unvanquished* 281), it may be assumed that she lived in the city during the war but was forced out when the Union invaders destroyed her house. She arrives in Jefferson at Christmastime in 1867 (*Unvanquished* 271) or 1869 (*Sartoris* 10 and "There was a Queen") with colored glass she has salvaged from the ruins (*Unvanquished* 217). Old Bayard remembers that her husband of "a few nights . . . had been killed at the very beginning of the War, by a shell from a Federal frigate at Fort Moultrie" (*Unvanquished* 263). This character is mentioned also in *Sartoris* and "There Was a Queen." Fort Moultrie is the outermost of three fortified islands, including Sumter, that were built at the time of the Revolution to defend the city against attack by sea. It had fallen into disuse in the meantime, and its sunken ramparts were considered inadequate to resist an assault on the Federal troops stationed there. When it became apparent late in 1860 that General Beauregard was about to send armed units from Charleston to seize Moultrie, the Federal commanders decided to abandon it and to evacuate its troops to the more secure garrison of Fort Sumter. The rebels, among whom Faulkner placed the unfortunate DuPre, seized Fort Moultrie in late December 1860 and engaged its batteries in the shelling of Sumter the following April. DuPre, it is told, was killed when Union gunboats fired on Moultrie in a attempt to disable its artillery.

As a characteristic name, "DuPre" rings true enough for a military unit commanded by a Beauregard and led by a deSaussure (captor of Fort Moultrie), but there were no fatal casualties on either side in the firing on Fort Sumter. (Two Federal soldiers were killed accidentally after the battle was over when the powder they were to use for a parting salute to their flag exploded.) One reason why this action was virtually bloodless was that the Federal naval ships sent to relieve Sumter never arrived. Both DuPre's death and the shell that caused it are therefore fictions that collapse under the weight of the very appeal to history that Faulkner makes to support them. On the other hand, if the character DuPre and his impossible demise are passed off as insignificant lapses, and if their outright collision with fact leads Faulkner's reader merely to the conclusion that he was careless at moments, or that he was an indifferent historian, or that such errors are really inconsequential, then there can be little possibility of identifying Faulkner's central pattern of the April fatality that occurs in connection with an apparently successful Civil War offensive carried out by the South. Other aspects of this pattern—the solo actor, his premonitory death, the shifting of narrative focus toward the earlier phases of the war—are implied by what would appear to be the cause of Faulkner's mistaken history of Fort Moultrie: his conflation of a Federal naval assault on the Charleston forts in April 1863 and the original attack. In their attempt to recapture them, Union ironclads managed to enter the harbor and fire a few salvoes, but the Confederate artillery either drove them back to sea or disabled them. It was another easy victory for the Confederates. Their sole fatality was a gunner at Fort Moultrie who was killed when his own flagstaff fell on him, knocked down by a round from one of the Union warships. The death of this extraordinarily unlucky man—Private J. S. Lusby, Company F, First South Carolina Infantry (Anderson 163)—and the two flag-related Union casualties in 1861 appear to have entered into Faulkner's ironic consciousness as he created a character for "Flags in the Dust" whose passing, in circumstances both honorable and absurd, marked the war at its otherwise hopeful beginning.

The luxuriance of Jenny DuPre's style as a raconteur grows as the post-war years accumulate, dramatizing her steady retreat from historical fact. By 1919, at age seventy-nine, fifty-eight years after her husband's death, it is not surprising that many of the crucial connections between her narratives and recorded history are broken. The setting of her earliest story is Baltimore in 1858, when she claims to have been a dancing partner of Jeb Stuart "with his crimson sash and his garlanded bay and his mandolin" (*Sartoris* 19, 357). Stuart was in fact stationed with the First

Cavalry at Fort Riley, Kansas throughout 1858 and was nowhere near Baltimore until a six-month leave took him to Washington late in the following year (Thomas 52–53). In this instance, the error may appear simply to be a lucky inadvertence on Faulkner's part, illustrating a plausible inaccuracy in the memories of an elderly character who, like her creator, tends at times to predate past events to a happier time. The account of her husband's death, on the other hand, plainly contradicts Faulkner's evident commitment to historical verisimilitude. It reveals his and his characters' general tendency to constellate actual events around the tragic moment when the illusion of victory for the South reached its most cruel intensity—a day, as he repeatedly imagined it, in April.

A particularly striking example of Faulkner's tendency to detach events of the Civil War from their positions in time and allow them to gravitate toward an earlier point occurs in *Intruder in the Dust* (1948). As the central character, Chick Mallison, hears Gavin Stevens tell the story of the Battle of Gettysburg, he imagines being "there in the instant when it's still not yet two o'clock on that July afternoon in 1863." This is the moment when Lee has positioned his brigades for the calamitous charge on the Federal positions along Cemetery Ridge: "the furled flags are already loosened to break out" and "there is still time for it not to begin" (194–95). The imagined moment is not quite frozen—the flags are "loosened"—and it hovers in Chick's imagination as an action perpetually removed from the disastrous onrush of time. It marks a history that is always just beginning to unfold. As he transposes himself imaginatively not only backward in time but out of chronology altogether, Chick has a sense of the fixations that deaden so many of Faulkner's characters. Fortunately, he is able to let this fantasy lapse and to live with equanimity in relation to both the present and the past.

Chick Mallison is one of a handful of characters in Faulkner's stories who find a partial solution to the problem of the consoling revisions of Civil War history. These were the stories that Faulkner heard—and evidently believed, according to Joseph Blotner—when he was young. Blotner reveals that members of his family and the courthouse loafers he befriended passed on many of these folklorish improvisations to him; others came more authoritatively from his teacher, Ella Wright (171). Although he soon acquired a taste for more formal and scholarly historical studies such as those in the library of his Oxford friend, Phil Stone, it is clear that these early vernacular accounts of the war had a permanent shaping influence on his imagination. One of the Oxford legends that Blotner cites involves a window in an old house on South Street: "In one of the window-panes, faintly scratched there by a diamond ring, was a name: Jane Taylor Cook." Oxford tradition has it that this young woman put her name on the glass "during the dark days of 1863" as she watched the 7th Tennessee Cavalry pass in front of her house, presumably retreating from the Battle of Hurricane Creek in 1864. She burst out of her house and cursed the passing cavalrymen for "running from the bluecoats." One of the officers, Captain William Montgomery Forrest, the general's son, admired her spirit so greatly that he resolved to return to Oxford after the war and marry her. And so, the story goes, he did (138).

Faulkner adapted this story twice in his novels. First, briefly, in *The Unvanquished*, Bayard remembers that "one day General Forrest rode down South Street in Oxford where there watched him through a window pane a young girl who scratched her name on it with a diamond ring: Celia Cook" (17). This version associates the girl with the charming, blind, virginal Saint Cecilia; the love interest fades; and the general of the cavalry is once more in Faulkner's spotlight. Then, in the later historical prologues of *Requiem for a Nun*, Faulkner elaborates the story further. "Cecilia Farmer" replaces Cecilia Cook and the original Jane Taylor Cook, and both Forrests give way to a nameless love-struck cavalryman who reappears in town on furlough after Appomattox, proposes to the girl, marries her, and carries her off to restore his devastated farm in Alabama. (Her new husband's curiously urgent and impetuous manner recalls Thomas Sutpen's frenzied effort to rebuild Sutpen's Hundred after the war—an evil omen for this young bride.) At this point, Faulkner's narrator assumes the role of a guide reciting tourist information: the girl was the daughter of the county jail-keeper; the house with the inscribed window pane was the jail; she scratched her name with her grandmother's ring; the present occupants use the room as a kitchen; and so on. Cecilia Farmer, he adds, did not shout abusively at the Confederates; she only gazed out the window, standing immobile "where, so it seemed to the town, she had been standing ever since" (200). She commemorated the event by engraving an oddly anachronistic date after her name: "April 16th 1861" (197). Reworking the legend in this way, Faulkner's imagination moved in opposite directions— toward a moment that is both palpably historical and curiously outside of time. While the narrator's meticulous factuality seems to give Cecilia Farmer's story the weight of a report by a municipal historical society, he also tends to de-historicize her identity by spiritualizing her first name and by omitting the dramatic anecdote of her clash with the retreating cavalry. The effect is to transform this inert, monitory figure who silently witnesses and records their defeat into an apotheosized Woman of the South traumatized by the spectacle of loss. To the modern-day Jeffersonian, she has become a sibylline emanation from the past, taking on a pan-historical, mythological significance:

demon-nun and angel-witch; empress, siren, Erinys: Mistinguett, too, invincible possessed of a half-century more of years than the mere three score or so she bragged and boasted, for you to choose among, which one she was—not *might* have been, nor even *could* have been, but *was*. (225)

Here Faulkner's local tour guide becomes a prophet—a visionary whose "truth and dream" emerge from the mere "rubble-dross of fact and probability." From the same vantage of victorious contempt for historical fact that dates Cecilia Farmer's signature, he projects an impossibly ancient Mistinguett, the French actress who was in fact seventy-five years old when Faulkner wrote this.

The narrator of *Intruder in the Dust* seeks to resolve the conflict between "truth" and "fact" by skewing the fact itself, offering a more or less plausible reference to a particular historical moment while at the same time displacing it from the rubble of history. Nothing that a conventional historian would consider momentous happened on April 16, 1861, the date on the window pane. The Federal defenders of Fort Sumter had already departed after their surrender three days before; Lincoln had issued a call for volunteers; and military leaders throughout the nation were preparing for the fighting that would break out later in the spring. The narrator identifies the date broadly as the "moment [when] the destiny of the land, the nation, the South, the State, the Country, was already whirling into the plunge of its precipice," as though it does in fact refer to the time of the war's inception; but no actual moment in time can contain such a cataclysmic whirling and plunging. Rather, the moment itself is severed from the chronology and drawn violently into the maelstrom of history. Faulkner recasts this image of radical dislocation in time in the spatial metaphor that follows:

not that the State and the South knew it, because the first seconds of fall always seem like soar; a weightless deliberation preliminary to a rush not downward but upward, the falling body reversed during that second by transubstantiation into the upward rush of earth; a soar, an apex, the South's own apotheosis of its destiny and its pride. (197–98)

No longer perceivable as a fixed point of reference in the past, the sixteenth day of April 1861 is substantially transformed into a turbulent action perpetuated in Jefferson's communal memory. Because the date has no history it remains as changeless as the glass it marks; and "the town's composite heritage of remembering" entombs its historical reality by mournfully recollecting "the old dead date in April almost a century ago" (219). Finally, the date on the window pane expresses Cecilia Farmer's "undistanced voice," saying, "*Listen, stranger; this was myself; this was I*" (225). *Was* and *is* are the same; chronology is abolished.

Because of her association with a date that both fixes and transcends one of the first days of the war, Cecilia Farmer gains for Faulkner's narrator the stature of a "progenitress" of all "the women, the ladies, the unsurrendered, the irreconcilable, who even after another thirty-five years [following Jenny DuPre's dedication of the Confederate memorial in Jefferson on Decoration Day, 1900] would still get up and stalk out of the picture houses showing *Gone With the Wind*" (207). Faulkner's characters—even those born after 1865—are particularly susceptible to this sort of emotional fixation, brought on by bitter memories of the war and its legends. It is mainly in the later works that his characters—all male—manage to free themselves of the obsessions that threaten to trap them in the past. In the earlier novels, Gail Hightower, Quentin Compson and Bayard Sartoris are to some extent successful in this struggle, but the women who survive the war seem destined to relive their experiences forever. This is most poignantly true of Jenny DuPre. In the concluding narrative of *Sartoris*, even though she finally overcomes the compulsion that drives her to repeat and elaborate her story of Bayard's death, she substitutes an identical fixation on her great-nephews, John and Bayard (each third Sartoris so named). John is wounded fatally in World War I, and Bayard becomes a suicidal victim of its traumas. She believes they died not in a separate war but in a continuation of the Civil War into this century, with the inevitable deadly consequences for the men of her family. When she unveils the soldier's statue in Jefferson, she does not register its southward gaze expressing the communal belief that "the old war was dead" (207). For Jenny, the war is dead but not yet buried. Like all of Faulkner's characters who are imprisoned in the past, she commemorates her dead as restless ghosts who never finish dying. She acquiesces as they draw their vitality from hers like vampires.

In his paper for the Salamanca conference, "'A Furious Beating of Hollow Drums Toward Nowhere': Faulkner, Time, and History" (Coy Ferrer and Gresset 77–95), André Bleikasten calls Faulkner a "heretic historian" who subverts the process of historical analysis by "regressing to the suspended moment when history is not yet written down, not yet fixed in the letter of an authoritative text. . . . He furrows and fractures, frustrating our wish for a well-ordered, meaningful discourse." In his attempt to summarize Faulkner's vision of Southern history, Bleikasten finds no clear, firm conclusions—not even in the relentlessly philosophical *A Fable* (1954). Time reveals nothing but its dynamism: "All we can know about history is its turbulence and its impetus; the headlong rush, the frantic race." We sense "the fever, the fury, the sheer urgency of most of Faulkner's tales." His literary style conforms to this quality of time as it "confronts us with the turbulence of an ongoing narration . . . without ever coming to rest." These, Bleikasten concludes, are identifying attributes of the "apocalyptic tradition" in American literature (79, 89, 93–94).

Since Bleikasten's observations on the Faulknerian historical sense are mainly correct, it would be useful to modify his formula of the "suspended moment" since it implies a contradictory notion of arrested time. A concept of arrested motion—of memory and feeling—is inadequate to characterize Faulkner's dynamic clusters of moments, whose essence is a sensation of overwhelming and unsuspended movement. Bleikasten's argument appears to revert inappropriately to the traditional critical discourse on the Joycean epiphany, the evanescent moment when *kinesis* is resolved to *stasis*, resulting in an instant of consciousness purified of kinetic desire and loathing. This is evidently the basis for his notion of Faulkner's "arrested, memory-ridden time" (80). For the Joycean character, the moment of "arrested" consciousness usually arrives as an authentic but fleeting *self-perception* that shatters a sentimental illusion. Faulkner's post-war characters, to the contrary, tend to remain in the grip of their illusions, so that—to revert to Joyce's terms—they cannot achieve a positive moment of *stasis* because their consciousness is overcome by kinetic obsessions: unbridled desire for a romantic, even apocalyptic history of the Civil War, unmitigated loathing of the South's defeat and ruin. It is the characters and not the moments that are frozen. Their war is an endless action—an action of dying. It persists as an illusion of consummate, violent movement that acts on their memories like a gravitational field or vortex. It draws even recorded historical events to its center and tends to compact the war's entire story in an ahistorical tragic April day when a young Confederate cavalry officer rides endlessly toward his extinction.

For young Ike McCaslin, as he broods on the war stories told in *Go Down, Moses* (1942), "those old times would cease to be old times and would become a part of [his] present, not only as if they had happened yesterday but as if they were still happening" (171). At first, because he is young, he is easily captivated by the adventure and strangeness of these narratives; but as an older man he learns to recognize them as emotional traps. This realization comes to him as it comes to old Bayard Sartoris in *The Unvanquished* soon after World War I:

> old men had been telling young men and boys about wars and fighting before they discovered how to write it down: and what petty precisian [sic] to quibble about locations in space or in chronology, who to care or insist: *Now come, old man, tell the truth: did you see this? were you really there?* Because wars are wars: the same exploding powder when there was powder, the same thrust and parry of iron when there was not—one tale, one telling, the same as the next or the one before. So we knew a war existed: we had to believe that, just as we had to believe that the name for the sort of life we had led for the last three years was hardship and suffering. Yet we had no proof of it. (107)

Bayard recalls that his feeling of isolation from the scenes of warfare not only deprived him of proof, but actually led to the "obverse of proof." This was his main sensation at those moments when his father would return from the fighting with "no flags nor drums . . . no poste and riposte of sweat-reeking cavalry which all war-telling is full of, no galloping thunder." Colonel Sartoris would reappear without notice or fanfare, his men looking "like tramps" in their shabby uniforms, astride the "crowbait horses" on whose bony backs they seemed to be "actually almost sneaking home" with nothing in their demeanor to confirm the old men's tales of gallantry and glory. These memories are so intolerable to Bayard that he turns instinctively to a narrative of Southern valor such as the old men would tell, but one he believes to be verifiable. It is the story of the Confederate soldiers who are said to have stolen a railroad locomotive in Union hands at Chattanooga and eluded pursuing Federal troops in a frantic chase along the line to Atlanta. Drusilla Hawk, who marries Colonel Sartoris after the war, has told him this story. Her fiery, ecstatic narration "congealed into an irrevocable moment . . . the sorry business which had dragged on for three years now" (107–12). She claims the authority of an eye-witness, and Bayard trusts her as a loyal family relative. Her tale offers Bayard an anecdote from history that he can use to mediate his sense of the war's reality between the older Jeffersonians' fabrications and his father's humiliating homecomings.

Perhaps inevitably, Drusilla's seemingly authentic history is riddled with errors. It accordingly frustrates Bayard's attempt to place his memory on firm ground between the immediately brutal facts of hardship and suffering and the distant triumphs of warfare. Drusilla actually reverses the principal facts of the historical "Great Locomotive Raid," sometimes referred to as "Andrews' Raid." James J. Andrews was an officer of the Union army, not of the Confederate. He and some twenty of his men went behind enemy lines in northern Georgia, made off with a railroad engine they seized in an Atlanta roundhouse, and raced for ninety miles toward safety in Chattanooga. For a while they outran an engine the Confederates sent after them, but, unlike Drusilla's heroes, they were captured in the end. The incident occurred on the twelfth day of April 1862, exactly one year after the outbreak of the war. Northern propagandists exploited it to the full, casting Andrews and his raiders as actors in a providential drama that atoned for the fall of Fort Sumter. Although Andrews and some of his men were executed as spies, those who survived were treated as heroes and became the first soldiers of the United States Army to be awarded the Medal of Honor. From a historian's point of view, Drusilla's version of this story is simply a lie. It not only portrays the Confederates falsely as heroes who avoid being caught after yet another astonishing rebel raid, but it also resituates the Atlanta-Chattanooga railroad to the west in Alabama, where she claims she saw the locomotives steaming toward Atlanta along the rails near her home.

Although April is demonstrably the month in Faulkner's "heretical" history when all things can happen, the zero point toward which his wartime is drawn, it rarely does so by means of such gross distortions of the simple facts that made him so restless. Accordingly, as with the account of the death of Jenny DuPre's husband at Fort Moultrie, other distorting pressures from Faulkner's history of the war external to the story itself can be brought to bear in order to locate it in a general pattern of transposed history. Such distortion can be understood as a constructive act of the imagination rather than a mere tall tale, or a factual error, or a lie. Even Drusilla Hawk's fabrication contains an element of such a construction. Among the fictional events that are related to the "Great Locomotive Raid" in ways that do not affront the historical record, Drusilla's fiancé, Gavin Breckbridge, is killed at Shiloh a week before. The news would have reached her, plausibly, within hours of the raid. While it would be simplistic to attribute her wild untruths to deranged grief, it is likely that Faulkner saw a connection between the distortions of her story and the disfiguring obsessions that rule her behavior following Breckbridge's death. As Bayard states it, "Drusilla had deliberately tried to unsex herself by refusing to feel any grief at the death in battle . . . of her affianced husband" (217). She nevertheless resolves "to try to look and act like a man after her sweetheart was killed" (218), and she persuades her future husband John Sartoris to let her join his cavalry regiment. In this way she achieves twice what Bayard terms "the highest destiny of a Southern woman—to be the bride-widow of a lost cause" (219). She gradually takes on the quality of androgynous, feverish impotence that Faulkner usually portrays in his female war victims. Finally, when John Sartoris is killed in "An Odor of Verbena," the concluding section of *The Unvanquished*, she becomes, like the "progenitress" Cecilia Farmer before her, an abstracted mythological emanation of the war and its lethal heritage. Her role transforms her into a "Greek amphora priestess of a succinct and formal violence," wholly absorbed into the obsessional patterns of Faulkner's war. She is martyred by her own exultant and spurious visions of the unvanquished South—necessary falsehoods such as her story of the band of transcendent railroad hijackers rushing forever beyond the reach of their destroyers. "Only not gone or vanished either," concludes the deluded Bayard, "so long as there should be defeated or the descendants of defeated to tell it or listen to the story" (112).

Drusilla Hawk Sartoris is an epitome of the Faulkner character who willfully—Bayard says "voraciously"—surrenders his or her historical identity to a tyrannous nostalgia. At the same time, Bayard views her as "the incorrigibly individual woman" (263); and, indeed, she displays many of the traits of Faulkner's female characters whose stories are set in the twentieth century: she is, or becomes, sexually indistinct; domestic routine bores her; and she is temperamentally at odds with such domestic values as filiality, marriage to an "acceptable young man" and child-rearing. She spurns all of this joyously in the excitement of the coming war, declaring, "Thank God for nothing" (114–15). The war offers her a means of escape from Southern social tradition, a free passage from its confining history to the "nothing" of war where all seems possible. Her illusion of liberation, however, is a snare; by welcoming "nothing" she becomes nothing, and in the long aftermath of defeat her character disintegrates into a cadaverous ruin embalmed in memory. Memories carry her out of historical time into a melodramatic void. In this she resembles another archetypal victim, Rosa Coldfield in *Absalom*, who declares that "there is a might-have-been that is more true than truth" (178). Faulkner shared this romantic sentiment, but he tempered it with the ironic imaginative mediation that imparts historic resonance to his otherwise abject remark, "there is no such thing as *was*— only *is*" (Merriwether and Millgate 255).

"Memory believes before knowing remembers. Believes longer than recollects, longer than knowing even wonders. Knows remembers believes"—the various modes of memory are really one action that precedes and outlasts consciousness of historical fact. The meditative murmur that opens the sixth chapter of *Light in August* (111) is Faulkner's prologue to his inquiry into the origins of Joe Christmas, a character whose past is largely unknown, even to himself. Because he has no means of knowing who his father was, the agonized question of his racial identity never finds a certain answer. Rumor further confuses the question by suggesting that he is half "Spanish." What Joe "knows" and "recollects" extends backward in time no further than the orphanage where he was placed, and the Bible-crazed janitor (Joe never learns that this is his maternal grandfather) who watches him ceaselessly. These scraps of memory are overshadowed by the figure of the dietitian who surprises him in her closet and calls him a "little nigger bastard" (144), thus giving birth to Joe's hesitating but nonetheless inescapable belief in his mixed blood. It becomes an obsessive conviction that torments him until his death at the hands of Percy Grimm, who castrates him:

> the pent black blood seemed to rush like a released breath. It seemed to rush out of his pale body like the rush of sparks from a rising rocket; upon that black blast the man seemed to rise soaring into their memories forever and ever. They are not to lose

it, in whatever peaceful valleys, beside whatever placid and reassuring streams of old age, in the mirroring faces of whatever children they will contemplate old disasters and newer hopes. It will be there, musing, quiet, steadfast, not fading and not particularly threatful, but of itself alone serene, of itself alone triumphant. (440)

Joe Christmas is one of Faulkner's latter-day casualties of the old fratricidal Civil War. Its immemorial denial of the brotherhood of white and black condemns him to a death that is recollected persistently—one of the perpetual actions engrossing the historical consciousness of Jefferson. The memory of his murder is like a soaring rocket that never falls or explodes. It is redeemed by a quality of martyrdom that absorbs all of history—the war included—into a moment, both in and out of time, that is "quiet . . . steadfast . . . serene." Placed in a narrowly historical perspective, Joe's death is neither more nor less than another lynching perpetrated in Mississippi in the 1930s. It belongs equally in the non-chronological dimension of the Holy Week of April, recorded in *The Sound and the Fury*, when Dilsey Gibson finds consolation for the historical ruin of the Compson family in her untroubled recollection of the Blood of the Lamb.

In William Faulkner's writing the modernist temperament sometimes betrays its exasperation with the literalness of reality embedded in time. At such moments it is prone to lapse into nostalgia and denial, exposing a complex regressive tendency that is also evident in the work of Joseph Conrad, James Joyce, F. Scott Fitzgerald and, as we shall see, Ernest Hemingway. What ultimately and ironically shields their work from the worst consequences of this inclination is their inability to define a desired alternate reality clearly enough to escape into it. In this respect they may be thought to recapitulate the old Gnostic heresy, with its certainty that the Creation is replete with error and evil, and with its belief in a collateral reality that is as spiritually whole as it is unknown. Faulkner's account of the American Civil War is at times deeply erroneous, but his errors are part of the fictions of time that have the potential to liberate as well as to paralyze his characters.

CHAPTER FIVE

Literary Hemingway:
Subversion and Influence

If the literary quality of writing is perceived in terms of an author's evident preoccupation with the work of others, then Ernest Hemingway must be considered one of the most literary writers of the modern period. That he always used the word *literary* with a measure of contempt only points to a central irony that underlay his belief that the act of writing "truly" was as authentic, vital and arduous as any distinguished human achievement could be. It was performed not as a solitary, passive reflection of the world's significant realities, but rather as a way of participating in them directly. His sense of the immediacy of the writer's art accordingly conferred great importance on the literature he read, and he always sought to include himself, not always convivially, in the dynamic community formed by its authors, present and past, great and obscure. His changing adaptations of their work in his novels divide his career into three phases. The early work culminating in *A Farewell to Arms* (1929) tends to be confrontational, parodying narrative patterns of previous writers by inversion. With *For Whom the Bell Tolls* (1940) the literary model becomes a kind of quarry whose materials Hemingway extracted, re-configured and assimilated. The later work is inclined to deteriorate into a mechanical, deferential paralleling of conspicuous sources. At its strongest, then, Hemingway's fiction displays a radical reworking of received narrative patterns; in decline, it is absorbed by them.

The reflexive allusions to the writer's craft in Hemingway's stories of warriors, bullfighters, sportsmen and lovers are meant not as analogies but as equations. Critics who ridiculed Hemingway for his refusal to separate those who write from those who act typically provoked a response on his part that was less polemical rebuttal than theatrical enactment of the role of the writer as battler. The best example of this is his behavior during the famous interview by Lillian Ross for the *New Yorker* in 1950. Taking on the manner of a pugilistic buffoon, he portrayed himself as a top contender among the champion prize-fighters of Western Fiction: "I started out very quiet and I beat Mr. Turgenev [*sic*]. Then I trained hard and I beat Mr. de Maupassant. I've fought two draws with Mr. Stendhal, and I think I had an edge in the last one. But nobody's going to get me in any ring with Mr. Tolstoy unless I'm crazy or I keep getting better" (Weeks 23). Hemingway paints much the same figure of the contentious young writer in his more sober 1935 article for *Esquire*, "Monologue of the Maestro: A High Seas Letter." The aspiring writer, he holds,

> should have read everything so he knows what he has to beat. . . . There is no use writing anything that has been written before unless you can beat it. What a writer in our time has to do is write what hasn't been written before or beat dead men at what they have done. The only way he can tell how he is going is to compete with dead men. The only people for a serious writer to compete with are the dead that he knows are good. (White 218)

Hemingway's notion of writing as a contest was a defensive screen to conceal his deep conviction that his achievements in *In Our Time* (1925) and in a dozen or so of his later stories were greater than anything by two of the best French authors of short stories in the nineteenth century; that his treatments of love and war in *A Farewell to Arms* and *For Whom the Bell Tolls* were at least on a par with *Le Rouge et le Noir* or *La Chartreuse de Parme*; but that an achievement of the magnitude of *Anna Karenina* or *War and Peace* was admittedly greater than his own. This, he feared, was particularly the case with the forthcoming *Across the River and into the Trees* (1950), a novel whose manifold weaknesses warned Hemingway that he was not "getting better."

He was of course hardly unique among writers for his feeling of combative rivalry with others whose reputations were rising or were already securely established; nor was he uniquely ungenerous when he gloated over what he supposed to be their defeat at his hands. What is characteristic about his way of expressing this competition, however, is his intense sense of engagement. His love of boxing, coarsely parodied in the Ross interview, explains only one rudimentary aspect of this feeling of immediacy; more important is his conviction that he and other writers of fiction past and present formed a vigorous, often turbulent and contentious community at the heart of contemporary life. He responded to them and to their writing with the camaraderie, admiration, envy, scorn and rage characteristic of other close relationships. For Hemingway it was, in a word, personal.

Hemingway's critics, biographers and acquaintances have sometimes given rather severe interpretations of this rough playfulness. Among his contemporaries, the American writer Nathan Asch, for example, himself the victim of an actual knock-out punch thrown by Hemingway in Paris, sought to explain his opponent's recurrent quarrels with Ford Madox Ford by surmising that he "could not function unless he fought and destroyed older men" (Reynolds, *Paris Years* 184). Similar charges followed the publication of *The Torrents of Spring* (1926), his remorseless parody of Sherwood Anderson's novel *Dark Laughter*. In more recent biographical studies such as Kenneth Lynn's *Hemingway* (1987), it has become common to view this behavior as a symptom of some deep emotional disorder. While much of the psychoanalytic work on Hemingway is plausible up to a point, it tends to oversimplify the complex, ambiguous motives of a man who was dead set on making his way—sometimes using elbows and fists— in the society of writers of his day. As he put it with typical bluntness in the daybook he kept at the outset of his career, "the more meazly & shitty the guy, i.e. Joyce, the greater the success in his art" (Reynolds, *Paris Years* 220).

It is true, on the other hand, that Hemingway's painfully assertive manner sometimes betrays a sense of uneasiness about his standing among the *literati*. The note of insecurity sounds with varying intensity in all of his work, and it is particularly evident in the self-consciously literary manner of Jake Barnes, the narrator of his first novel, *The Sun Also Rises* (1926). Most of Jake's male acquaintances are professional writers of some sort, and his two closest friends, Robert Cohn and Bill Gorton, have published books in America. Their success galls him more than he is ready to admit. The decline of both friendships, reaching a low point in the drunken violence at the fiesta in Pamplona, reveals not only Jake's personal limitations in close relationships but also his failure to accommodate the literary values implicit in his friends' work. As a newspaperman whose material is evidently little more than gossip (early in the novel he asks Cohn if he has heard any "dirt" for his dispatch [9]), he repeatedly misses or evades opportunities to fill the emptiness of journalistic tattle with more worthy work of the literary kind he pretends to despise. This is apparent in the Spanish fishing scene with Bill Gorton in chapter 12 (112–26). Jake has an easy, joking rapport with his American friend, and he admires his achievements as a writer on nature and as a sportsman. Bill's recent publishing success in New York shows no signs of having corrupted him, and his satirical thrusts at the literary posturing he has witnessed in America keep its artificialities at a distance from the natural setting of the Irati River. Nevertheless, in their retreat from the unnatural life of New York and Paris, Jake can't escape the knowledge that Bill is more securely at home in the sportsman's world they have turned to than he is. The truer angler, Bill takes his fly rod downstream from the dam where Jake remains to fish indolently with worms. Bill calls him a "lazy bum" (112) in a tone that would convey nothing more than rough male camaraderie if it were not for his tendency to dwell, albeit humorously, on Jake's shortcomings. "Nobody that ever left their own country ever wrote anything worth printing," he jeers, parodying the literary chauvinism he has encountered in New York and Chicago, and adds, "Not even in the newspapers." Then he pauses to sip his coffee and consider whether he may have offended his friend, but Jake appears to be enjoying his humor too much to be pained by it. Bill then stumbles onto the subject of impotence and falls silent again; even at this juncture Jake manages to keep his composure despite his sexually incapacitating war wound: "I was afraid he thought he had hurt me with that crack about being impotent. I wanted him to start again" (115). His levity notwithstanding, Bill has drawn a connection between journalism and impotence. He calls Jake a bum again (121), then decides not to risk teasing him further.

Because Bill Gorton plays only a minor role in the sordid drama at Pamplona after the fishing trip, he preserves the innocence that has contributed to his success as a writer. He has what Hemingway calls "the real thing" in *Death in the Afternoon* (1932), referring to the authentically portrayed emotions that were "beyond" him, as it is beyond Jake, in his early career as a journalist (2). Bill stays mainly on the sidelines as Jake, Robert Cohn and Mike Campbell skirmish over Brett Ashley; and when he leaves for America, he is virtually unscathed, having been drawn only briefly into the drunken quarreling. Of the four male characters who cluster around Brett, Bill is the most wary of her, and he alone is spared the most painful effects of her behavior.

Lady Brett Ashley is a hostile alien in Hemingway's world of emerging literary value. When Mike Campbell talks glibly about the amount of reading he does at home, her sneering rejoinder, "You'll be writing next" (143), expresses the sort of derision that Jake the newspaper man half-suspects of himself. As *The Sun Also Rises* concludes, Brett stays in character by becoming an abject parody of a writer with her stagy telegram to Jake in San Sebastian: "COULD YOU COME HOTEL MONTANA MADRID AM RATHER IN TROUBLE BRETT." Jake the writer manqué responds in kind and is ashamed of the false romantic role he allows himself to play: "That seemed to handle it. That was it. Send a girl off with one man. Introduce her to another to go off with him. Now go and bring her back. And sign the letter with love. That was it all right. I went in to lunch" (238–39). By juxtaposing the behavior of Bill Gorton and Jake Barnes in their relation to Brett Ashley and to the natural order that she contaminates, Hemingway dramatizes his conviction that the character who acts and the character who writes are one.

Another instance of Jake's fumbling approach to literary value occurs during the fishing trip:

> It was a little past noon and there was not much shade, but I sat against the trunk of two of the trees that grew together, and read. The book was something by A. E. W. Mason, and I was reading a wonderful story about a man who had been frozen in the Alps and then fallen into a glacier and disappeared, and his bride was going to wait twenty-four years exactly for his body to come out on the moraine, while her true love waited too, and they were still waiting when Bill came up. (120)

Jake's tone always turns sour when he uses the expression "true love"—as it does in his sneering reference to Brett Ashley's "true love" who succumbed unromantically to dysentery during the Great War (39). His snide synopsis of Mason's story allows him to strike the comfortable pose of the hard-boiled realist facing down literary sentimentality. He consequently projects a conclusion onto the story that is quite different from the one that Mason actually wrote. The story is "The Crystal Trench," one of twelve included with a short play in Mason's 1917 volume, *The Four Corners of the World*. Jake interrupts his reading at the point where the widowed Stella Frobisher approaches the end of the long period of mourning that she enters after the death of her husband in a climbing accident during their honeymoon in the Alps. Her "true love" is Dennis Challoner, an English bachelor on holiday at the Frobishers' hotel. As Stella's sole countryman present, he agrees to break the news of her husband's death to her. Then he and a party of climbers try to bring the body down from the mountain, but they lose it in a glacial crevasse; Stella learns subsequently that twenty-four years must pass before it will emerge above the terminal moraine. For reasons that Mason fails to make entirely clear, she resolves to remain celibate—"devoted . . . as a nun to her service"—while she waits for the glacier to give up her husband's remains. Challoner, who proposes marriage to her during this time and is accepted, agrees to wait with her and to honor her chastity.

It is perhaps understandable why a reader such as Jake might become impatient with this tale, but the ominous mood that Mason sustains hardly supports Jake's evident assumption that the final pages promise nothing to turn the lovers from their implausible fidelity to the dead man. Yet the conclusion to "The Crystal Trench" in fact subverts the theme of "true love," for the lovers find that Frobisher's body, when it finally emerges on the glacial moraine, bears a locket enclosing a picture of another woman. They see, suddenly and horribly, that they have sacrificed their lives to a delusion; and this is the revelation that Jake, because of his misreading, has no chance of experiencing and comparing to his obsession with Brett Ashley.

To a greater extent than Bill or Brett, Robert Cohn brings out Jake's anxiety over his position in the world of writers. Both Jake and Robert have left America for Paris in order to practice their profession as writers, and in their different ways both are making little progress. In his sketch of Cohn's life, Jake dwells maliciously on the setbacks his friend's literary career has suffered. He relishes Cohn's disappointment at the failure of an American "review of the Arts" which he edited after he finished his studies at Princeton (4–5); he refers to the "very poor" novel that he published subsequently (6); and he silently gloats over Cohn's present difficulties with a second novel. At the same time, he becomes uncomfortable whenever he feels drawn into an alliance with Cohn's adversaries. As he witnesses the scene that Frances Kline makes in Paris when she discovers that Cohn intends to leave her and return to New York in pursuit of his literary and sexual interests, Jake believes she is performing partly for his benefit. This is a consideration he hardly welcomes since it implies that he shares her disdain for Cohn's ambition. Like Brett, Frances uses Jake as an impotent foil for the performance of her private sexual drama. She complains to him bitterly about Cohn's treachery, but Jake can only reply with virtually the same words he uses in responding to Brett's sexual malaise: "And of course there isn't anything I can do" (48).

Jake tries to dispel Cohn's notion—evidently inspired by a book—that a trip to South America will solve his problems, revealing "what life holds." The book, a novel by W. H. Hudson titled *The Purple Land* (1904), has evidently obsessed Cohn. Jake has read it, and he deplores the "sinister" effect of its romantic characterization:

> It recounts splendid imaginary amorous adventures of a perfect English gentleman in an intensely romantic land, the scenery of which is very well described. For a man to take it at thirty-four as a guide-book to what life holds is about as safe as it would be for a man of the same age to enter Wall Street direct from a French convent, equipped with a complete set of the more practical Alger books. Cohn, I believe, took every word of "The Purple Land" as literally as though it had been an R. G. Dunn report. You understand me, he made some reservations, but on the whole the book to him was sound. (9)

As with his impulsive rejection of Mason's "The Crystal Trench," Jake automatically assumes a stance of resistance to romantic fictional narrative and in doing so he again reveals his inadequate reading. The story that William Henry Hudson tells in *The Purple Land* (1885) conveys the mainly painful and decidedly unromantic adventures of the English expatriate Richard Lamb in Argentina and Uruguay in the late 1860s and early 1870s. Lamb's manner usually displays a conventional mid-Victorian gentility, but he is hardly Jake's "perfect English gentleman." He elopes, for instance, with an under-age Argentine girl, and her father eventually has him jailed. Although he marries her and remains technically faithful until she dies during his imprisonment, her scandalous circumstances cause him to struggle repeatedly with a bad conscience. He finds respectable lodgings for her in Montevideo, then wanders into the wild ranchlands of the Uruguayan interior, looking for work.

The "intensely romantic land, the scenery of which is very well described" that Jake recollects appears infrequently in *The Purple Land*. Hudson uses it mainly as a backdrop to the coarseness, monotony and violence that Lamb encounters among the natives. Although he occasionally displays a naturalist's interest in his surroundings, his narrative for the most part carries out the intentions of his statement, "I might fill dozens of pages with descriptions of pretty bits of country . . . but must plead guilty to an unconquerable aversion to this kind of writing . . ." (84). Among his lapses from gentlemanly comportment during this time, he remorselessly shoots a man to death, consorts only half-reluctantly with rum-besotted brawlers, and runs away from a battle he joins briefly in the Uruguayan civil war. His behavior with the women he meets at the cattle ranches is courtly, and he repeatedly allows their blandishments to delay his return to his wife. The "splendid imaginary amourous adventures" that Jake recalls are for the most part limited to Lamb's stilted and narcissistic displays of gallantry. In the presence of the beautiful young Margarita, for example, he feels "a magnetic power drawing my heart; a something that is not love, for how can a married man have a feeling like that towards anyone except his wife? No, it is not love, but a sacred eternal kind of affection . . ." (52). This sort of effusion is typical of Lamb's reaction to women who fall in love with him, as they do almost invariably, but it characterizes Hudson's portrayal of a resolutely faithful Victorian husband rather than an amorous adventurer. He actually strays no further from his marriage vows than the shamefully "disloyal sigh" (113) he heaves for the intoxicating Dolores, whom he kisses spasmodically, then flees, expressing remorse for his "insane passion" (146).

Hudson's chief interest in *The Purple Land* lies in closely observed naturalistic portraiture of the Uruguayan ranchers. His convincing skill in shaping this material makes his novel a book far different from the one Jake Barnes believes he has read, and a far better one. Not only is it unrecognizable as the silly romance that has seized the imagination of Robert Cohn, but it also appeals to little that is central to Cohn's urbane personality. Because the flat contradictions of his portrait reflect the inadequacy of his reading, Jake Barnes' authority as interpreter—of character and of literature—wanes. *The Purple Land* therefore emerges as another misconstrued subtext of the main narrative. As with "The Crystal Trench," Jake's ingrained suspicion of the emotional appeal of a literary work actually blinds him to the kind of unadorned truth-telling that he likes to think he values.

As the relationships of the characters in *The Sun Also Rises* break down during the Spanish fiesta, Jake's approach to literary texts continues in a parallel pattern of declining authority. Having abandoned Mason during the fishing trip, in Pamplona he turns to a story in Ivan Turgenieff's *A Sportsman's Sketches* (1847–51). Unlike Mason and Hudson, Turgenieff appears to be a writer whom Jake admires without reservation. (Hemingway characterized his own admiration during this period thus: "Turgenieff to me is the greatest writer there ever was. Didn't write the greatest books, but was the greatest writer" [*Selected Letters* 179].) The unnamed story is one he has read before, but this later reading is severely impaired by his drunkenness. He uses the text only to steady his mind and to keep his hotel room from appearing to spin around him. The stratagem evidently works, but Jake's alcohol-induced vertigo only gives way to his old enemy, insomnia. Accordingly, he then puts Turgenieff to use as a soporific, and this succeeds also, as he finally falls asleep toward daylight. During this reading, Jake thinks, oddly, "I knew that now, reading it in the oversensitized state of my mind after too much brandy, I would remember it somewhere, and afterwards it would seem as though it had really happened to me. I would always have it. That was another good thing you paid for and then had" (147, 149). This boozy nonsense is an example of the "bilge" that Jake realizes he is inclined to "think up at night." It is typically Barnesian bilge in that it implies not only that inebriation improves memory but also that his recollection of a story he read while he was intoxicated will be so intense that he will virtually become one of its characters. Here is the kind of delusion that makes him so impatient with Robert Cohn's book-reading when he is sober; and it further exposes his naïve over-commitment to the idea that reading shapes character and consequently determines behavior. He is not being entirely facetious when he warns against Hudson's "dangerous" novel, nor is he merely glib when he says that Cohn "read too much at Princeton," that he acquired his dislike of Paris "possibly from Mencken," and that his notion that "South America could fix it" was "out of a book." By overestimating literary influence, Jake betrays the self-conscious awkwardness that causes his fumbling with Mason and Hudson. It is the uneasiness of the literary outsider, the friend whom Bill Gorton calls a "good guy," whereas Henry James is a "good writer." He is the mere journalist who is Cohn's "tennis friend" but not, like the editor, Braddocks, his "literary friend" (116).

Only when Jake retires to the extra-literary texts of journalism does he show his competence as a reader. The two bullfight newspapers that arrive in his Paris mail allow him to experience the insider's self-assurance that eludes him in the world of literary writing. As his passionate involvement in the matador's performances at Pamplona shows, bullfighting is a clearly circumscribed milieu where Jake can hope to achieve something like a complete, tragic literary vision. As he reads *Le Toril*, he judges, with the discrimination of the *aficionado*, that it is the better of the papers, even though "both have the same news." He reads it "all the way through, including the Petite Correspondance and the Cornigrams" (30), the latter presumably word puzzles that he solves with his command of the technical language of the bullfight.

Outside the bull ring, on the other hand, newspapers provide no more than a brief distraction from the unsolved puzzles of his life, as he realizes when the "old grievance" of his war wound brings back his insomnia. Newspapers, in fact, commonly figure in scenes that show the futility of Jake's life among the expatriates. Robert Cohn uses the pretext of going to buy one to take Jake aside and ask him to stop talking in the presence of Frances about the "swell girl" he knows in Strasbourg (6). Later, Jake nervously buys and opens a copy of the *Paris Times* when Frances starts to berate Cohn (46). In Pamplona he spreads a newspaper for Brett to sit on as she begins to lure him into her scheme to seduce his favorite matador, Pedro Romero. Bill Gorton, to the contrary, displays his freedom from Jake's troubled insomniac's ordeal by napping with a newspaper over his face during the fishing trip. Moreover, for all of Jake's involvement in journalism—he reads the newspapers in nearly every episode of *The Sun Also Rises*—he shows very little concern with current events. A rare instance of his awareness of contemporary political realities is his glib remark to Bill about the "jam" that the Spanish dictator Primo de Rivera has "gotten into in the Riff" (114). He also mentions the death of William Jennings Bryan ("I read it in the paper yesterday" [121]), but he is otherwise silent about the turbulent world of the summer of 1925. It is a part of the radical irony of his condition that newspapers mainly serve the purpose of disengaging Jake Barnes from history and from all value external to his search for a private code.

At the conclusion of the story of Jake Barnes as reader, he finally abandons the effort to enter the domain of the literary. As he attempts to recover at San Sebastian from the ordeal of Pamplona, the only reading he mentions by title is the French sporting magazine, *L'Auto*. A group of bicycle-racers has left copies scattered in the reading room of his hotel, and, with nothing better to do, he gathers them up and takes them out into the sun. Although he has unpacked his books in his room, *A Sportsman's*

Sketches, begun in Pamplona, is forgotten as Jake decides instead "to read about and catch up on French sporting life" (238). His tone is heavy with ironic realization of his frivolous life and his disgrace among the Spanish *aficionados*; and he appears to recognize how painfully appropriate it is to divert himself with the journalistic litter discarded by true sportsmen.

When Brett's telegram summoning him to Madrid prevents him from finishing even this trivial reading and causes him to send back his insincere "love" as he sets out on yet another sentimental errand, Jake's descent from literary value nearly reaches bottom. Only his pained self-consciousness saves him from full complicity in Brett's melodrama. To the extent that he acknowledges his incapacity for the autonomous emotional experience that literature conveys, Jake becomes not a tragic character but one who comes to understand that his life is incapable of tragedy. He is at his best at the bullfight—a witness of a tragedy whose emotional purity eludes him elsewhere but might nonetheless lead him beyond sentimentality, self-pity and all that is falsely "literary." The tragic drama of the bullfight gives rise to the equanimity that enables him finally to resist Brett's romantic illusions. He does so without rancor because he can see his own condition in her crippled emotions and can therefore say to her with muted and chastened affection, "Isn't it pretty to think so?" (247). He can't reach this point of resolution of his feelings for his friend Robert Cohn, however, because the literary dimensions of Cohn's character are beyond his powers of perception.

Because the works of literature that Jake encounters in *The Sun Also Rises* all exist historically outside his narrative, they constitute a separate presence in the novel, potentially imposing themselves on a reader's imagination in proportion to the degree of inadequacy that Jake's reading betrays. If his critical authority should dwindle in this manner, the works he misreads would be transformed reflexively into important sources of value in a novel that was written in search of value. This is one way Hemingway's writing achieves its literary density; as he distances himself and his reader from a character's flaws, he subtly cultivates values that to some extent compensate for them. This process, to the extent that it is discernible by a reader, is an ironic equivalent of the more overt ascendancy of the bullfighter Pedro Romero in Jake's world. Romero's character is not finally corrupted or debased in any sense as a result of Jake's inadequate interpretation of the values of the *aficionado*. Rather, it is because of the futility of Jake's collusion in Brett Ashley's seduction of the matador that he embodies the incorruptible and "unattainable" (168) ideal that Jake has pursued in his unsteady, contradictory way.

Hemingway's travesty of Sherwood Anderson's *Dark Laughter* (1925) in his next book, *The Torrents of Spring*, has often been taken as a gratuitous attack on a writer who had not only done nothing to provoke it but had on several occasions been its author's benefactor. In this assessment, Hemingway appears as a cynical ingrate, scheming to terminate his contract with Anderson's publisher, Boni and Liveright, by offering them a book they could not possibly accept. Meaner motives have been imputed to him, notably by Kenneth Lynn, who sees *The Torrents of Spring* as part of Hemingway's strategy for leaving his first wife, who didn't like it, for his second, who did (305–306). However plausible such explanations may be, they have nothing to do with the literary quality of Anderson's novel. Shortly after its publication, Hemingway privately called *Dark Laughter* "a pretentious fake with two or three patches of real writing" (*Selected Letters* 174); and in his last work, *A Moveable Feast* (1964), he held to this view, describing it as "so terribly bad, silly, and affected that I could not keep from criticizing it in a parody" (25). Because of its nearly unrelieved contempt for Anderson's novel, the tone of *The Torrents of Spring* bears few traces of the countervailing irony that undercuts Jake Barnes as a critic in *The Sun Also Rises*. Consequently, in contrast to the positive transformations that result from Jake's misreadings, the main narrative patterns of *Dark Laughter* are more simply re-configured by inversion. In Anderson's story, for example, the main character, Bruce Dudley, leaves his bohemian-journalist wife, Bernice, in Chicago and makes his way to Old Harbor, a small town on the Ohio River. Hemingway's Scripps O'Neil, to the contrary, finding that his wife has left *him* in the small Michigan town of Mancelona, sets out for Chicago (but gets no further than Petoskey, on Lake Michigan). Bruce works briefly in a car wheel factory, then is hired as a gardener by the owner's wife, who commences an affair with him; when she becomes pregnant they run away. Hemingway counters with the erotic rebirth of Yogi Johnson, Scripps O'Neil's co-worker at the Petoskey pump factory. Yogi, who had been unmanned by a love affair in Paris (sinister things happen to Anderson's characters in Paris), is revitalized by the arrival of an unclothed Ojibway woman in Petoskey. He disappears with her on a fine spring evening in a bathetic deflation of Bruce's hope-filled departure toward his new life and love at the conclusion of *Dark Laughter*.

Meanwhile, Scripps marries Diana, a waitress at Brown's Beanery, but he soon leaves her for Mandy. He makes this switch not because Mandy's person is more appealing but because her literary tastes are more refined than Diana's (she engagingly repeats Ford Madox Ford's literary anecdotes). Hemingway develops this pattern of changing partners out of a naïve curiosity about art and literary value to satirize Anderson's pretentious interlacing of Dudley's questions about love, sexuality and marriage with his inarticulate ruminations on the artistic life. The following is a sample:

> If a man got so he could use his own thoughts, his own feelings, his own fancies as Sponge could use a paint brush, what then? What would the man be like? Would that be what an artist was? It would be a fine to do, if he, Bruce, in running away from Bernice and her crowd, from the conscious artists, had only done so because he wanted to be just what they wanted to be. Men and women in Bernice's crowd were always talking of being artists, speaking of themselves as artists. Why had men, like Tom Wills and himself, a kind of contempt for them? Did he and Tom Wills secretly want to be artists of another sort? Was that what he, Bruce, had been up to when he lit out from Bernice and when he came back to Old Harbor? Was there something in the town he had missed as a boy there—he wanted to find—some string he wanted to pick up? (123)

Anderson put a great deal of this sort of thing in *Dark Laughter*, and he did so without evident irony. It nevertheless brought Anderson his greatest commercial success, mainly because Bruce Dudley's maundering style was received critically as the sort of straight talk about art that the common man could understand. This popularity indicated to Hemingway that *Dark Laughter* was not going to parody itself into oblivion, so he accordingly set out to construct a curved mirror image that would expose Anderson's pretensions. Charging him not only with "sloppy thinking" but also with "borrowed thinking" (*Selected Letters* 262), Hemingway gave the finishing touch to his parody by blatantly borrowing his title from Turgenieff.

The Torrents of Spring therefore constitutes something more interesting than a mean-spirited gesture of hostility toward Anderson. It expresses Hemingway's seriousness about entering the contentious arena of champions and contenders that he had constructed from his reading. He clearly understood the need to purge his style of the mannerisms that early works such as "Up in Michigan" (1921) and the first Nick Adams stories had acquired from Anderson. Hemingway knew he had achieved a much more fully individualized style in *The Sun Also Rises*, and he was angered by the persistence of critical comparisons of his work with that of a writer who was capable of the bad writing in *Dark Laughter* (*Selected Letters* 173).

As he became more certain of his own success, Hemingway became more generous and discriminating in his response to the writing of other novelists and poets as he sought ways to develop his self-consciously literary manner. He appears also to have taken some sly advice on the question of literary influence from Ezra Pound in the mid-1920s: "Be influenced by as many great artists as you can," said Pound, "but have the decency either to acknowledge the debt outright, or try to conceal it." This prompted Hemingway's note to himself, "Imitating everybody, living and dead" (Reynolds, *Paris Years* 29). By means of these strategies, Hemingway was able to refine the burlesque manner of *The Torrents of Spring* and the blatant parodies of *The Sun Also Rises*, experimenting with more subtly implicit paralleling structures of the kind that James Joyce had used in *Ulysses* (1922). In that work, the presence of the *Odyssey* is unlike Jake Barnes' books in that it is latent, entering in no sustained way into the consciousness of Joyce's characters or his narrating voices. Freed of this limitation, Homer's narrative serves as a far more richly reflective framework for Joyce's modern reworking of his heroic story than literary sources are able to provide for Hemingway's early writing. Joyce and Pound showed him that his encounters with other writers need not always be so confrontational.

A *Farewell to Arms* (1929) contains features of a later stage in Hemingway's art of imitation. These are usually so understated as to remain conjectural, and it is perhaps necessary to see them less as conscious models—although that is clearly possible—than as counter-examples of Hemingway's modern fiction of warfare and expatriation. They serve, in other words, to highlight Hemingway's radical reconfiguration of conventional narrative patterns. In the case of *A Farewell to Arms* the principal patterns are those of the classical military epic.

Michael Reynolds suggests that Hemingway based his description of the Italian retreat from Caporetto in Book Three of *A Farewell to Arms* on the story of Napoleon's withdrawal from Waterloo as told by Stendhal in *La Chartreuse de Parme* (*Hemingway's First War* 154–58). It is similarly possible that the broad outlines of Hemingway's plot, and the principal characters as well, were drawn from the *Aeneid* of Virgil. Like *The Torrents of Spring*, *A Farewell* inverts the structure of an antecedent narrative, but the effect is no longer satirical. Hemingway's title itself suggests a reversal of Virgil's opening line, "*Arma virumque cano*," providing an initial hint that the stories of Frederic Henry's story and Aeneas are in some way to be read antithetically. The *Aeneid*, for example, opens as *A Farewell* concludes, with the exile of the hero and the death of his wife (Catherine Barkley enjoys playing the married role with Henry). During his flight from the destruction of Troy, Aeneas has a passionate affair with Queen Dido of Carthage, who dies as a result. He then goes on to Italy where he wages war victoriously and makes possible the founding of the city of Rome. Hemingway tells this segment of the story backwards as well. Henry travels to Italy to study architecture—an unusually sedate activity for a Hemingway character—and presumably learns about the construction of the capital. Then he serves in a disastrous war from which he retreats, bidding farewell to arms and to Italy, and seeking a "separate peace" (243) in his love affair with Catherine. In Lausanne she and their son die in childbirth, leaving Henry desolate.

Although Aeneas loses his wife in the destruction of Troy, he succeeds in saving his son, Ascanius, and his father, Anchises. Anchises dies during their journey, and Aeneas commemorates the anniversary of his death with ritual sacrifices and games in Sicily. Ascanius, on the other hand, survives to fight heroically against the Latins in the struggle to gain a new national identity for his father's people. Henry's story of family and nationality follows a contrary pattern of dissolution, developing no positive theme of restoration comparable to Virgil's. It begins with his estrangement from his family and from America (only his grandfather communicates with him and sends him sight drafts), then leads to his vaguely motivated participation in the Italian campaign against Austria, and culminates in his stateless, solitary isolation in Switzerland.

Hemingway's clear intention in his reversed *Aeneid* was not to deflate Virgil but to dispel the illusions of martial glory in his own time. Generally, his method had become Joycean by becoming more implicit, but there are two exceptional instances of overt literary reference that revert to his earlier technique. They occur as Henry discusses books with his old friend, Count Greffi, at the Grand-Hotel in Stresa, where he joins Catherine in his flight from the war. He refuses to discuss the fighting:

> "You don't want to talk about it? Good. What have you been reading?"
> "Nothing," I said. "I'm afraid I am very dull."
> "No. But you should read."
> "What is there written in war-time?"
> "There is 'Le Feu' by a Frenchman, Barbusse. There is 'Mr. Britling Sees Through It.'"
> "No, he doesn't."
> "What?"
> "He doesn't see through it. Those books were at the hospital."
> "Then you have been reading."
> "Yes, but nothing any good."
> "I thought 'Mr. Britling' a very good study of the English middle-class soul."
> "I don't know about the soul."   (260–61)

As abruptly as Jake Barnes, Henry dismisses as worthless two of the earliest and best-received novels to treat the Great War. In 1916 the French Socialist writer Henri Barbusse published *Le Feu (Journal d'une Escouade)*, translated as *Under Fire, The Story of a Squad*. He adapted it from a diary he kept during the artillery duels of the previous year in Artois and Picardy. Although Barbusse lapses at moments into fine writing as he strains toward an optimistic vision of human progress *via* warfare, elsewhere *Le Feu* achieves the harsh naturalism that characterizes the best fiction about the war written by somewhat later novelists, including Erich Maria Remarque, Ford and Hemingway himself. Barbusse describes the destruction caused by a German artillery barrage targeted on the French positions:

> the woods are sliced down like cornfields, the dug-outs marked and burst in even when they've three thicknesses of beams, all the road-crossings sprinkled, the roads blown into the air and changed into long heaps of smashed convoys and wrecked guns, corpses twisted together as though shoveled up. You could see thirty chaps laid out by one shot at the cross-roads; you could see fellows whirling around as they went up, always about fifteen yards, and bits of trousers caught and stuck on the tops of the trees that were left. (214)

There are comparable passages in *Le Feu* that Hemingway, unlike his character, would have commended for their uncompromised reporting. Reynolds, while referring to Hemingway's disparagement of Barbusse for his "hysterical" tone, helps to distance his judgment from Henry's summary dismissal by quoting his comment on his reading in Paris just after the war: "There were very many interesting books about the war, & I read them with pleasure" [*Hemingway's Reading* 18]. Henry's judgment accordingly takes on some of the leveling effect of Jake Barnes' scornful rejection of Mason and Hudson. In both cases, the painful experiences of war partly account for their extreme reactions.

Henry's expression of contempt for the second work Count Greffi mentions is easier to justify. The novel by H. G. Wells, *Mr. Britling Sees It Through* (also 1916), whose title the Count inverts—another display of Hemingway's primal impulse—is more wishfully optimistic than *Le Feu*; and it has the additional handicap of being written from a non-combatant's point of view—always a damaging factor in Hemingway's estimation of war fiction. At the climax of Wells's narrative, when the son of the English Mr. Britling is killed in France, he consoles himself by writing a letter to the parents of a German soldier who has also died in the fighting. He asserts that the fabric of war is becoming so threadbare that "at a thousand points the light is shining through" it. As "dreadful" as the war may be, he concludes, the lessons it teaches may lead to "the establishment of a new order of living upon earth." Therefore, he concludes, the "two sons have died not altogether in vain" (418, 421). Sonorities such as these are examples of the wartime rhetoric that Henry terms "obscene":

> I was always embarrassed by the words sacred, glorious and sacrifice and the expression in vain. We had heard them, sometimes standing in the rain almost out of earshot, so that only the shouted words came through, and had read them, on proclamations that were slapped up by billposters over other proclamations, now for a long time, and I had seen nothing sacred, and the things that were glorious had no glory and the sacrifices were like the stockyards at Chicago if nothing was done with

the meat except to bury it. There were many words you could not stand to hear and finally only the names of places had dignity. Certain numbers were the same way and certain dates and these with the names of places were all you could say and have them mean anything. Abstract words such as glory, honor, courage, or hallow were obscene beside the concrete names of villages, the numbers of roads, the names of rivers, the numbers of regiments and the dates. (184–85)

In this passage the pattern of inversion that shapes the narrative and the critical tone of *A Farewell* extends also to its language. Eloquent patriotic words are transformed grotesquely into their antonyms, obliterating their own meaning; they are cleansed and dignified by self-nullification. The language that is left intact after this radical purgation preserves only words that are least susceptible to abstraction. These appear as names on maps and road markers, and as printed numbers and dates. They convey a paradoxically anti-literary view of language that ultimately would reduce speech, writing and reading to a consciousness of nothing but the most fundamental phenomena of time and space.

The extreme nature of Henry's revulsion requires Hemingway to subtly undercut his authority as he did Jake Barnes's. Henry, after all, acts inconsistently when he summarily rejects the literary judgment of Count Greffi, to whom he willingly defers in other intellectual matters. His repudiation of wartime writing is, at least in part, a function of his deep disillusionment, itself a kind of illusion. He reveals this as he tries to withdraw from the warring world into an alexic fantasy that excludes even newspapers: "I had the paper but I did not read it because I did not want to read about the war. I was going to forget the war. I had made a separate peace" (243). Despite his air of stolid renunciation, as the deaths of Catherine and their child in neutral Switzerland make clear, the notion of a "separate peace" is not essentially different from the romantic literary illusions that he and Jake so proudly despise. In their extravagant reactions to the idea of heroic warfare, to romantic love and to the "literary," they regress into another, darker romantic fiction that taints their essentially innocent characters.

Ezra Pound's indulgence of concealed and even unacknowledged literary sources doubtlessly fortified Hemingway's determination to write literary prose without appearing to do so. In the note on "imitating everybody" he further describes his strategy as "relying on the fact that if you imitate someone obscure enough it will be considered original. Education consists in finding sources obscure enough to imitate so that they will be perfectly safe" (Reynolds, *Paris Years* 29). The writer/narrator of *Green Hills of Africa* (1935) restates this idea from a more authoritative perspective: "a new classic does not bear any resemblance to the classics that have preceded it. It can steal from anything that it is better than, anything that is not a classic, all classics do that. Some writers are only born to help another writer to write one sentence" (21). This was Hemingway's best answer to the question of literary influence; eventually it enabled him to put inferior or neglected work to positive use rather than subjecting it to the destructive parodic impulses of his early novels.

In this light it is interesting to consider the role that a lesser author such as W. H. Hudson may have played in Hemingway's writing after *A Farewell to Arms*. That he admired much of Hudson's work is plainly evident in the fourteen titles in addition to *The Purple Land* listed by Reynolds as those he read. Reynolds also states that Hemingway recommended Hudson's *A Traveller in Little Things* to Ezra Pound for its style of "the simple statement" (*Hemingway's Reading* 138–39). Among other Hemingway characters with literary interests, the writer David Bourne in *The Garden of Eden* (1986) remembers that "the books of W. H. Hudson had made him feel rich" (95). Indeed, that problematic novel, *The Purple Land,* appears to have occurred to Hemingway as a usable, "perfectly safe" model for *For Whom the Bell Tolls* (1940). The two works resemble one another in numerous ways that suggest this connection. Here was a familiar, flawed, and, as we have seen, already oddly seminal work that Hemingway could engage anew without the old reflexive antagonism. Hudson had died in 1922, and his works had begun to fade into obscurity sufficiently to serve Hemingway's purposes by the time he began to write his story of the Spanish Civil War.

Hudson and Hemingway tell stories about expatriates of English or American origin who try to fashion a new identity among Hispanic people. The narratives center on their support for the losing side in a civil war. When Hemingway's Robert Jordan senses that he is treated as an alien in the band of Spanish Republican guerrillas he joins, he protests, "That I am a foreigner is not my fault. I would rather have been born here" (15). In the same rueful way but in the florid manner of his time, Hudson's Richard Graves broods on his feeling of separation from the Uruguayans and their cause: "I wished that I had been born among them and was one of them, not a weary, wandering Englishman, over-burdened with the arms and armour of civilisation, and staggering along, like Atlas, with the weight of a kingdom on which the sun never sets on his shoulders" (52). Graves reveals little about his resented English origins—probably a reflection of Hudson's own uncertain sense of nationality. (Hudson's parents emigrated from New England to take up cattle ranching in Argentina, a change that contributed to the mood of exile that hangs over his novel. He became an English citizen in 1900.) Hemingway could readily have recognized his own dimmed sense of nationality in Hudson's; it is echoed clearly in Robert Jordan's dismissive, sketchy references to his American birth.

The inchoate political convictions held by Richard Graves are analogous to the imperfect ideological development that complicates Robert Jordan's participation in the cause of the Spanish Republic. The actions of both characters on behalf of armed struggles against military dictatorships are much less strongly motivated by ideology than by personal feelings of sympathy with the people and of affinity with their land. An emotional attachment of this kind has brought Jordan to Spain more than once before the war, and he has written a book about his experiences there. Like Hudson's wanderer, who joins the rural Blancos against the Colorados based in Montevideo, he sides with a popular front in its resistance to an authoritarian military force—Francisco Franco's Fascists—seeking control of the government.

The principal military action that each character participates in is a fiasco that proves to be a disastrous turning point in the war. In *The Purple Land,* Graves rides in a badly organized cavalry assault at San Paulo led by the Blanco General San Colomas. His force is routed by the superior Colorados, whose success effectively brings the rebels' threat to an end. Hemingway similarly places the crucial military scenes of his story in the Republican effort against Franco's forces in the mountains north of Madrid in the spring of 1939. Their planned surprise attack fails totally, making Jordan's bridge-blowing mission tactically pointless. At the novel's conclusion Fascist gunfire kills his horse and he is about to be killed as the guerrillas retreat; but the others, including his young lover Maria, escape because of his self-sacrifice. Hudson's conclusion anticipates Hemingway's: Graves accepts the dangerous task of escorting the young Demetria, imperiled by a menacing Colorado sympathizer, to safety in Buenos Aires. Although, unlike Jordan, he carries out his mission without physical harm to himself, he is eventually arrested and jailed, as he had feared he would be, by the father of his wife, who dies in misery during his imprisonment. His flight from the war thus takes on an aspect of fatality that appears to prefigure Robert Jordan's.

Hudson's alert, intelligent reportorial manner and his naturalistic portraits of the rough-hewn male characters Lamb meets at the ranches of the Uruguayan interior surely appealed to Hemingway no less than his story of the expatriate who seeks an authentic sense of self in the national struggle of another people. One of Hudson's most effective devices for dramatizing this attraction is his imitation of the elaborate and ironic civilities of speech of the gauchos; it appears to be quite as skillful and convincing as anything Hemingway achieved comparably in his portrayal of Castilian peasants. Both writers were drawn to the coarse vigor and even the corruption of these characters. Some of Hudson's are "robbers and cut-throats" (141) whose war-time conduct exposes them to be "horsemen and little else" (150). These terms would adequately describe Pablo, the demoralized leader of Hemingway's band of guerrillas. Lamb's grateful appreciation of their songs and poems, free of the "worn-out, stilted, artificial" manner of the Europeans (22), is a sentiment Hemingway expressed or inferred in everything he wrote about Spain. Hudson's female characters, on the other hand, are almost invariably abstracted—as are Hemingway's to a great extent in *For Whom the Bell Tolls*—in an attempt to highlight the grace and dignity of their "Spanish origin" (204); he finds their beauty "strangely captivating" (19), and he notes with approval their "sweet . . . primitive simplicity" (52). Language similar to this conveys Hemingway's portrayal of Maria, who, despite his efforts to round out her character as Jordan's lover, functions narrowly as an incarnation the violated but resilient innocence of the Republic. Equally, Pilar—a Spanish *Marseillaise*—is anticipated by Hudson's Dolores, who is less a convincing character than a voice of propagandistic fervor that exhorts the vacillating Lamb "to help a suffering people cruelly oppressed by wicked men who have succeeded by crimes and treachery and foreign aid in climbing into power" (134). Although both writers draw these female characters awkwardly, their presence injects great emotional energy into the narration. The main effect is to give the principal characters a sense of personal identification with their people and their countries even though they are unable to become fully committed to their causes. In much the same way that Pilar senses Jordan's personal attachment to her people, Hudson's rebel leader, General Colomas, says to Lamb, "you were made for an [Uruguayan], only nature at your birth dropped you down in the wrong country. . . . you are in heart one of us" (145).

The success of *For Whom the Bell Tolls* is partly attributable to the satisfactory answer to the question of literary influences that Hemingway appears to have found in the safe obscurity of background works such as *The Purple Land*. In no other novel of his are the themes of solidarity, reconciliation, ideological commitment and even romantic love treated so positively or with equal confidence. It is as though Hemingway had achieved an enabling equanimity with his increasingly secure place in a literary community populated by many more Hudsons than Tolstoys. The old wariness about the "literary" still appears at moments—Robert Jordan scolds himself for "making dubious literature" by idealizing the Spanish peasants and their cause: "Don't lie to yourself, he thought. Nor make up literature about it" (287)—but it does not lead to the distorting reflex reactions that are common with his earlier characters. Jordan, after all, has already made his mark with the book he has written about Spain, and he intends matter-of-factly to write another (134). He and his cause fail, but his position in the company of writers is not in question.

Hemingway continued to work with the technique of the implicit literary parallel in his later fiction, increasingly adapting Joyce's technique of the highly conspicuous "classic" model. Mainly for this reason, the results are for the most part unconvincingly mechanical. In *Across the River and into the Trees* he shaped the narrative and characterization after Dante's *Inferno*, perhaps considering, as he appears to have done in *A Farewell to Arms,* that an Italian story needed an Italian model. Carlos Baker first noted the general pattern of derivations from Dante in the story of Colonel Richard Cantwell's doomed love affair in Venice: "It is a rough and tender fable of an earthly paradise, with some few inscapes of an earthly inferno along the way. If the idiom is Hemingway's, the mood is Dantesque" (*Writer as Artist* xix). Later studies include a chapter in Gerry Brenner's *Concealment in Hemingway's Works*, "A Dantesque Imitation: *Across the River and into the Trees*" (151–63). Because of the failure of his military career and of his marriage, Baker reasons, Cantwell "has known castigation, and though he can draw Inferno-circles and populate them with his enemies as unjustly as Dante did, there is still room for love" (*The Writer as Artist* 269). That Hemingway was considering Dante as a model during the period when he wrote *Across the River* is suggested in his letter of 17 September 1949 to John Dos Passos: "Since trip to Italy have been studying the life of Dante. Seems to be one of the worst jerks that ever lived, but how well he could write! This may be a lesson to us all" (677). Hemingway's acute sense of responsibility for trouble in his fourth marriage during this period lay behind this not entirely glib sense of identification with Dante, and he gave expression to it in Cantwell's self-portrayal as a Dantesque character who viciously condemns people to their earth-bound hells but at the same time retains his capacity for affection and compassion.

Hemingway signals the correspondences between *Across the River* and *Inferno* most overtly in scenes dominated by Cantwell's humorous self-perceptions. He calls himself "Mister Dante—for the moment," the name proposed by his young Italian lover, Renata. The idea occurs to her when he jokes about his plan to post armed guards at the gates of hell so that the phonies won't be able to follow him there: "he drew all the circles. They were as unjust as Dante's but he drew them" (232). He plays the three principal infernal roles—Virgil the guide, Dante the embittered exile and lover in spite of himself, and a doomed character engulfed in hellish misery. The Virgilian Cantwell emerges in the opening five chapters as he travels from Trieste with his young driver, Sgt. Jackson, to meet Renata in Venice. Just east of the city, he tells Jackson to turn off the main road— Dante opens by telling how he lost the straight path (*"la diritta via era smarrita"*)—and drive to the shore of the Venetian lagoon. There he plays the sage guide to his chauffeur's pilgrim, pointing out the principal islands and explaining their character and history. In Venice he combines the personal role of Renata's lover and Dante's role as the backslider who opens his poem by telling of the time he had strayed into a dark woods. The effect is to evoke Cantwell's miserable wartime memory of leading his infantry unit to its destruction in the Argonne forest. In their pained reunion, the two resemble the calamitous lovers, Paolo Malatesta and Francesca da Rimini, who appear in Dante's fifth canto among the "more than a thousand shades / departed from our life because of love" and are condemned to be blown around forever by infernal winds. Hemingway's pair is correspondingly "lashed at" by the winter wind that blows in from the lagoon, disheveling Renata's hair and swirling around Cantwell's room in the Gritti Palace (he insists on keeping the window open); "inside the hotel, there was no wind" (194), an otherwise needless observation that appears to allude to the moment in Canto V when the wind pauses, enabling Dante to hear Francesca's sorrowful story.

This final meeting of Cantwell and Renata takes place in the tenth chapter, which is the fifth of the thirty-four chapters that Hemingway set in Venice, evidently in imitation of Dante's thirty-four cantos. (The later Venetian chapters tend to be quite brief and at times insubstantial, adding little to the narrative except another unit of this total.) Similarly, he appears to represent the nine circles of Dante's hell directly by having Cantwell enter his windy hotel room nine times, either in fact or in memory and fantasy. The frozen Cocytus of the ninth circle is reached more graphically in the last six chapters, in which Cantwell leaves Renata and joins a duck hunting party on an icy river east of Venice. Then, at the conclusion, Hemingway breaks the parallel: whereas Dante moves on to the spiritual renewal of Purgatory and reunion with his beloved Beatrice in Paradise, Cantwell, separated from his love, suffers a fatal heart attack as he returns to Trieste.

Hemingway's determination to rid his fiction of false sentiment required him again in *Across the River and into the Trees*, as in the earlier novels, to avoid a conclusion that would cast his central character as merely a broken-hearted lover. He makes it plain that the long-term effects of Cantwell's war injuries and his alcoholism, rather than lovelorn grief, are the primary causes of his death at fifty (the half-century reflecting Dante's opening, "*Nel mezzo del cammin di nostra vita*," noted by the fifty-year-old Hemingway during his Italian trip in 1949). He endures his farewell to Renata in a mood as austerely resigned as that of any Hemingway character, and he accepts the death that follows without flinching. This is a recurring critical moment of characterization that Hemingway had great difficulty in portraying convincingly. In the instance of Cantwell, because his self-conscious posturing tends to belie his air of impassivity, Hemingway infuses his end with the pathos of *Inferno* awkwardly at best. Yet his image of Venice seeks to some extent to humanize Dante's medieval hell, not through some impossible reprieve for the lovers, but by allowing their suffering to end. Paolo and Francesca's great misery arises from their ironic knowledge that they must remain together as guilty lovers forever. Francesca tells Dante, "There is no greater sorrow / than thinking back upon a happy time / in misery" (Mandelbaum V, 121–23). She can hope neither for relief nor for release. The shock of this knowledge causes Dante to fall into a swoon like death, as though the fact of endless suffering were nearly fatal to contemplate. Because of Hemingway's incomplete transformation of such scenes, *Across the River and into the Trees* fails to draw powerfully on their emotional vitality.

The latent literary parallel offered Hemingway the advantage of deniability. It allowed him to dismiss as professorial wool-gathering those readings that saw such "literary" dimensions to his writing. Philip Young discovered this when he suggested in 1953 that a cluster of symbols in "The Snows of Kilimanjaro" was derived from Flaubert and Dante (Baker, *A Life Story* 509). Hemingway's denials were part of a strategy to guard his deeply divided but nonetheless exploratory approach to the possibilities of self-consciously literary techniques. Even in the case of the doggedly naturalistic *To Have and Have Not* (1937), a work that appears to be written at a very far remove from literary artifice, he concludes with a female monologue that is clearly a tribute to Joyce. In the case of *Across the River*, Dante rises toward the narrative surface by means of a handful of explicit allusions in the dialogue and in a collateral narrative development, but he is finally kept at too great a distance and becomes no more than a potential source of the tragic feeling that Cantwell's story, as narrated, represses. In this way Hemingway tried to have it both ways with Dante—to be literary but not in the sense of the term as he thought it was misunderstood by people who learn everything, therefore nothing, from books.

The last novel published in his lifetime, *The Old Man and the Sea* (1953), strongly suggests that Hemingway was tired of the struggle to sustain an enlivening tension between his narrative and what appears to be its principal model—the New Testament account of the death of Jesus. Instead of reconstructing it through some transmuting process as he had attempted to do earlier, his story of old Santiago's ordeal with the enormous fish only parallels the biblical story in a bald, mechanical way. As Santiago retires from his futile battle to save the fish from sharks, an episode narrated with redundant images of the Crucifixion, he must make his way painfully past the principal Stations of the Cross: "Then he shouldered the mast and started to climb" (Station Two: Jesus takes up the cross); "He started to climb again and at the top he fell and lay for some time with the mast across his shoulder" (Station Three: Jesus falls the first time); "Finally he put the mast down and stood up. He picked the mast up and put it on his shoulders and started up the road. He had to sit down five times before he reached the shack" (further stations conflated); "Then he lay down on the bed . . . and he slept face down on the newspapers with his arms stretched out straight and the palms of his hands up" (Stations Eleven and Twelve: The Crucifixion: earlier, trying to stay awake in his boat, he drives a nail through his hand and "into the wood" [134, 118]). When Santiago expresses his agony in echoes of the Seven Last Words—Now it is over, he thought. . . . "he knew that it was over" (130–31)— Hemingway's narrative is virtually engulfed by the prior text. The Passion overwhelms the story rather than engaging it because there is no convincing connection of its vital energy to Santiago's abject suffering. As was the case to a lesser extent with *Inferno* and *Across the River and into the Trees,* the "classic" model is simply too imposing, too resistant to a reconfiguring disguise. As he might have put it with his rueful humor, he got into the ring with Mr. Tolstoy. Perhaps something of this sense of being overmatched in *The Old Man and the Sea* is felt in Santiago's words of resignation toward the end of the story: "Now they have beaten me. . . . They beat me. . . . They truly beat me (124, 137).

The literary quality of Hemingway's fiction reached its highest levels when he was most sure of his ability to reshape the narrative models he used, to mold them anew in his tactile manner. The concept of writing as literary engagement offers another way of recognizing and accounting for the relative superiority of his earlier achievement, culminating in *For Whom the Bell Tolls*, and it provides insight into the general decline in the quality of the work that followed. As a theoretical formulation of Hemingway's development, it recalls in some respects the main argument of Harold Bloom's *The Anxiety of Influence: A Theory of Poetry* (1973). In his figure of the "strong" poets locked in an agonized Oedipal struggle with their great precursors, battling against a fear of "belatedness," of drowning in the tides of influence, and of merely repeating what has been accomplished already, we may recognize the main pattern of Hemingway's contentious literary attitudes and relationships. His attack on Sherwood Anderson in *The Torrents of Spring* can be partly understood in the light of Bloom's characterization of the poet who exposes his guilty ingratitude by "turning his precursor into a fouled version of the later poet himself. But that too is a self-deception and a banality, for what the strong poet thus does is to transform himself into a fouled version of himself, and then confound the consequences with the figure of the precursor" (62).

Elsewhere, as in the ambiguous parodies of the romantic strain in *Mason and Hudson*, Hemingway resembles Bloom's poets of "reductiveness" who perpetrate "a radical misinterpretation in which the precursor is regarded as an over-idealizer" (69).

A more positive view of Hemingway's divided response to his literary inheritance is suggested by Bloom's idea of the mature poet who both affirms and at the same time achieves the "undoing" of a precursor's poems (83). In this double role the poet acts as one who "knows only himself and the Other he must at last destroy . . . yet who remains formed by actual past poems that will not allow themselves to be forgotten" (121–22). Hence "the mature [John] Ashberry of *Fragments* subverts and even captures the precursor [Wallace Stevens] even as he appears to accept him more fully" (145). This analysis might serve as a summary of the relationship that developed between Hemingway and Hudson. In his role as the clowning pugilist of the *New Yorker* interview, victorious over Turgenieff and Maupassant, and the proven equal of Stendhal, Hemingway gains authority as one of the writers whom Bloom perceives in late maturity, "confronting the imminence of death" by seeking "to subvert the immortality of their precursors, as though any one poet's afterlife could be metaphorically prolonged at the expense of another's" (151).

The Anxiety of Influence posits the drastic conflicts of the Freudian "family romance" as a paradigm for its analysis of the conflicts between poetic generations; but his literary families include only the "strong" poets. Considering none but the literary giants, Bloom precludes their "weak" precursors as potential agents of influence, except in cases of essentially "strong" poets caught in "weak" moments—those lapses, for example, in which "Stevens sounds rather too much like Ashberry" (142). The struggle against belatedness, for Bloom a matter of poetic life and death, is so dire that the "strong" poets' responses to their precursors leave no place for affirmative emotions of generosity, gratitude or admiration. Their anxiety must suppress communal and collegial feeling because such sentiments as these, Bloom insists, expose a poet's weakness. Those who see their writing as a means of fighting their way into the "canon" can experience only the anxiety and never the ambivalence, least of all the equanimity, of influence. Bloom's drama of literary kinship accordingly becomes too exclusively an affair of a contentious elite to provide roles for the authors of most works of literature.

Hemingway's fullest and best-known statement on the question of literary influence appears in *Death in the Afternoon*:

> Every novel which is truly written contributes to the total of knowledge which is there at the disposal of the next writer who comes, but the next writer must pay, always, a certain nominal percentage in experience to be able to understand and assimilate what

is available as his birthright and what he must, in turn, take his departure from. If a writer of prose knows enough about what he is writing about he may omit things that he knows and the reader, if the writer is writing truly enough, will have a feeling of those things as strongly as though the writer had stated them. The dignity of movement of an ice-berg is due to only one-eighth of it being above water. (192)

Hemingway's conception of the authentic work of fiction finds only a partial equivalent in Bloom's "strong" poem. The literary "birthright" required to make such writing possible is assimilable only in the experience of strenuous rivalry between the "next writer" and others whose claims to authorship of "truly written" prose are often a matter of intense, sometimes ferocious dispute. The key to the art of this writing is subversive disguise—not only through reliance on implication and indirection of statement, but also through the protective, at times seemingly deceptive and contradictory concealment of the writer's private voice. This carefully calculated strategy permits the writer to "omit things" in order to avoid being attacked as sentimentally romantic, derivative or speciously literary. If he succeeds, he assumes an increasingly parental, dominating role in the literary family whose lesser members he thus surpasses. His tactics are at times violent, but his goal is communal as well as familial. His creativity, departing from Harold Bloom's internecine, Oedipal warfare among the canonical poets, is an alternative to the "anxiety of influence." The poet Thomas Kinsella, similarly differing from Bloom, makes this distinction:

> No: the function of influence is a fructifying one; it helps, if the poet has the capacity to enlarge the influenced poet. It is also, however, a very predatory thing on the part of the influencée. He will take what suits him. . . . In another way, it's a way of getting started. You can see this pretty clearly in Pound: before you have found your own voice—manufactured your own version of the language—you cast around for various aids, and if you find a voice that more or less gets things said for you, you seize upon it with delight. The same applies to the borrowing of a point of view, borrowing an attitude toward form—toward all these enabling things. It really is a stepping stone to the discovery of your own methods. Either way of handling influence seems to me an expanding one: it opens out possibilities for the receiver, and makes him the more active partner, in the exchange of influence. (O'Hara 5)

Writers of "truly written" books will therefore be capable of recognizing their own limited successes, of agreeing that their works include some that are less true because of their kinship with the "weak" as well at the "strong." Hemingway's iceberg metaphor implies the writer's consciousness of obligations to precursors both celebrated and obscure. The submerged preponderance of experience that is felt but not expressed overtly includes the prior texts that he may appear in his maturity to have left behind, whereas he has mainly sought to make them unrecognizable through distortion and dissimulation. In this way the writer protects and preserves his literary birthright. It includes the lesser works that provide the strength to accept a degree of failure with dignified grace. Hemingway's conclusion to *Death in the Afternoon* is a case in point: "No. It is not enough of a book, but still there were a few things to be said" (278). He implies again that the things that are unsaid are the main ones. An iceberg, truly depicted, has the appeal of a massively inverted object. As it moves and dissolves, its invisible bulk gives it mass, momentum, stability, the appearance of solitary greatness and an illusion of permanence.

CONCLUSION

A Community of Writers:
Modernists, Realists, Postmodernity

The myriad departures of modern fiction from the realistic conventions of the nineteenth century tend to expose not only the frailties of literary language but also the uncertain artistry of its users. As the world of historical fact became an increasingly hostile reality from which the literary imagination was impelled to stray or retire, writers of fiction were inclined to regard the criterion of factuality as an incitement to deviance and regression. With varying degrees of deliberation, they established a virtual anti-convention of error. They understood that realism had placed an exaggerated confidence in the ascertainability of the Real, and they exposed the doubtful epistemology underlying its methods. Its creators were nonetheless accorded merit by a critical tradition that measured their literary achievement on the basis of an ostensible commitment to lifelike social portraiture. The canonical writers of the realist tradition were accordingly identified as those in whose writing the assumption of factuality was virtually a given. A typical, capably stated example of this widespread critical deference to illusionist dexterity is Mary McCarthy's essay, "The Fact in Fiction" (1960), which commends the socially conscious novelist's "deep love of fact, of the empiric element in experience." This strong emotion is what protects novelists against the infections of romance and supernaturalism, distinguishing their work by a totality of technical mastery. Jane Austen's "clear locative sense," for example, reassures a reader of this fidelity, displayed in the "painstaking census-taking" that scrupulously lets us know, say, "exactly how much money the characters have" in *Pride and Prejudice.* Lacking such accuracy, "the novel is discredited," McCarthy argues, raising the nearly unthinkable possibility that "if Tolstoi was all wrong about the Battle of Borodino or the character

of Napoleon, *War and Peace* would suffer." The celebrated steady hands of
Austen and Tolstoy, by achieving their meticulously observed solidity of
characterization and setting, produce an appearance of veracity that often
eludes the modernist writers, with their perplexed narrative points of view.
Significantly, the achieved accuracy of the great realists is an unexamined
donné for McCarthy, who includes the erratic William Faulkner among
those with a "passion for fact in a raw state."

The clash of imaginative freedom and factual necessity in modern
fiction generates forms of subversion in consequence of which it tends to
reduce the supposedly verifiable realities of time and space, and the
language that conveys them, to fundamental units. For Joseph Conrad and
James Joyce the language of the writer of fiction, submitted to the
"destructive element" of modernity, suffers a loss of expressive energy and
fades into the muteness of things. The settings of F. Scott Fitzgerald
dissolve analogously into an American Nowhere, and William Faulkner's
history is distilled into a virtual moment that can never be fixed in his
chronologies. Ernest Hemingway, spurning a belletristic literary tradition,
subjected its conventions to a series of fictive reconstructions that at first
vitalized his writing, and then vitiated it. In every case, modern literature
was commonly said, by Ihab Hassan and others, to recede into a sacred
silence.

The main stream of literary criticism that had established the modernist
canon by the 1970s, represented in the previous chapters by the work of
Hassan and Hugh Kenner among others, has produced images of a
paradoxical heroism of the authors it includes, and of those who succeeded
them. Samuel Beckett, the most celebrated of their inheritors, "comes
closer than any other writer to piercing the heart of the Muses," writes
Hassan, with his "pure and terrible art" and his devotion to the modernist
"sacramental language of silence" (*Dismemberment* 221, 237, 251). For
Kenner, Beckett's withdrawal from the modernist competition with reality
leads to the idea that "art is the perfect not-doing of what cannot be done"
(*Stoic Comedians* 76). As a descendent of the modernists, and a herald of
postmodernity, Beckett is thus presented as a propagator of the tradition
that exalts consummate artistry as a trophy won in drastic contests with
historical forces of disintegration. The ironic condition into which that
tradition has devolved is expressed famously by Beckett in his "Three
Dialogues" thus: "to be an artist is to fail, as no other dare fail, that failure
is his world . . ." (Weeks 21). Characteristically, what appears at first to be
an abject disavowal of artistic sovereignty on Beckett's part becomes a
manifesto, with its pure and unequaled renunciation, its gesture toward an
inverted spirituality.

Because of the superlatives that critical rhetoric has so often chosen to characterize these writers' responses to the aesthetic crises of the modern condition, their work has been burdened heavily with the visionary functions of prophecy and spiritual disclosure. Their fiction has been encased in the presupposition of a departed plenitude that *almost* appears in the fissures of their fragmented images and in their characters' enigmatic consciousnesses. In *Ruin the Sacred Truth: Poetry and Belief from the Bible to the Present*, Harold Bloom provides a fairly late instance of this hagiological reading, once again placing Samuel Beckett in the role of saint: "Beckett's Cosmos resembles, if anything at all, the Demiurge's creation in ancient Gnosticism. . . . It is the world ruled by the archons, the *kenoma*, nonplace of emptiness. . . . Beckett's enigmatic spirituality quests (though sporadically) for a void that is a fulness" (200). Bloom's carefully qualified assertion of Beckett's religious impulse is virtually contradicted in his subsequent admission that Beckett's work is entirely lacking in the Christian Gnostic knowledge of a transcendent reality and the potential to release the spark or *pneuma*—vestige of the deepest, original self—to re-enter the lost fulness of the Pleroma (201). Bloom does not concede, however, what is apparent—that Beckett, because of this agnostic position, along with his modernist precursors, belongs not only among the Gnostics but also among the *somatics*, those condemned and excluded from the *gnosis* because of their engrossment in the temporality and materiality of the false Creation.

Joyce, as we have seen, explicitly resumes and at the same time parodies the Gnostic doctrine equating the Creation with the Fall. He sees language reduced to somatic matter as the literary artist reverts to an infantile paradise. The other writers who figure principally in this study re-enact the Gnostic nullification of their fallen world by imaginatively exposing its susceptibility to subversion. Conrad invokes the Alexandrian cosmology of the Gnostic heresiarch Valentinius as a metaphor for the "inconceivable history" that may one day be written, but only if the history that is known does not lead to a chaos of indifferentiation. Fitzgerald's transfiguring energy fleetingly glimpses a collateral world that recalls the Gnostics' Pleroma, as does Faulkner's unseizable day of release from a disastrous chronology. In a more immediately historical sense, Hemingway may be said to reconvene the Gnostic elite through his faith in a community founded on the antithetically "truly written" book. His uncertainty about his enduring inclusion among this company of the elect points to another modernist departure from the Gnostic paradigm—its lack of certain knowledge of the alienated Creator who fell with man and who dwells in a collateral but unascertainable exile. As Bloom says in his latest religious study, *Omens of Millennium*, as an enlightened Gnostic "you *know* yourself as having affinity with the alien, or stranger God, cut off from this world" (252). Without such knowing, or conscious only of faint traces and vague intimations of its truth, the art of modernism remains a fragmentary phenomenon of a lesser Creation.

The process of literary subversion—involving the hazardous and at times haphazard inversions, transpositions, reductions and disfigurations of conventional materials, techniques and themes—need not lead solely to this disconsolate reality. It also suggests that it is not history alone but also idiosyncratic artistic limitations that preclude a satisfying, sustained contact with a super-historical spiritual reality. To be an artist, in this sense, is to fail as others have dared to fail, and that post-heroic failure leads from aesthetic solitude toward an inclusive sense of artistic community.

WORKS CITED

Introduction

deMan, Paul. *Blindness and Insight: Essays on the Rhetoric of Contemporary Criticism.* Rev ed. Minneapolis: U of Minnesota P, 1983.

Eagleton, Terry. *Against the Grain: Essays 1975–1985.* London: Verso, 1986.

Ellmann, Richard. *James Joyce.* New York: Oxford UP, 1982.

Ellmann, Richard and Charles Feidelson, eds. *The Modern Tradition.* London: Oxford UP, 1965.

Erlich, Victor. *Russian Formalism: History, Doctrine.* London: Mouton, 1965.

Esslin, Martin, ed. *Samuel Beckett: A Collection of Critical Essays.* Englewood Cliffs: Prentice-Hall, 1965.

Flaubert, Gustave. *Madame Bovary.* Tr. Mildred Marmur. New York: New American Library, 1964.

———. *Madame Bovary.* Paris: Garnier, 1960.

———. *Selected Letters.* Ed. Francis Steegmuller. New York: Vintage, 1957.

Givens, Seon, ed. *James Joyce: Two Decades of Criticism.* New York: Vanguard, 1948.

Hassan, Ihab. "The Culture of Postmodernism." *Theory, Culture and Society* 2, 3 (1985): 119–31.

———. *Rumors of Change: Essays of Five Decades.* Tuscaloosa and London: U of Alabama P, 1995.

Joyce, James. *Stephen Hero.* London: Jonathan Cape, 1956.

———. *Ulysses.* New York: Random House, 1986.

Kenner, Hugh. *The Stoic Comedians: Flaubert, Joyce, and Beckett.* Berkeley: U of California P, 1974.

Larkin, Philip. *The Less Deceived: Poems.* Hessle, East Yorkshire: Marvell, 1955.

Nicholls, Peter. *Modernisms: A Literary Guide.* Berkeley: U of California P, 1995.

Proust, Marcel. *Jean Santeuil.* New York: Simon and Schuster, 1956.

Troyat, Henri. *Flaubert.* Tr. Joan Pinkham. New York: Viking, 1992.

Woolf, Virginia. "Mr. Bennett and Mrs. Brown." *The Captain's Death Bed and Other Essays.* New York: Harcourt, Brace, Jovanovich, 1950. 94–119.

———. *A Room of One's Own.* San Diego: Harcourt, Brace, 1981.

Chapter One: Conrad's Blank Maps

Adelman, Gary. *Heart of Darkness: Search for the Unknown*. Boston: Twayne, 1987.

Baines, Jocelyn. *Joseph Conrad: A Critical Biography*. New York: McGraw-Hill, 1960.

Bierman, John. *Dark Safari: The Life Behind the Legend of Henry Morton Stanley*. New York: Knopf, 1990.

Conrad, Joseph. "Geography and Some Explorers." *Last Essays*. Ed. Richard Curle. Garden City: Doubleday, 1926: 1–21.

———. *Heart of Darkness*. Ed. Paul O'Prey. New York: Penguin, 1983.

———. *Lord Jim*. Ed. Cedric Watts and Robert Hampson. New York: Penguin, 1986.

———. *Notes on Life and Letters*. Garden City: Doubleday, 1923.

———. "An Outpost of Progress." *Tales of Unrest*. Garden City: Doubleday: 1925.

———. *Under Western Eyes*. Garden City: Doubleday, 1925.

———. *Within the Tides*. Garden City: Doubleday, 1925.

Darras, Jacques. *Joseph Conrad and the West: Signs of Empire*. Totawa: Barnes and Noble, 1982.

Driver, Felix. "Henry Morton Stanley and His Critics: Geography, Exploration and Empire." *Past and Present* 133 (Nov 1991): 165-66.

Erdinast-Vulcan, Daphna. *Joseph Conrad and the Modern Temper*. Oxford: Clarendon, 1991.

Goonetilleke, D.C.R.A, ed. *Heart of Darkness*. Peterborough, Ont.: Broadview, 1995.

———. *Joseph Conrad: Beyond Culture and Background*. New York: St. Martin's, 1990.

Hall, Richard. *Stanley: An Adventurer Explored*. Boston: Houghton, 1975.

Karl, Frederick. *Joseph Conrad: The Three Lives*. New York: Farrar, Straus and Giroux, 1979.

Kermode, Frank. *The Art of Telling: Essays on Fiction*. Cambridge, Mass.: Harvard UP, 1983.

Kimbrough, Robert, ed. *Heart of Darkness: An Authoritative Text, Backgrounds, and Sources, Criticism*. New York: Norton, 1988.

Mallarmé, Stéphane. *Poems*. Tr. Roger Fry. New York: Oxford UP, 1939.

Meyers, Jeffrey. *Joseph Conrad: A Biography*. New York: Scribner's, 1991.

Sherry, Norman. *Conrad's Western World*. Cambridge: Cambridge UP, 1971.

Smith, Iain R. *The Emin Pasha Expedition 1886–1890*. Oxford: Clarendon, 1972.

Spittles, Brian. *Joseph Conrad: Text and Context*. New York: St Martin's, 1992.

Stanley, Henry M. *Despatches to the New York Herald 1871–72*. Ed. Norman R. Bennett. Boston: Boston UP, 1970.

———. *How I Found Livingstone*. New York: Scribner, 1872.

———. *In Darkest Africa*. 2 vols. New York: Scribner's, 1890.

———. *Through the Dark Continent*. 2 vols. New York: Harper's, 1878.

Watt, Ian. *Conrad in the Nineteenth Century*. Berkeley: U of California P, 1979.

White, Andrea. *Joseph Conrad and the Adventure Tradition: Constructing and Deconstructing the Imperial Subject*. Cambridge: Cambridge UP, 1993.

Chapter Two: Joyce's Material Language

Atherton, James. *The Books at the Wake: A Study of Literary Allusions in James Joyce's Finnegans Wake*. Carbondale: Southern Illinois UP, 1959.

Beckett, Samuel, et al. *James Joyce/Finnegans Wake: A Symposium*. New York: New Directions, 1972.

Bishop, John. *Joyce's Book of the Dark: Finnegans Wake*. Madison: U of Wisconsin P, 1986.

Boyle, Robert, S. J. *James Joyce's Pauline Vision: A Catholic Exposition*. Carbondale: Southern Illinois UP, 1978.

Brivic, Sheldon. *Joyce the Creator*. Madison: U of Wisconsin P, 1985.

Chasseguet-Smirgel, Janine. *Creativity and Perversion*. London: Free Association Books, 1985.

Chatman, Seymour, ed. *Literary Style: A Symposium*. New York: Oxford UP, 1971.

Ellmann, Richard. *The Consciousness of Joyce*. New York: Oxford UP, 1977.

———. *James Joyce*. New York: Oxford UP, 1982.

———. *Ulysses on the Liffey*. New York: Oxford UP, 1972.

Forster, E.M. *Aspects of the Novel*. New York: Harcourt, Brace, 1954.

Freud, Sigmund. *The Standard Edition of the Complete Psychoanalytical Works of Sigmund Freud*. Ed. James Strahey. London: Hogarth, 1953–57.

Gifford, Don and Robert J. Seidman. *Ulysses Annotated: Notes for James Joyce's Ulysses*. Second ed. Berkeley: U of California P, 1988.

Gose, Elliott B., Jr. *The Transformation Process in Joyce's Ulysses*. Toronto: U of Toronto P, 1980.

Hart, Clive and David Hayman, eds. *James Joyce's Ulysses: Critical Essays*. Berkeley: U of California P, 1974.

Herring, Phillip. *Joyce's 'Ulysses' Notesheets in the British Museum*. Charlottesville: UP of Virginia, 1972.

Joyce, James. *The Critical Writings of James Joyce*. Ed. Ellsworth Mason and Richard Ellmann. New York: Viking, 1959.

———. *Dubliners: Text, Criticism, and Notes*. Ed. Robert Scholes and A. Walton Litz. New York: Penguin, 1996.

———. *Finnegans Wake*. New York: Viking, 1939.

———. *Letters*. Vol. 1. Ed. Stuart Gilbert. New York: Viking, 1957.

———. *A Portrait of the Artist as a Young Man: Text, Criticism, and Notes*. Ed. Chester G. Anderson. New York: Penguin, 1977.

———. *Ulysses*. New York: Random House, 1986.

Joyce, Stanislaus. *My Brother's Keeper*. New York: Viking, 1958.

Kenner, Hugh. *Ulysses*. Rev. ed. Baltimore: Johns Hopkins UP, 1987.

Lawrence, Karen. *The Odyssey of Style in Ulysses*. Princeton: Princeton UP, 1981.

Lewis, Wyndham. *Time and Western Man*. London: Chatto and Windus, 1927.

MacCabe, Colin, ed. *James Joyce: New Perspectives*. Bloomington: Indiana UP, 1982.

———. *James Joyce and the Revolution of the Word*. New York: Harper and Row, 1979.

McHugh, Roland. *Annotations to Finnegans Wake*. Baltimore: Johns Hopkins UP, 1980.

Nicholls, Peter. *Modernisms: A Literary Guide*. Berkeley: U of California P, 1995.

Norris, Margot. *Joyce's Web: The Social Unraveling of Modernism*. Austin: U of Texas P, 1992.

Pecora, Vincent P. "'The Dead' and the Generosity of the Word." *PMLA* 101 (March 1986): 233–45.

Power, Arthur. *Conversations with James Joyce*. New York: Harper and Row, 1974.

Robinson, Fred Miller. *The Comedy of Language*. Amherst: U of Massachusetts P, 1980.

Roughley, Alan. *James Joyce and Critical Theory: An Introduction.* Ann Arbor: U of Michigan P, 1991.

Schlossman, Beryl. *Joyce's Catholic Comedy of Language.* Madison: U of Wisconsin P, 1985.

Vico, Giambattista. *The New Science of Giambattista Vico.* Tr. Thomas Bergin and Max Harold Fisch. Garden City: Doubleday, 1961.

Wells, H. G. "James Joyce." *New Republic* 10, 123 (March 19, 1917): 156–58.

Chapter Three: Fitzgerald's New World

Allen, Joan M. *Candles and Carnival Lights: The Catholic Sensibility of F. Scott Fitzgerald.* New York: New York UP, 1978.

Bryer, Jackson, ed. *F. Scott Fitzgerald: The Critical Reception.* New York: Burt Franklin, 1978.

Bruccoli, Matthew. *Some Sort of Epic Grandeur: The Life of F. Scott Fitzgerald.* New York: Harcourt, Brace, Jovanovich, 1981.

Dos Passos, John. *Manhattan Transfer.* New York: Harper, 1925.

Fitzgerald, F. Scott. "Absolution." *All the Sad Young Men.* New York: Scribner's, 1926. 109–32.

———. *The Beautiful and the Damned.* New York: Macmillan, 1986.

———. *Correspondence of F. Scott Fitzgerald.* Ed. Matthew Bruccoli and Margaret Duggan. New York: Random House, 1980.

———. "The Diamond as Big as the Ritz." *Babylon Revisited and Other Stories.* New York: Scribner's, 1932. 74–113.

———. *The Great Gatsby.* Ed. Matthew J. Bruccoli. New York: Macmillan, 1991.

———. *The Great Gatsby.* Ed. Matthew Bruccoli. (The Cambridge Edition of the Works of F. Scott Fitzgerald). New York: Cambridge UP, 1991.

———. "Homage to the Victorians." *New York Tribune* 14 May 1922: 7.

———. *The Last Tycoon.* Ed. Edmund Wilson. New York: Scribner's, 1941.

———. "May Day." *Babylon Revisited and Other Stories.* New York: Scribner's, 1932. 25–73.

———. "My Lost City." *The Crack-Up.* Ed. Edmund Wilson. New York: New Directions, 1956. 23–33.

———. Preface. *The Great Gatsby.* New York: Modern Library, 1934.

———. "The Sensible Thing." *All the Sad Young Men.* Scribner's: New York, 1926: 217–38.

———. "The Spire and the Gargoyle." *The Apprentice Fiction of F. Scott Fitzgerald.* Ed. John Kuehl. New Brunswick: Rutgers UP, 1965. 105–14.

———. *Tender Is the Night.* New York: Scribner's, 1933.

———. *This Side of Paradise.* New York: Macmillan, 1986.

Pendleton, Thomas A. *I'm Sorry about the Clock: Chronology, Composition, and Narrative Technique in The Great Gatsby.* Selinsgrove, PA: Susquehanna UP, 1993.

Turnbull, Andrew. *Scott Fitzgerald.* New York: Scribner's, 1962.

———, ed. *The Letters of F. Scott Fitzgerald.* London: Bodley Head, 1964.

Chapter Four: Faulkner's Civil War

Anderson, Bern. *By Sea and by River: The Naval History of the Civil War.* New York: Knopf, 1962.

Blotner, Joseph, *Faulkner: A Biography.* New York: Random House, 1974.

————, ed. *Selected Letters of William Faulkner.* New York: Vintage, 1978.

Brooks, Cleanth. *William Faulkner: The Yoknapatawpha Country.* New Haven: Yale UP, 1963.

Catton, Bruce. *Grant Moves South.* Boston: Little, Brown, 1960.

Cowley, Malcolm, ed. *The Faulkner-Cowley File: Letters and Memories, 1944–1962.* New York: Viking, 1968.

Coy Ferrer, Javier and Michel Gresset, eds. *Faulkner and History.* Salamanca: Ediciones Universidad de Salamanca, 1986.

deMan, Paul. *Blindness and Insight: Essays in the Rhetoric of Contemporary Criticism.* Rev. ed. Minneapolis: U of Minnesota P, 1983.

Faulkner, William. *Absalom, Absalom!* New York: Vintage, 1986.

————. "Evangeline." *Uncollected Stories of William Faulkner.* Ed. Joseph Blotner. New York: Random House, 1979. 583–609.

————. *Go Down, Moses.* New York: Random House, 1942.

————. *Intruder in the Dust.* New York: Random House, 1948.

————. *Light in August.* New York: Vintage, 1972.

————. "My Grandmother Millard and General Bedford Forrest and the Battle of Harrykin Creek." *Collected Stories of William Faulkner.* New York: Random House, 1950. 667–99.

————. *Requiem for a Nun.* New York: Vintage, 1975.

————. "A Return." *Uncollected Stories of William Faulkner.* Ed. Joseph Blotner. New York: Random House, 1979. 547–74.

————. *Sartoris.* Ed. Douglas Day. New York: Vintage, 1974.

————. *The Sound and the Fury.* New York: Vintage. 1990.

————. "There Was a Queen." *Dr. Martino and Other Stories.* New York: Smith and Haas, 1934.

————. *The Unvanquished.* New York: Vintage, 1966.

Hartje, Robert G. *Van Dorn: The Life and Times of a Confederate General.* Nashville: Vanderbilt UP, 1967.

Henry, Robert Selph. *'First with the Most': [Nathan Bedford] Forrest.* Indianapolis: Bobbs-Merrill, 1944.

Joyce, James. *Ulysses.* New York: Random House, 1986.

Merriwether, James, and Michael Millgate, eds. *Lion in the Garden: Interviews with William Faulkner, 1926–1962.* New York: Random House, 1968.

Moreland, Richard C. *Faulkner and Modernism: Rereading and Rewriting.* Madison: U of Wisconsin P, 1990.

Nevins, Allan. *The War for the Union.* 2 vols. New York: Scribner's, 1960.

Taylor, Walter. *Faulkner's Search for a South.* Baltimore: Johns Hopkins UP, 1983.

Thomas, Emory M. *Bold Dragon: The Life of J.E.B. Stuart.* New York: Harper and Row, 1986.

Waggoner, Hyatt. *William Faulkner: From Jefferson to the World.* Lexington: U of Kentucky P, 1959.

Chapter Five: Literary Hemingway

Anderson, Sherwood. *Dark Laughter*. New York: Boni and Liveright, 1925.
Baker, Carlos. *Ernest Hemingway: A Life Story*. New York: Scribner's, 1969.
————, ed. *Ernest Hemingway: Selected Letters 1917–1961*. New York: Scribner's, 1981.
————. *Hemingway: The Writer as Artist*. 3rd ed. Princeton: Princeton UP, 1963.
Barbusse, Henri. *Under Fire, The Story of a Squad*. Tr. W. Fitzwater Wray. London: Dent, 1955.
Bloom, Harold. *The Anxiety of Influence: A Theory of Poetry*. New York: Oxford UP, 1973.
Brenner, Gerry. *Concealment in Hemingway's Works*. Columbus: Ohio UP, 1983.
Hemingway, Ernest. *Across the River and Into the Trees*. New York: Scribner's 1950.
————. "A Clean, Well-Lighted Place." *The Snows of Kilimanjaro*. New York: Scribner's, 1955. 29–33.
————. *Death in the Afternoon*. New York: Scribner's, 1932.
————. *A Farewell to Arms*. New York: Scribner's, 1969.
————. *For Whom the Bell Tolls*. New York: Scribner's, 1940.
————. *The Garden of Eden*. New York: Macmillan, 1986.
————. *A Moveable Feast*. New York: Scribner's, 1964.
————. *The Old Man and the Sea*. New York: Scribner's, 1952.
————. "The Snows of Kilimanjaro." *The Snows of Kilimanjaro*. New York: Scribner's,1955. 3–28.
————. *The Sun Also Rises*. New York: Scribner's, 1970.
————. *To Have and Have Not*. New York: Scribner's, 1937.
————. *The Torrents of Spring, A Romantic Novel in Honour of the Passage of a Great Race*. New York: Scribner's, 1972.
Hudson, William Henry. *The Purple Land*. NewYork: Three Sirens P, 1904.
Lynn, Kenneth S. *Hemingway*. New York: Fawcett, 1987.
Mandelbaum, Allen, tr. *The Divine Comedy of Dante Alighieri: Inferno*. New York: Bantam, 1982.
Mason, Alfred Edward Woodley. *The Four Corners of the World*. New York: Scribner's, 1917.
O'Hara, Daniel. "An Interview with Thomas Kinsella." *Contemporary Poetry* 4, 1: 1–18.
Reynolds, Michael. *Hemingway: The Paris Years*. London: Blackwell, 1989.
————. *Hemingway's First War: The Making of A Farewell to Arms*. London: Blackwell, 1987.
————. *Hemingway's Reading 1910–1940: An Inventory*. Princeton: Princeton UP, 1981.
Weeks, Robert P., ed. *Hemingway: A Collection of Critical Essays*. Englewood Cliffs: Prentice-Hall, 1963.
Wells, H. G. *Mr. Britling Sees It Through*. London: Hogarth, 1985.
White, William, ed. *By-Line: Ernest Hemingway; Selected Articles and Dispatches of Four Decades*. New York: Scribner's, 1967.

Conclusion: A Community of Writers

Bloom. Harold. *Omens of Millennium. The Gnosis of Angels, Dreams and Resurrection.* New York: Riverhead Books, 1996.

———. *Ruin the Sacred Truth: Poetry and Belief from the Bible to the Present.* Cambridge, Mass.: Harvard UP, 1989.

Hassan, Ihab. *The Dismemberment of Orpheus: Toward A Postmodern Literature.* New York: Oxford UP, 1971.

Kenner, Hugh. *The Stoic Comedians: Flaubert, Joyce and Beckett.* Berkeley: U of California P, 1964.

McCarthy, Mary. "The Fact in Fiction." *The Humanist in the Bathtub: Selected Essays from Mary McCarthy's Theatre Chronicle 1937-1962, and On the Contrary.* New York: Signet, 1964. 173-94.

INDEX

–A–

Achebe, Chinua, 31
Aiken, Conrad, 68
Alighieri, Dante, 43, 57, 148–51
Allen, Joan M., 86
Anderson, Sherwood, 131, 138–41, 151
Andrews, James J., 125
Appomattox, 121
Aquinas, Thomas, 49
Aristotle, 58
Asch, Nathan, 131
Ashberry, John, 152
Atherton, James, 52, 60
Augustine, Saint, 50
Austen, Jane, 156

–B–

Baines, Jocelyn, 20
Baker, Carlos, 148, 150
Bakunin, Mikhail, 34
Balzac, Honoré de, 59
Barbusse, Henri,
Barthes, Roland, 45
Barttelot, Major Edmund, 26, 28
Baudelaire, Charles, 8, 9, 10
Beauregard, P. G. T., 100, 118
Becker, Charles, 77–78
Beckett, Samuel, 2, 157
Belmer, Hans, 62
Bennett, Arnold, 5
Bible, 59, 85, 150–51
Bierman, John, 19, 21, 28
Bishop, John, 42-43, 45, 54
Bishop, John Peale, 68
Blake, William, 97
Bleikasten, Andrè, 123–24

Bloom, Harold, 4, 67, 151–53, 157–58
Blotner, Joseph, 109, 120
Boyle, Fr. Robert, 49
Brenner, Gerry, 148
Brivic, Sheldon, 44, 50
Brooks, Cleanth, 98–99, 107, 109
Bruccoli, Matthew, 75
Bruno, Giordano, 56, 60
Bryan, William Jennings, 137
Burton, Richard, 13

–C–

Chalmers, James R., 103–105, 107
Chasseguet-Smirgel, Janine, 62
Chickamauga, Battle of, 101
Conrad, Joseph, 4, 8, 11, 67, 128,
   157
   "The Ascending Effort", 40
   Congo Diary, 20, 29
   Heart of Darkness, 14–36, 39, 40
   Last Essays, 14–16, 25
   Lord Jim, 33
   The Nigger of the Narcissus, 16
   "An Outpost of Progress," 28
   Under Western Eyes, 16, 32–40
   Within the Tides, 13
   Youth, 16
Cohan, George M., 77
Cowley, Malcolm, 97
Coy Ferrer, Javier, 97, 98, 123

–D–

Dada, 5, 10
Darras, Jacques, 16, 31

daVinci, Leonardo, 59–60
deMan, Paul, 8
Dos Passos, John, 73, 148
Dreiser, Theodore, 81
Dumas (*père*), Alexandre, 106

–E–

Eagleton, Terry, 11–12
Eliot, T. S., 1, 3, 42
Ellmann, Richard, 3, 5, 42-44, 54, 59, 63, 65
Emin Pasha, 14, 17, 18, 21, 22, 27
Erdinast-Vulcan, Daphna, 31
Erlich, Victor, 10

–F–

Faulkner, William, 2, 6, 96, 157
  Absalom, Absalom!, 4, 98, 100, 101, 112–16, 127
  A Fable, 123
  Go Down, Moses, 124
  Intruder in the Dust, 120, 122
  Light in August, 113–14, 127–28
  "My Grandmother Millard and General Bedford Forrest and the Battle of Harrykin Creek," 104–106, 111
  Requiem for a Nun, 97, 99, 104, 107, 121
  "A Return," 113
  Sartoris, 99, 100, 110–13, 115, 118–19, 123
  The Sound and the Fury, 128
  "There Was a Queen," 118
  The Unvanquished, 99–101, 107, 109, 112, 116, 118, 121, 124, 126–27
Fay, Msgr. Cyril S. W., 86
Feidelson, Charles, 3
Fitzgerald, F. Scott, 6, 98, 128, 157
  "Absolution," 91–93
  The Beautiful and the Damned, 68, 72–76, 81, 87, 92
  Correspondence, 68, 69, 85, 88
  "The Diamond as Big as the Ritz," 93–95
  The Great Gatsby, 4, 68–87, 91–93
  The Last Tycoon, 81, 87, 89–91, 93
  Letters, 69
  "May Day," 73
  "My Lost City," 75–76, 96
  "The Sensible Thing," 72, 95
  "The Spire and the Gargoyle," 72, 75
  Tender Is the Night, 88. 91, 93
  This Side of Paradise, 68, 72–73, 76, 86–87
Fitzgerald, Zelda Sayre, 69, 70, 72, 85
Flaubert, Gustave, 6–10, 150

Fleishman, Avrom, 36
Ford, Ford Madox, 131
Forrest, Nathan Bedford, 102–109, 115, 117, 121
Forrest, William Montgomery, 121
Forster, E. M., 42
Fort Moultrie, 118–19, 126
Fort Sumter, 118–19, 122, 125
Franklin, Battle of, 101
Franklin, Sir John, 1
Freud, Sigmund, 59–60, 62

–G–

Galsworthy, John, 5
Gettysburg, Battle of, 101, 118, 120
Givens, Seon, 3
Gnosticism, 57, 128, 157–58
Gone With the Wind, 123
Goonetilleke, D.C.R.A., 31
Gose, Elliott B., Jr., 43–44
Grant, Ulysses S., 100–103, 113–14
"Great Locomotive Raid," 125–26
Gresset, Michel, 97, 98, 123
Guesclin, Bertrand du, 115
Guys, Constantin, 8, 9

–H–

Haggard, H. Rider, 16
Hall, Richard, 19, 28
Hardy, Thomas, 98
Hart, Clive, 52
Hassan, Ihab, 2, 67
Hayman, David, 52
Hemingway, Ernest, 4, 6, 69, 96, 128
  Across the River and Into the Trees, 130, 148–51
  Death in the Afternoon, 132, 152–54
  A Farewell to Arms, 129, 141–45
  For Whom the Bell Tolls, 129, 145–47, 151
  The Garden of Eden, 145
  Green Hills of Africa, 144
  In Our Time, 130
  A Moveable Feast, 139
  The Old Man and the Sea, 150–51
  Selected Letters, 136, 139, 140
  "The Snows of Kilimanjaro," 150
  The Sun Also Rises, 131–32, 136–41
  To Have and Have Not, 150
  The Torrents of Spring, 131, 138–41
Henry, Robert Selph, 103, 106
Herring, Phillip, 0
Homer, 43, 141
Hood, John B., 101

Hudson, W. H., 134–37, 143, 145–47, 152

–J–

Jackson, T. J. "Stonewall," 100, 112, 117
James, Henry, 3, 137
Jameson, James, 26, 28
Johnston, Joseph E., 101, 102, 108–109, 112
Jolas, Eugene, 5
Jousse, Père Marcel, 63
Joyce, James, 3, 5, 8, 11–12, 124, 128, 131, 157
  Critical Writings, 57
  Dubliners, 53–54, 58
  Finnegans Wake, 10, 43–45, 50, 53–65
  Letters, 48, 50, 52, 58
  A Portrait of the Artist as a Young Man, 41, 46–50, 55, 58
  Stephen Hero, 9–10
  Ulysses, 4, 42, 49–54, 58, 65, 97, 141, 142, 150
Joyce, Stanislaus, 48

–K–

Kenner, Hugh, 2, 42, 67
Kermode, Frank, 35
Kimbrough, Robert, 18, 20
Kinsella, Thomas, 153
Kipling, Rudyard, 16
Klein, Georges Antoine, 18
Kropotkin, Peter, 34

–L–

Lardner, Ring, 68–69
Larkin, Philip, 1, 5
Lawrence, Karen, 51, 52
Lee, Robert E., 100, 112, 118, 120
Leopold II, 16, 40
Lewis, Sinclair, 81
Lewis, Wyndham, 2, 42
Livingstone, David, 13–15, 19, 28, 31
Longstreet, James, 100, 102, 112
Lynn, Kenneth, 131, 139

–M–

MacCabe, Colin, 53–54
Mallarmé, Stéphane, 36
Manassas, Battles of, 109–12, 117
Mandelbaum, Allen, 150
Mannes, Marya, 80
Mason, A. E. W., 133, 137, 143, 152
Maupassant, Guy de, 130, 152

McCarthy, Mary, 156
McClellan, George B., 117
McClintock, Leopold, 13
Mencken, H. L., 68, 79, 137
Merriwether, James, 97, 127
Millgate, Michael, 97, 127
Mistinguette, 122

–N–

Nevins, Allan, 111
Nicholls, David, 8, 9
Nietzsche, Friedrich, 38
Norris, Margot, 45

–O–

O'Hara, Daniel, 153
Oxford, Battle of, 102–108

–P–

Park, Mungo, 13
Pendleton, Thomas, 81
Perkins, Maxwell, 68, 69, 70
Pitavy, François, 99
Pope, John, 113
Pound, Ezra, 10, 42, 140, 141, 144, 145, 153
Power, Arthur, 5
Proust, Marcel, 10

–R–

Remarque, Erich Maria, 143
Reynolds, Michael, 131, 141, 143, 144, 145
Rivera, Primo de, 137
Robinson, Fred Miller, 43, 51
Rosenthal, Herman, 77–78
Ross, Lillian, 130
Rothstein, Arnold, 78
Rousseau, Jean Jacquqes, 39

–S–

Sade, Marquis de, 62
Said, Edward, 31
Schlossman, Beryl, 44
Shelley, Percy Bysshe, 59
Sherman, William Tecumseh, 101–103, 112
Sherry, Norman, 20
Shiloh, Battle of, 101, 102, 108, 109, 113, 126
Smith, A. C., 103–107
Smith, Iain, 19
Spittles, Brian, 16
Stanley, Henry Morton, 14–31, 34

Stendhal, 130, 141, 152
Stevens, Wallace, 152
Stone, Phil, 120
Stuart, J. E. B., 100, 110–12, 117–20

–T–

Terrail, Pierre de, Seigneur de Bayard, 115
Thomas, Emory, 111–12, 120
Tolstoi, Leo, 130, 147, 151, 156
Troyat, Henri, 8
Turgenieff, Ivan, 130, 136, 137–38, 152
Turnbull, Andrew, 68, 76

–V–

Valentinius, 157
Van Dorn, Earl, 113–17
Vicksburg, Siege of, 101, 108–109

Vico, Giambattista, 56–57, 60, 64
Virgil, 57, 59, 141–42, 148

–W–

Waggoner, Hyatt, 98
Washburn, Cadwallader, 103–104
Watt, Ian, 16
Wells, H. G., 5, 44, 143
Wilde, Oscar, 59, 62
Wolfe, Thomas, 67
Woolf, Virginia, 5, 10–11, 42
World War I, 1, 4, 123, 133, 142
Wright, Ella, 120

–Y–

Yeats, William Butler, 48
Young, Philip, 150